C0-ATA-959

THE GAELIC VISION IN SCOTTISH CULTURE

The Gaelic Vision in Scottish Culture

MALCOLM CHAPMAN

CROOM HELM LONDON

McGILL-QUEEN'S UNIVERSITY PRESS
Montreal

U638638 53991

© 1978 Malcolm Chapman
Croom Helm Ltd, 2-10 St John's Road, London SW11

British Library Cataloguing in Publication Data

Chapman, Malcolm
Gaelic culture.
1. Highlands of Scotland – Civilization
I. Title
941.11 DA880.H7

ISBN 0-85664-752-7

McGill-Queen's University Press
1020 Pine Avenue West, Montreal H3A 1A2

ISBN 0-7735-0506-7

Legal deposit first quarter 1979

Bibliotheque Nationale du Québec

Printed in Great Britain by
Biddles Ltd, Guildford, Surrey

CONTENTS

063863 53991

ACKNOWLEDGEMENTS

This book has grown out of a thesis submitted to Oxford University for the degree of B.Litt. in 1977. I am grateful to all at the Institute of Social Anthropology in Oxford who have helped to provide the intellectual and social context within which I have worked. I am indebted especially to all those concerned with and contributing to the *Journal of the Anthropological Society of Oxford*, which has provided a focus of discussion that I have found invaluable.

In particular, Maryon McDonald and Roger Rouse have helped me both in discussion and with early drafts of this work. Edward Condry, with whom I have shared an interest in the Highlands, has helped me in many ways to sustain and further this interest. Alasdair Duncan, Graham Chapman, Elizabeth Grimshaw and Leonard Barkan have all provided, in different ways, friendly and sceptical commentaries on my enthusiasms. John MacInnes, of the Edinburgh School of Scottish Studies, who examined this work in its thesis form, has made several helpful and sympathetic suggestions for its improvement. Many people have helped me, in various ways, to learn such Gaelic as I can command. My family has provided sustained and invaluable moral support, and James Drummond and Sons have allowed me to use their photocopier. I am grateful to them all.

My principal debt, however, is to my supervisor, Edwin Ardener, who has taught me much of the Gaelic that I know, and most of the anthropology. The benefits of my discussions with Mr Ardener are manifest throughout this book, in far more ways than any specific reference might suggest.

I acknowledge with thanks the financial support of the Social Science Research Council. I am also indebted, for permissions received to cite the various Gaelic poems contained within, to Canongate Publishing Ltd, and to Gairm Publications.

For all defects and misunderstandings in this work, the responsibility is mine.

Mr. Crotchet. 'The sentimental against the rational, the intuitive against the inductive, the ornamental against the useful, the intense against the tranquil, the romantic against the classical, these are great and interesting controversies, which I should like, before I die, to see satisfactorily settled.'

Thomas Love Peacock
Crotchet Castle, 1831

'He's dreaming now,' said Tweedledee: 'and what do you think he's dreaming about? . . . Why, about *you*! And if he left off dreaming about you, where do you suppose you'd be?'

'Where I am now, of course,' said Alice.

'Not you!' Tweedledee retorted contemptuously. 'You'd be nowhere. Why, you're only a sort of thing in his dream!'

'If that there King was to wake,' added Tweedledum, 'you'd go out–bang!–just like a candle!'

'I shouldn't!' Alice exclaimed indignantly. 'Besides, if *I'm* only a sort of thing in his dream, what are *you*, I should like to know?'

Lewis Carroll
Through the Looking Glass

1 INTRODUCTION: HISTORY AND THE HIGHLANDS

The Highlands and Islands of Scotland occupy a place in Scottish history whose importance is out of all proportion to their economic significance, or to the small population that now occupies these remote and infertile regions. The face that Scotland turns to the rest of the world is, in many respects, a Highland face. When Scottish identity is sought, it is often by the invocation of Highland ways and Highland virtues that it is found. At the same time, both the Gaelic language and the Highland way of life have suffered persecution at the hands of their southern neighbours. Indeed, the history of Scotland since the Reformation reads in many ways as a sustained confrontation of the Highlands and the Lowlands.

This work is an attempt to show how the Highlander has come to occupy this paradoxical place in Scottish and British history. I have not, however, attempted a history of the Highlands, or of Gaelic culture and life. The place that the Highlander occupies in the Lowland imagination cannot be understood by a simple reading of Highland history. This is not to deny the importance of this history, but rather to recognise that the importance it assumes is something we need to explain. Every country has its minorities, its histories of lost opportunity and its vanished and vanishing traditions, few of which come to dominate their history in the way that the Highlander looms in the Scottish imagination. The past only offers its message at the enquiry of the present, and it is the nature and structure of that enquiry, as it has been turned towards the Scottish Gaidhealtachd,[1] that I attempt to examine and explain here.

This is an often tortuous exercise, and it does not produce results that can be laid out in chronological sequence, although for conventional convenience the chapters are laid out in roughly such a sequence. History might be said to make itself forwards, but it is always written backwards, and within this tension we have always to be looking both ways. Yesterday's commentary leads to today's, and is then re-interpreted in the light of the latter. It is not only the consciousness of the historian that we are concerned with here, however. The very objects of study, the Highlanders themselves, have long been conscious of their place in our history, and in acting with such knowledge further tangle the relationship of the present to the past, of fact to fiction, and of 'reality' to the mere 'printed word'. Each chapter within this work has complicated and sometimes only implicit repercussions in others, and the ideas here discussed play themselves out through one another in a way that defies simple linear exposition. This is not an academic pretension, nor an apology for lack of clarity. Ideological structures, by their very existence, show themselves to have a multifold capacity for self-validation and self-regeneration, and the power that inheres in their complexity must make us shy of too readily reducing them to step-by-step explanation.

The history of the Gaels and Gaelic in Scotland is easily accessible in several publications, notably J.L. Campbell (1950) and K. MacKinnon (1974). In spite of the frequency with which this history is referred to in speaking of the Gael, it is in many respects curiously irrelevant to an understanding of the position that the modern Gael occupies. I only intend to give here the barest outline, partly as conventional background, and partly to establish the claim to national antiquity that the Scottish Gael can make (more detailed information on the early history of the Scots in Scotland can be found in, for example, J. Bannerman, 1969, 1974; M.O. Anderson, 1973).

The Gaelic language was introduced into Scotland by settlers from Ireland in the early centuries of the first millennium AD. These Irish settlers came from the kingdom of Dalriada in Northern Ireland, and the date at which they assumed political importance in Scotland is generally reckoned to be about 500 or 600 AD. By 844 the Gaelic king Kenneth Mac Alpin had emerged as ruler of the Picts and the Scots, inhabiting a kingdom united north of the Forth/Clyde line. By the eleventh century the Gaelic language was at its most widespread, spoken throughout most of the area covered by modern Scotland. It is commonly felt that it was at this period that Scottish nationhood was first fully realised, under the Gaelic-speaking monarch Malcolm Canmore. Smout has said of the Scotland of this period that 'it would be wrong to think of it in any sense as a state, Celtic or otherwise' (T.C. Smout, 1975, p. 20). It can also be said, however, that 'The kingdom had therefore a strong Irish-Celtic emphasis, for it had been men of Dalriada who proved themselves strongest in arms and subtlest in diplomacy' (ibid.).

The memory of this Gaelic hegemony has not been entirely lost, and modern Gaelic speakers can claim, even if for many it is a claim retrospectively established by scholars rather than one handed down by tradition, that Scotland belongs *de jure* to the Gael, and that the *de facto* occupancy of the Anglo-Saxon and his tongue is an injustice that history might one day be expected to repair.

Malcolm Canmore went to the English royal house for a bride, and his prize, the 'great, formidable and religious English queen, Saint Margaret' (ibid., p. 21) brought both English religious forms and southern nobility with her. After this, the Gaelic language began a slow decline in prestige and influence, and the successors of Malcolm Canmore and Margaret 'held the values of European civilisation more dear than the traditions of Celtic Alba' (ibid.). Independent Gaelic power survived for much longer in the near-autonomous Gaelic/Norse Lordship of the Isles which was established by Somerled in the twelfth century, and which comprised the Western Isles and Coastlands northwards from Kintyre. The Lordship of the Isles was forfeited in 1493, and attempts by Clan Donald to re-establish it in the sixteenth century failed.

With the departure of James VI to London in 1603, and the parliamentary Union of 1707, Gaelic culture lost all contact with its claim to legitimate power and greatness. Gaelic politics henceforth became a rather scrappy and bloody affair, as internal loyalties and disloyalties were exploited and manipulated by distant powers. Even so, however: 'a rich and varied world existed behind the clouds of political and military turbulence that for most people represents the "history" of Gaelic Scotland' (J. MacInnes, 1976, p. 59).

Gaelic-speaking Highlanders have exercised considerable if fleeting political power at various times in recent centuries, when their antipathy to government from the Lowlands coupled with the martial prowess of a pastoral mountain people were recruited to serve a political cause within a larger Scottish or British context. We can mention here the campaigns of Montrose in the civil wars of the seventeenth century, the campaign of Claverhouse that culminated in the battle of Killiecrankie in 1689, or the risings provoked by the exiled Stuart monarchy in 1715 and 1745. This military prowess did nothing, however, to effect any reversal in the fortunes of the Gaelic language, which was probably widely regarded by non-speakers who knew of its existence with the same contempt as that expressed in the Statutes of Iona[2] of 1609, where it is described as 'one of the chief and principall causis of the continewance of barbaritie and incivilitie amongis the inhabitantis of the Iles and Heylandis' (cited K. MacKinnon, 1974, p. 35). The military prowess of the Highlander was, indeed, his undoing, since it provoked severe repressive and retributive measures by the central authorities. Smout says: 'From the point of view of London the main problem after the Union was the Jacobites, whose stronghold in the hills beyond the Tay might yet have proved the Achilles heel of the whole British Protestant Establishment' (T.C. Smout, 1975, p. 206). This diseased member of the body politic was ruthlessly cauterised after the ''Forty-five', and the martial ambitions of the Highlanders were diverted into the service of the legitimate Crown: 'The raising of Highland regiments, upon commissions granted to their chiefs, took sullen and resentful men away from their despoiled glens, and used them in the creation of an imperial Britain' (J. Prebble, 1973, p. 302).

The Gaelic language has been subject to persecution, denigration and neglect, both officially and unofficially, since the early seventeenth century. This has been particularly operative within the field of education, and as a consequence an unfavourable attitude towards Gaelic as representative of ignorance, old-fashioned ways, and the like, is still prevalent among many Scottish people, both Gaelic- and non-Gaelic-speaking. Recent years have seen, however, a resurgence of interest in Gaelic throughout Scotland. Evening classes in Gaelic are popular and well attended throughout the Lowlands, and Gaelic publication is in a stronger position than it has ever been, in spite of the continuing steady decline in the number of native speakers.[3] John Prebble says of the Scottish Gaels: 'The Scots of Dalriada gave the land its name and its kings, the spirit of its history and the substance of its dreams, but their language would die with them' (ibid., p. 31).

The image of the Gaelic world as the ever-departing spiritual substance of Scottish life is very compelling, and while we might wonder about the 'spirit of history' and the location and status of the dreams of a nation, and question the inevitability of fate when it asks for the disappearance of the Gaelic language, Prebble's imagery here is of a type that we find again and again in discussions of Scottish history. We are faced with the problem that a language not understood by over 98 per cent of the Scottish people, with a modern literary tradition that only begins to assume any importance in the late eighteenth century and is still very small (although substantial enough considering the size of the community from which it springs), and spoken by a people who have been regarded for centuries by their southern neighbours as barbarians, should now be regarded as the quintessence of Scottish culture. As Billy Wolfe, the chairman of the SNP, says: 'I want to learn Gaelic. I see that as a symbolic assertion of my being Scottish' (B. Wolfe, 1973, p. 161).

Today this is often explained as a waning of the influence of things English, as the virtues of Scottish nationhood are reasserted, and Scotland sees itself as 'the Scotshire Ghost of itself left by the corrosive "Union"' (T. Scott, 1970, p. 9). The suppression of Gaelic is often judged, popularly if not always in considered judgement, to have been due, in some sense, to 'English' oppression and influence. The easy association of the English language, by which Gaelic was replaced, with the kingdom of England and its institutions, makes it possible to deny Scottish political and moral responsibility for the suppression of Gaelic culture and language. This denial gives to the high esteem in which Gaelic is now held a place in a newly coherent and continuous Scottish history, uninterrupted and untroubled except by outside influence.

The paradoxical position of Gaelic in Scotland today, as both spiritual substance of the nation and struggling minority language, cannot be explained by simply looking to the history of the Gaels, and attempting objectively to assess their importance in Scottish history. We must remember that the fact that Prebble can speak, along with many, of the Celtic spirit of Scottish history as a continuing and vital thread unbroken since the Gaels of Dalriada first set foot on Scottish shores, does not mean that this thread has always been recognised or highly valued. James VI and I and his courtiers would surely have found little value in the notion, and to the majority of the inhabitants of eighteenth-century Edinburgh it would have been an incomprehensible claim to an ancestry best hidden.

Since the eighteenth century, however, the Scottish people have increasingly looked to the Highlands to provide a location for an autonomy in which they could lodge their own political, literary and historical aspirations. They have thereby been allowed to reap all the benefits of Union, while at the same time retaining a location for all the virtues of sturdy independence. This has of course occurred over a period when Highland society was being reduced and scattered by clearances and forced emigrations, and by religious and cultural imperialisms of various kinds. We can illustrate this paradox in various ways. Traditional Highland dress was proscribed by a governmental decree of 1747, but two generations later George IV was visiting Edinburgh and making Highland dress fashionable by wearing it himself. The Highlands have long been derided as the barbarous antithesis of southern civilisation and sophistication, but they have at the same time become the location of all the virtues that civilisation has felt itself to lack. Gaelic has long been kept from the lips of Gaelic-speaking schoolchildren by derision and by the threat of corporal punishment, and the place of Gaelic in the education of such schoolchildren is still tenuous, yet at the same time more and more people throughout Scotland are learning Gaelic. The economy of the Highlands is now, and has been for a long time, depressed and depressing, and yet many thousands of people go there to take their holidays, and to look for a secure and changeless way of life.

It is not only the holidaymaker and the Gaelic-learner that can find fascination in the Highlands. Martainn Domhnallach, in a recent issue of the *West Highland Free Press*, complains of another regular visitor:

> An tug sibh an aire cho deidheil 's a tha sgoilearan – neo co-dhiubh feadhainn a tha ag gabhail orra fhein a bhith 'nan sgoilearan – air fas air a bhith a' rannsachadh 's ag cnuasachd feadh na Gaidhealtachd bho chionn ghoirid? Cha mhor nach eil iad cho lionmhor ris a' mheanbh-chuileig agus a cheart cho feumail! (M. Domhnallach, 1978, p. 2)

> Have you noticed how enthusiastic scholars – or at least people that claim to be scholars – have been getting recently about researching and investigating in the Gaidhealtachd? They are almost as plentiful as midges, and about as useful! (my translation)

It is often claimed by aggrieved Highland scholars that Scottish schoolchildren are taught to regard the Highlander as a violent and feckless barbarian. As MacLean complains:

> Now that Gaelic is no longer spoken, the use of Gaelic sounds in English speech must be avoided at all costs. There is nothing worse than having the epithet 'Heilant' hurled at one. That is one of the results of the Scottish educational system. There has always been some subtle insinuation that Highland and barbaric are synonymous. Formal Scottish historians did not quite say so. Nevertheless, they implied as much (C. MacLean, 1959, p. 41)

At best the Highlander is credited with a peripheral glamour; at worst children are taught to view him as a mere stumbling block on the road to civilisation and Union. J.L. Campbell has written that 'The official history of Scotland used in schools today, even in Gaelic-speaking areas, is that of the late Professor Hume Brown, whose sympathies were strongly Whig and anti-Gaelic' (J.L. Campbell, 1950, p. 12). The relationship between what is actually written in the textbooks and the impression that schoolchildren get from reading them is by no means simple. Such pedagogic processes operate as much through tacit oral suggestion as through the printed word, and are not very susceptible to demonstration. It is perhaps worth noting that Campbell's complaints about the education of Scottish children cannot, at least from my own school experience, be extended to English schools. Scottish history was largely ignored as a separate study, it is true, but I managed to acquire, through what process of tacit suggestion and private reading I am not sure, a view of the Highlands and of Scotland in general that gave them every credit. England and its people seemed pale and lifeless by comparison.

There is, I think, little doubt where the majority of public sympathy lies in looking at the civil wars between 'Cavalier' and 'Roundhead' in the seventeenth century (see, for example, *1066 And All That*, W.C. Sellar and R.J. Yeatman (1930), 1976, pp. 71-88). Although eclipsed temporarily by the constitutional rectitude of William of Orange, by the time Culloden came round the Stuart dynasty was thoroughly restored to its dashing and cavalier place. Opposed to the dull and faceless Electors (not even proper kings) of Hanover, the Bonny Prince of the 'Forty-five takes all the sympathies. My early appreciation of Scottish history was informed by a keen regret that his gallant enterprise had failed. I do not think that I was alone in this. J.L. Campbell admits, in writing his history of Gaelic in Scotland, that his 'personal sympathies are Jacobite' (J.L. Campbell, 1950, p. 12). I think that I can add, on behalf of my primary school colleagues, that ours were as well, although we little knew what exalted company we were keeping – 'George IV himself had Jacobite sympathies' (D. Daiches, 1973, p. 324).

Exactly who among the population of the British Isles has been taught to view Highland culture as barbarous and worthless must remain a matter for impression and conjecture. Even so, the vehemence with which Highland scholars will deny this judgement makes it difficult to avoid the conclusion that several generations of Highlanders have been so taught. It is also clear that this apparent self-denigration was externally orientated, and that southern ways were held up as a model for emulation. We can readily understand that those who found no virtue in this emulation would interpret it as an imposition from the south. On the other hand, it should be emphasised that those who gave to the Highlands their enviable place in our literature were predominantly Lowlanders, and that many of those who have been foremost in deriding the old Highland ways have been young and laudably ambitious Highlanders, impatient of 'Tìr nan Òg'. We should also note that the old lore and customs of the nineteenth century are available to us as much through the efforts of cosmopolitan scholars as through the efforts of Highlanders, and that it was a clergy drawn from the Highlands that was foremost in consigning to the moral and historical rubbish heap the old customs of their people.

Not only do Highland scholars claim that their culture and manners are derided by the Lowlander. They also, by a geographical implication, expect the same from the Englishman. This expectation is indeed only one example of a fairly common Scottish notion, operative in a variety of contexts, that England is simply more Lowland than the Lowlands in its attitude towards the far north. There are very clear symbolic and geographical reasons why this should seem an easy and appropriate assumption to make. It might seem obvious, for example, that if the populace of Edinburgh can find it in their sophisticated and urbane hearts to despise the Highlander for his rusticity and barbarity, then the population of London, that much bigger, more sophisticated, more urbane and more southerly, must despise him that much more. This extension is not, however, entirely justified. The populace of the south of England (and the north as well, but the point is better made with the south) do not, on the whole, think about the Scottish Highlander very much. When they do, it is not usually with any overtly political intent, but rather within the simple symbolic ethnology that renders the Highlander the bold, kilted and thoroughly admirable occupant of the distant and romantic north. While it might be argued that this very ignorance and indifference manifests a particular political relationship, it is one much less potent and engaged than that within which the Lowlands and Highlands of Scotland confront one another.

I have several times, at first to my considerable surprise, and then to my increasing interest, been remonstrated by partisan and trainee Gaels for holding a low opinion of the Highlander and his life. I think that we must accept that such complaints, in spite of this notionally appropriate outward direction, have an internal rationale. If the aspirant to social status in the Highlands chooses to ape Lowland ways and deride his own, then a contemporary understanding of such activity is to be found in the Highlands, and not in the Home Counties. If the Scottish Lowlanders, particularly the articulate middle class, choose to use 'English' manners and modes of expression in order to establish a social primacy, or to distance themselves from the Highlander or the rustic Scot, this is not in any simple sense the fault of the English. The 'Englishman' of Scottish resentment is in many respects the product of a purely internal dialogue – a product that it is a convenient falsity to locate elsewhere. It is a common Scottish Nationalist jibe that the English view Scotland as a mere 'Scotshire', an unimportant northern county. We can, I think, with both justice and gravity, turn the resentment around, and point out that England is not merely a southerly extension of the Lowlands of Scotland, however much it might seem to be so from Inverness.

The significance of this rather polemical note will gradually become clearer. One of the results of the treatment to which Gaeldom has been subjected is that it has become, in its own eyes and in the eyes of Britain, a particular kind of half-world. As a consequence of this the Gaidhealtachd, now entirely bilingual, can seek to establish its political place by invoking linguistic, political and symbolic dualities that can be laid out on a north–south axis between the Highlands and Edinburgh/

London. Scotland in general, and the Gaidhealtachd in particular, are thus allowed to offload elsewhere many political problems that they contain within themselves in their entirety. This often leads to a political and intellectual dishonesty that obscures, in spite of sometimes commendably radical claims, the problems that it seeks to expose. I return to this point in the conclusion.

There is no doubt, however, that there is a long and strong tradition of commentary on the Highlands wherein the Highlander becomes the reckless and destructive opposite of Lowland civility. We can readily understand the impatience that such criticism generates among Highland scholars. It is not, however, difficult, in the 1970s, to find virtue and strength in simple and marginal societies. Indeed, a distaste for the cultural imperialism that political centralisation can bring is now part of liberal stock-in-trade. Faced with urban blight, mass-media culture, pollution and heart disease, the rural fringes of our society offer us ready salvation. I could have written of all those writers that have dismissed Highland life as barbarous and primitive, and I could have shown them wrong by invoking the manifest cultural and social virtues of that society. This would not have been difficult. It would also not have needed saying. It is now very unfashionable to deride the rural peasant, and the mere disapproval and disavowal of such derision leaves many basic concerns untouched. Campbell regrets, along with many, that Highlanders have been regarded as 'barbarous in manners and uncouth in speech' (J.L. Campbell, 1933, p. xviii). He would prefer to argue, on the contrary, that the Gaels have 'an ever-present sense of the reality and existence of the other world of spiritual and psychic experience' (J.L. Campbell, 1960, p. 24). Different as these statements are, it can nevertheless be argued that they are statements of the same order, in that both owe their organising rationality to the discourse of the dominant English-speaking majority. I have therefore largely left aside all those critics who would abuse and belittle Highland society in overt and obvious ways.

I have been interested in a more general explanation that would subsume the simple fact that different groups in society will often hold unfavourable opinions of one another. I am not, of course, thereby denying the significance of such opinions. We all know that when one group in society is much more powerful than another, then such opinions can become unpleasant, destructive and lethal. In this context the Highland Clearances spring to mind, and some idea of the pointless brutality and breathtaking self-righteousness of the landlords and their agents can be had from several publications – notably A. Mackenzie

(1887) and J. Prebble (1969). The problem has more dimensions than any model of political ill-will or economic disequilibrium could simply accommodate, however.

Since the eighteenth century, the Celtic fringes have posed for the urban intellectual as a location of the wild, the natural, the creative and the insecure. We can often find it said, with warm approval, that the Celts are impetuous, natural, spiritual and naïve. I try in what follows to make it clear that such an approval is drawing on the same system of structural oppositions as is the accusation that the Celt is violent (impetuous, emotional), animal (natural), devoid of any sense of property (spiritual), or without manners (naïve). I include the bracketed terms as effective synonyms of the words that precede them, that we would use to praise rather than to deride. This will be made clearer in Chapter 4. We are dealing here with a rich verbal and metaphorical complex, and I have not thought it very important to distinguish between those who find a favourable opinion of the Gael within this complex, and those who dip into it to find the materials for derision. In both cases the coherence of the statements can only be found at their point of origin, the urban intellectual educated discourse of the English language, and not at their point of application, the Celt, the Gael, the primitive who is ever-departing, whether his exit be made to jeers or to tears.

I have already noted that the rising of 1745, the Battle of Culloden, and the figure of the Bonny Prince were pivotal in securing a place for Scotland in the skeletal pageant of kings and queens and victories and defeats that was schoolboy 'history'. Anyone reading rather more seriously into the subject of Scottish Highland history could not fail, I think, to confirm this first impression, and conclude that the eighteenth century did indeed represent some sort of meeting of the historical waters. Scholars of the nineteenth and twentieth centuries evoke the eighteenth century as the period from which a trajectory into the modern can be traced. The scouring of Highland society after Culloden, the Clearances of the late eighteenth century, the entry of utilitarian economics and the maximisation of gain – all these thresholds are invoked to lament a lost plenitude where a man's life was loyalty to his clan, where material rewards weighed not with him, where chief and clansman shared their blood, where warring clans were 'united in the strife that divided them' (cf. T.S. Eliot, 1969, p. 195; M. Gluckman, 1955; Evans-Pritchard, 1941), and where even bloodshed, theft and violence had their own capacity for effecting a meaningful integration of a bold and free humanity into its social world.

This originary feel that the eighteenth century has does not stem, I think, simply from a paucity of historical data from the preceding period. Nor does it stem from the fact that Highland society did indeed radically change course in the eighteenth century, although this is a popular enough notion, with events such as the 'Forty-five marking the change. Such an explanation is very much an artefact of history, and some works have marked the persuasive simplicity of this explanation by demonstrating the need to argue cogently against it (for example, Youngson, 1973). We look to the middle of the eighteenth century as a watershed in Highland affairs not primarily because of any change in those affairs, but rather because it was at this period that the outside world began to take an interest in the Highlander, and this interest is only very obliquely related to the significance and structure of events in a purely Highland history.

Perhaps the most significant intellectual trend of the eighteenth century was that towards what we now label 'Romanticism'. Within this often rather monstrous historical figment of retrospective definition, one of the commonest of theoretical concerns was to speculate on the nature of society, and on the nature of social development. Theories of man's primitive nature blossomed, and the Romantics looked both to nature and to this primal human essence for their poetic and intellectual inspiration.

At the same time as British intellectuals were becoming more and more interested in the nature of primitive man and primitive society, they had within their own national boundaries a fitting object for their attention. The Scottish Gael fulfilled this role of the 'primitive', albeit one quickly and savagely tamed, at a time when every thinking man was turning towards such subjects. The Highlands of Scotland provided a location for this role that was distant enough to be exotic (in customs and language) but close enough to be noticed; that was near enough to visit, but had not been drawn so far into the calm waters of civilisation as to lose all its interest. It is worth noting in this context that the early issues of the *Edinburgh Review*, published from 1802 onwards, have in their quarterly lists of new publications many travel books relating to the Highlands. These are gradually replaced over the early decades of the nineteenth century by works concerning increasingly accessible and more fashionable exotica overseas. By the time the *Edinburgh Review* first appeared, however, the sentiments of primitivism were thoroughly established, and Romanticism a fully fledged bird. The Scottish Highlander became accessible at a time when his role was, in a sense, written for him.

We do not, therefore, need to say that Highland society was undergoing greater change in the eighteenth century than ever before, nor do we need to argue that Highland society had never before been influenced, politically or economically, by the external world. It is, I think, proper to regard it as fortuitous that the intellectual world of the larger society became interested in the primitive at a time when the Highlander was peculiarly suited for the role, in a way that neither, say, the Lothian peasantry, who were too close, nor the South Sea Islander, who was too far away, could approach. The conceptual boundaries of civilisation were expanding fast, following on the great exploratory periods of the sixteenth and seventeenth centuries, and the strange and exotic were becoming elusive enough to merit lament for their absence. The Scottish Gael stood ambiguously in this world, at once a fit object for the location of primitive traits, and a fit object for taming, schooling and 'improving'.

The space that the Highlander came to occupy was, therefore, prepared in his absence and ready to be filled in the eighteenth century. When he came along to fill it, with the profoundly dramatic gesture of the 'Forty-five, it is not surprising perhaps that he acquired an instant and mythological reputation. We have scant means of knowing what the average Highlander who came 'out' in the 'Forty-five thought of the enterprise, but there is no doubt that, for Prince Charles at least, and probably for many of his noble supporters, the whole affair was a 'deliberately histrionic act' (D. Daiches, 1973, p. 132). At this level, the 'Forty-five may have been, at its very inception, informed by the intellectual structures through which it came to be interpreted.

The 'Forty-five occupies an enormously important place in the Scottish historical consciousness, and it hardly seems necessary to question why this should be so. We might, on the other hand, wonder that a relatively minor rising should have come to occupy such an important place. The battles were fought over a constitutional issue that had been irrevocably decided a century before. The military engagements were none of them great or glorious, and might be expected to fade into comparative insignificance before, say, the civil wars of the previous century, or the Napoleonic wars of the early nineteenth century. It must surely be argued that the enterprise was without any great chance of success, and that the constitutional threat was not nearly as great as history has made it. The 'Forty-five might have appeared to history, like the Duke of Monmouth's rebellion of 1685, as regrettable, unfortunate, unnecessary, and pointlessly bloody, and it might, like that rebellion, have fallen into historical obscurity. Instead it has become one of the few dates in the historical calendar that is commonly remembered, and its leader has become perhaps the figure in the whole historical pantheon with whom the word 'romance' is most easily associated.

The 'Forty-five was, of course, ill-received by the establishment. The *Scots Magazine* of 1745 spoke of the Young Pretender's army as:

> made up out of the barbarous corners of this country: many of whom are Papists, under the immediate direction of their priests; trained up to the sword, by being practised in open robbery and violence; void of property of their own; the constant invaders of that of others; and who know no law, but the will of their leaders. (p. 518)

The rising was brutally suppressed, by troops under the aptly named 'Butcher' Cumberland, and plans to de-Gaelicise the Highlands were rigorously enforced. At the same time, however, it seems that the rising struck a historical chord that is still ringing, and that once the political threat had been thoroughly expunged, the rising and the people were apt to become mythologised, in an intellectual climate that was ready for them.

Hence I think the lofty aspiration that has come to be located in the 'Forty-five. It is often difficult to avoid the impression that many Scottish intellectuals are glad that the 'Forty-five happened, however sordid and disastrous the consequences:

Feachd a' Phrionnsa

'Nuair a ràinig arm a' Phrionnsa ùir Shasuinn,
agus iad air an abhainn a chur as an déidh, thionndaidh iad,
rùisg gach fear a chlaidheamh, agus dh'amhairc iad gu
tosdach air Albainn car tacain.'

Nuair a chuir an t-arm an abhainn
s a sheas iad air ceud raointean Shasuinn,
thionndaidh iad gun ghlaodh, gun fhacal,
dh'amhairc iad le dùrachd dhainginn
air Albainn, s rùisg gach fear a chlaidheamh.
Bheachdaich iad 'nan tosd car tacain.

Sgrìoch na truaillean fo'n stàilinn,
dh'éigh a' phìob is lean am màrsal.

Tha an corr againn air chuimhne.

53991

Chaidh an gealladh sin a chumail
le ceuman sgìth s le lotan fuilteach.
Chuir iad Goliàt mór air uidil,
is, aon ri triùir, mu dheireadh thuit iad.

– Dhùin iad an greis a bhos le alladh –
Aon chuairt, aon chuairt gheibh sinn air thalamh
a nochdadh an fhaghairt a th'annainn,
a dheuchainn faobhar ar tapachd,
a chosnadh cliù do'r tir no masladh.

Is e bu chòir dhuinn stad is tionndadh,
amharc air ar tìr le dùrachd,
le gealladh blàth gun bhòsd, gun bhùitich,
is lann ar spioraid theth a rùsgadh,
seann lann lasairgheal ar dùthcha;
s a liuthad bliadhna meirg' is dùsail
a mhaolaich i san truaill dhùinte.
B'e'n dusal dubh e – so an dùsgadh.

The Prince's Army

'When the Prince's army reached the soil of England
after fording the river, they turned round, every man
unsheathed his sword and they looked silently on Scotland for
a while.'

When the army forded the river and they stood in the first
fields of England, they turned round without either a
cry or a word, they looked with steady purposeful devotion
on Scotland and every man unsheathed his sword. They
gazed silently for a while, and vowed to her their
strength and courage.

The sheaths scraped under the returning steel, the pipe
cried out and the march continued.

The rest of it is in our memory. That vow was kept
with weary steps and bloody wounds. They set great
Goliath rocking, and one against three they fell at last.

They closed their spell on this world with honour . . .
one spell, one spell only do we get on earth to show the
temper of the metal in us, to test the edge of our courage,
to win fame for our country or shame.

Now is the time when we should stop and turn, look upon
our land with affection and devotion, with a warm promise
without either boasting or threats, and unsheath the blade
of our hot spirit, the old flaming-white sword of our
country – so many years of rusting and slumber it has
been going blunt, set fast in its sheath.
It was a wretched slumber – this is the awaking.

Poem and translation are by George Campbell Hay (see 1946, pp. 14-15).

Celtic Ireland, Wales and Brittany do not in any clear sense have their Culloden. They do not have an apocalypse in which the threshold of the modern world was crossed. The drama that they can inject into their historical reconstruction of themselves is the poorer for the lack. History has welcomed this definitive struggle between old and new, Celt and Anglo-Saxon, primitive and sophisticate, Gael and guile. The Gaelic language is still retreating as a spoken tongue, as the old Highland ways depart before Anglo-American fashions. We cannot be surprised that it has become convenient to regard the 'Forty-five as 'the loss of Jacobite hopes and the end of the Stuart cause, . . . the devastation of the country and . . . the ending of an ancient civilisation and a unique way of life' (I.B. Cameron Taylor, 1968, p. 146). We are left only with 'the memory of that way of life and that Celtic heritage, which was lost to the Anglo-Saxon at Culloden' (ibid.). This struggle appears, therefore, like a historical watershed for a variety of interconnected reasons. And just as the 'Forty-five prepared the eighteenth-century mind to expect the epic from the mountain-dwellers of the north, so the epic was quite literally supplied, in the 1760s, by James Macpherson.

Macpherson published a series of prose poems that have come collectively to be known as 'Macpherson's Ossian'. They were Macpherson's own compositions, but he claimed that he had merely translated them from ancient Gaelic originals. The poems were extremely successful, and became involved in an argument about their authenticity that ranks as one of the greatest of literary controversies. It was through this controversy, and through the inauthenticity of Ossian, that the Scottish Gael found his way into the European imagination.

The same explanations that help us to account for the peculiarly

0638638

dramatic position that the 'Forty-five occupies in Scottish history can also to some extent be invoked to explain the meteoric success of Macpherson's Ossian. A Northern Odyssey and a Northern Homer were required, and Macpherson supplied both. The place on the shelf for Macpherson's Ossian was, as it were, ready to be filled. In Chapter 2, I try to show how Ossian, while ostensibly drawn from the alien Highland world, in fact drew its appeal from its suitability as a vehicle for debate within a European intellectual tradition.

At the same time as Macpherson's Ossian was taking Europe by storm, genuine Gaelic poets were producing what is now considered to be the finest flower of Gaelic verse. In Chapter 3, I discuss the two most notable poets of this period, Alexander Macdonald and Duncan Bàn Macintyre, and discuss the various relationships, direct and indirect, between these two poets and the English-language romantic tradition. I argue that the English-language discourse of which Ossian was a part has had an influence on the appreciation of these Gaelic poets of great importance, and that the inauthenticity of Ossian was part of a more general inauthenticity in the assessment of other cultures which is closely linked to the romantic aesthetic.

Chapter 4 is primarily concerned with the ethnologies of the Celt constructed by Ernest Renan and Matthew Arnold. The coherence of their construct is shown to be largely independent of the Celt as he lived in Wales, Brittany, Ireland and Scotland, and to derive rather from a system of metaphors of great generality which constantly recur in works concerning the Celts, while being by no means confined to them. Other occurrences of these metaphors are referred to, particularly in the assessment of the nature of science, and of the relative characteristics of 'man' and 'woman'. Renan's and Arnold's Celt can be regarded as a metaphorical hot-house plant – an ethnological fiction deriving from the internal logic of the same system of representation as that which allowed the construction of the ideal 'woman'. In so far as man and woman can serve as a model for the kind of definitional problems that arise, then of course we are talking about all societies. In so far as we are concerned with the economic rationality of Western thought looking to its rural fringes, then in an increasingly industrialised world we are entering a global dialogue (cf. M. McDonald, 1978). The example of Gaelic Scotland has also, needless to say, an interest entirely of its own.

This theme of the independence of commentary on the Gael from the Gael himself, and the relationship between these two dissociated phenomena, which begins in Chapter 2 with Ossian, is continued in Chapter 5, where the activities of folklorists right up to the present day are shown to derive their *raison d'être* within imagery with which we become familiar in the nineteenth century. The metaphorical dualities used to express the relative natures of folklore and its 'opposite' (for example, 'rational knowledge' or 'science') are shown to be substantially similar to those used to express the relative natures of Celt and Anglo-Saxon. Folklore studies themselves are argued to be largely inspired by a misapprehension of the potential of a scientifically conceived rationality to extend to all spheres of human activity.

Chapter 6 is mainly concerned with the works of five notable modern Scottish Gaelic poets. Certain aspects of their perception and literary expression of the Gaelic world are shown to derive from metaphorical dualities which a non-Gaelic-speaker would use to express the relative characteristics of, for example, rural and urban, or family and business, and the like. The basis of the continuing validity of this imagery is discussed.

A common problem confronting the modern intellectual Gael lies in deciding what attitude to adopt to the Calvinist Church of his native community. Using the works of these poets to demonstrate the unease provoked by this Church, I examine likely reasons for that unease, arguing that Calvinist philosophy represents, in practice, a subversion of most of the imagery which has been used to express the nature of Gaelic society. It should be noted that my appreciation of the poetry that I discuss in this chapter is still dependent to a considerable extent on translation by others. My temerity in subjecting to discussion poems which I cannot fully appreciate in their original form (although I can, at a simple and literal level, 'translate' them) is only excused in that my discussion, and the conclusions that I reach, are only very obliquely related to the poetic value of these poems, judgement on which is outside both my scope and my competence. Translations from the Gaelic throughout are by the original author unless otherwise stated.

Chapter 7 is concerned with the work that social anthropologists have carried out in the Gaelic-speaking areas of Scotland. The anthropological concerns which form the background to their work are discussed, and reasons suggested for the lack of continuity between the folkloric and anthropological traditions. The relationship of the anthropologist's model to the model of society that the people themselves have is discussed, and this relationship is projected into a brief consideration of the links between Gaelic society in the traditional Gaelic-speaking areas and the large urban Gaelic population in Glasgow. The main theme of this work, the way in which Gaelic life is symbolically subsumed by the majority society, is shown to be no merely literary phenomenon, but to have application at all levels of the relationship of the majority to the minority, and of the English language to the Gaelic language.

In Chapter 8, I conclude by drawing together again in a short discussion much of the imagery whose treatment recurs throughout, and briefly examine the validity and status of that imagery. A few methodological remarks and apologies follow, within which I suggest some of the potential for materially affecting the Gaelic community that 'mere literary imagery' has.

The topics covered by these different chapters appear, at first glance, to be widely disparate, and it is not easy to summarise the connecting themes in any simple way. I am tempted merely to request that the book be read as a whole, and to hope that the reader will find it as coherent in the reading as I have found it in the writing. I could, however, perhaps sum up one of the most important points in this way: the Highlands have been looked to as a source of a changeless fidelity to their own past (and, by extension, to the past of Scotland and to the past of mankind). Much of my argument lies in the paradox that the more this kind of fidelity to the past has been pursued, the more Highland life has become a mere facet of a world-view that is not its own. The more historical authenticity has been desired, the more the Gaelic world has responded by creating itself in an image imposed from without.

This work began as an attempt by someone trained in social anthropology to apply the insights and methods of his discipline to the Scottish Gaidhealtachd, its history, and its contemporary structure. It has certainly not turned out as I expected, and there is little discussion of social structure, division of labour, land tenure, or indeed any of the other subjects that a work from a sociological tradition might be expected to cover. I have, however, addressed myself to what seemed to me to be immediate concerns – concerns which can easily be ignored but which can, if they are not seriously broached, order all argument that we might engage in with a presumptive and self-validatory power that will rob our discussion of much of the analytical gravity it might otherwise have. My failure to treat of subjects like 'what Gaelic society is really like' does not therefore stem from a retreat into literary indulgence. On the contrary, I think that the simple empirical desire to 'see what the Gaidhealtachd is really like' cannot assume any truly radical or incisively inquisitive substance until the issues that I am concerned with in this work are thoroughly discussed.

I have not been explicitly concerned here with theoretical problems in social anthropology, although this work is in many ways in and about social anthropology. What theoretical discussion there is to be found here is made in and through the material with which it deals, and I think that it is best left there for those who wish to find it. I do not consider myself to belong to any particular school of anthropology, or to have a body of theory that I could apply to data, and express apart from that application. Belonging to an anthropological school is, in any case, largely achieved by not belonging to others, and I will again leave it to anybody that is interested to decide to what school, if any, this work belongs. This is not to say that I think that theoretical discussion is an ephemeral self-indulgence, to be dismissed in favour of some more robust ambition such as 'getting on with the job'. This work has come out of social anthropology at Oxford University, and there is simply not space here to do explicit theoretical justice to that origin. My more immediate intellectual debts are made clearer in my acknowledgements.

I should perhaps point out that the intellectual framework which I dissect in Chapters 4 and 5, the framework which permitted and required the Celt and Anglo-Saxon of the literature to gather their opposed personalities about them, is one that is still keeping alive old problems in the modern social sciences. My discussion of nineteenth-century ethnological problems is, therefore, quite immediately relevant. Much of the imagery employed in these constructs is still very much part of our everyday perception of the world. Many of these images can, of course, be 'derived' from an overtly philosophical tradition, and in this respect I have found many works helpful, notably H.-G. Gadamer (1975). I have tried briefly elsewhere to show the continuing relevance of this imagery, and the moral concerns that it provokes, to some aspects of the modern theoretical concerns of social anthropology (see M. Chapman, 1977). My attempt there to treat of the opposition between formalism and a more humane and moral approach to the human sciences is not entirely jocular in its comparison of this opposition with that between Anglo-Saxon and Celt.

I have tried throughout this work to relate the 'literary' and the 'historical' and 'sociological' material, and to show that we cannot find objective footing in any of these, nor by the same token dismiss any of them as irrelevant or rank them as essentially different kinds of evidence. Gaelic culture has been subject to a literary interpretation that has diminished and subsumed it, offering it a secure but ephemeral niche. The majority society has used Gaelic culture as a symbolic element in a process of defining itself, and consequently Gaelic culture is only present in English literary discourse in a shape that has been imposed upon it from without. Gaelic culture has been subject to what I term 'symbolic appropriation' at the hands of the majority and dominant culture. At the same time, the face that Gaelic culture is given within this appropriation is often persuasively apt, even for those within that culture. I would risk the assertion that Gaelic culture has to a considerable extent *become*, particularly in its more self-conscious moments, the literary interpretation to which it was initially subjected by an alien tradition. I hope it will be clear that in invoking the concept of symbolic appropriation to describe the relationship of the majority British population to the Gaelic-speaking minority, I do not thereby intend to denote anything insubstantial or ephemeral in the nature of the relationship, or in its effects (see also M. Chapman, 1978, on this point).

The field covered by this work is enormous, and if I have achieved no more than a clearance of the ground on which a more substantial edifice could be raised, that is, I think, no worse a fate than befalls many works which try to examine critically not only their overt subject matter (in this case, the Scottish Gael), but also the structure of the academic and literary treatments within which that subject is constituted for the eye of the reader. It should however be emphasised, as I hope will be evident, that the dissolution of an academic or literary object is not merely gratuitous violence, but is a route towards understanding the effectivity that discourse has in constituting its object, and towards understanding the manner in which groups within society subsume and manipulate one another to serve their own ends, both material and symbolic.

2 OSSIAN AND THE EIGHTEENTH CENTURY

At the beginning of the eighteenth century Edward Lhuyd, curator of the Ashmolean Museum in Oxford, published his *Archaeologia Britannica*, in which he attempted a comparative study of the Celtic languages and peoples. Other works concerning the Celts had preceded this, notably Paul-Yves Pezron's *L'Antiquité de la Nation et de la Langue des Celtes* of 1703, but Lhuyd was the first to formulate the philological and historical problems in a way that the modern scholar would recognise as valid. Oxford was not, however, ready for him. *Archaeologia Britannica* did not proceed beyond the first volume, published in 1707, and Lhuyd himself died soon after, in 1709. Interest in the subject in Oxford died with him, and his invaluable collection of Gaelic manuscripts, folklore, and philological material, much of which he had gathered himself in the Gaelic-speaking areas of Scotland and Ireland, was dispersed. Campbell and Thomson connect this lack of interest in Celtic matters to a more general picture of Anglo-Scottish relations in the eighteenth century. They speak of:

> Lhuyd's immense contribution to the study of Scottish Gaelic dialects, manuscript literature, and folklore at a time when interest in these subjects was only just beginning to awaken, and was soon to be extinguished again for another two generations by the political and sectarian passions aroused by the Union of Scotland and England in 1707, the foundation of the S.P.C.K. in Scotland in 1709 with the purpose of extirpating Catholicism and the Gaelic language from the Highlands and Islands, and the Jacobite risings (partly provoked by this Society's activities) of 1715, 1719, and 1745. When these passions subsided and interest in Gaelic language and literature revived, it was centred on the bogus compositions of 'Ossian' Macpherson and the bitter controversy between the upholders of their 'authenticity', on the one hand, and those who totally denied the existence of any Scottish Gaelic literature, on the other. (J.L. Campbell and D. Thomson, 1963, xxiii)

Lhuyd's scholarly preoccupations were not in any case likely to be shared by a very large public. However, it is probable that a work such as his would have achieved a limited popularity, had it been published later in the eighteenth century, by its appeal to a primitive Celtic past. Lhuyd was 'in several ways . . . nearly two centuries ahead of his time' (ibid., xiii). There are signs, however, shortly after Lhuyd's premature work had sunk into obscurity, that a new movement in literary taste was occurring – a movement within which we can place the poems of Ossian, the academic interest in the Scottish Highlands that they provoked, and the more general late-eighteenth-century vogue for things 'Celtic'.

Allan Ramsay published, in four volumes between 1724 and 1737, a collection of traditional songs and ballads entitled *The Evergreen*, which was the first of many such publications in eighteenth-century Scotland. Ramsay says in his preface to the first volume:

> When these good old 'Bards' wrote, we had not yet made use of imported trimming upon our Cloaths, nor of foreign embroidery in our writings. Their 'Poetry' is the product of their own country, not pilfered and spoiled in the transportation from abroad: Their 'Images' are native, and their 'Landskips' domestick; copied from those Fields and Meadows we every day behold (Allan Ramsay, 1724, vii).

He goes on to say, showing an early distaste for Classical iconography, 'The Morning rises (in the Poet's description) as she does in the Scottish Horizon. We are not carried to Greece or Italy for a Shade, a Stream, or a Breeze' (ibid., viii). A criticism of the 'Gentlemen' of Scotland is voiced, in sentiments felt ever since the Union of Crowns in 1603:

> yet such there are, who can vaunt of acquiring a tolerable perfection in the French or Italian Tongues, if they have been a Fortnight in Paris or a Month in Rome: But shew them the most elegant Thought in a Scots Dress, they as disdainfully as stupidly condemn it as barbarous. . . . for the most part of our Gentlemen, who are generally Masters of the most useful and politest Languages, can take Pleasure (for a Change) to speak and read their own (ibid., xi).

Daiches has written of this passage in his *The Paradox of Scottish Culture*, where Ramsay well exemplifies the paradox in question: 'This was written by the same writer who imitated Pope and quoted Prior and read the Spectator in order to model his life on the way of life there indicated' (D. Daiches, 1964, p. 27).

Ramsay was writing in a Scotland bitter about the blow to national pride represented by the Union of 1707, and in the emphasis on 'imported trimming' and 'foreign embroidery' we can detect the attempt to define clearly what was truly Scottish – a definition that the loss of nationhood seemed to make both more difficult and more necessary. Daiches says of the confrontation of native and imported art:

> Pretentious settings, overloaded with trills and other prettifications, were destroying the native vigour and simplicity of Scots song. Burns was to see this as Fergusson had seen it. . . . Still, it is a reflection of the impoverishment of Scottish Culture that the issue should have been between a native simplicity and an imported sophistication: older Scottish polyphonic music, which died after the migration of the Court to England in 1603, had been fruitfully responsive to continental influence (ibid., p. 34).

We can readily agree with the assessment that the inability to absorb external forms manifests a lack of strength, and argue that the nervousness about self-identity which characterises so much Scottish art, not least in the twentieth century, is evidence of the lack of a confident and robust identity as much as it is a means of producing it. However, the opposition of natural simplicity to civilised sophistication (whether imported or not) is a significant feature of much eighteenth-century literary discourse, and cannot simply be explained as a consequence of the peculiar political position of Scotland in the years after the Union.

Daiches says that in eighteenth-century Scotland 'there steadily developed a cleavage between genteel culture and popular culture, which adversely affected both' (ibid., p. 10). We can find an ambiguity, intentional or otherwise, in this formulation, that is itself built into the eighteenth-century experience. Does Daiches mean that the culture of the peasants and the culture of the gentry were once similar, but in the eighteenth century were growing apart? It is often implied that Scottish culture was once an ideal unity, and that differentiation only arose through 'Anglicisation' of the upper classes. This hypothetical homogeneity is, however, unlikely. We can, I think, more accurately interpret the cleavage of which Daiches speaks as a burgeoning interest among the cultured and literate in the relative qualities of the 'genteel' and the 'popular'. The opposition of gentility to peasanthood, of sophistication to the natural, and the like, were prominent features of the Romantic movement throughout Europe, and cannot be pinned to 'a split, or a series of splits, in the whole National ethos of Scotland, of which the Union was one significant cause' (ibid.). Nevertheless, concern with the Union may have given a political referent to these emergent literary dualities in Scotland that might, as Daiches argues, have given an energy to their expression in a

Scottish context that was lacking elsewhere.

What is clear, at least, is that there was throughout the eighteenth century a growing interest in native traditions on the part of the cultured in Scotland. It is ironic and probably not simply coincidental that this was occurring at a time when the new middle class of Edinburgh was becoming more and more cosmopolitan in its tastes and aspirations and, by more and less subtle means (not least their isolation in the splendour of the New Town of Edinburgh after 1770), more and more removed from contact with the simple native tradition in which it began to take such an interest. At the same time as such works as Ramsay's *The Evergreen* (1724), his later *The Tea Table Miscellany* (1730), and William Thomson's volume of Scots airs for the voice, *Orpheus Caledonius* (1725), were encouraging Scots to look to their native folk song for freshness and spontaneity, others were looking to both the distant past and contemporary savagery for just such qualities. This preoccupation with the 'Primitive', which merged towards the end of the century into what we now recognise as the Romantic movement, explains in part the position that the poems of Ossian came to occupy in eighteenth-century intellectual life.

The debate over primitive life revolved around two potentially contradictory theses. One argued that man in an early stage of society was in important ways more free, more spontaneous and more natural than civilised man, who had lost something irretrievable through his materialism, rationalism and sophistication. This thesis has come to be particularly associated with the works of Rousseau. The second argued that man, through society, was making continual progress towards a well-being and a level of achievement that only the leisured could produce, away from the desperate shifts of the savage living the life that Hobbes had called 'solitary, poore, nasty, brutish, and short' (T. Hobbes (1651), 1909, p. 97). These two theses did not necessarily exclude each other. Whitney gives an account of both the fertility and ambiguity of these ideas, referring to the:

> habit of keeping hold of as many fashions of thought at the same time as possible. I am referring . . . to the writers who clung to all the public favourites at once: who made their North American Indians creatures of sensibility, who made their characters of sensibility also utilitarians and rationalists, and who gave their perfectionists a passion for the simplicities of primitive life. (L. Whitney, 1934, p. 332)

The ideas of primitivism were much concerned with the state of art in savage and civilised society. Thomas Blackwell said of the age of Homer (with whom Ossian was later often compared) that it had 'natural and simple Manners: it is irresistible and inchanting; they best shew human Wants and Feelings; they give us back the Emotions of an arteless Mind' (T. Blackwell, 1736, p. 24). 'State and Form disguise Man; and Wealth and Luxury disguise Nature' (ibid., p. 25). He elaborates this:

> For so unaffected and simple were the Manners of these Times, that the Folds and Windings of the Human Breast lay open to the Eye; People were not as yet taught to be ashamed of themselves and their natural Appetites, nor consequently to dissemble them; They made no scruple of owning the Inclinations of their Heart, and openly indulged their Passions, which were entirely void of Art and Design. This was Homer's Happiness, with respect to Mankind, and the Living Part of his Poetry. (ibid., p. 34)

Dr Johnson stands as a figure to set against this exultation in the primitive life. Johnson, the rationalist, intellectual and arch-conservative, sums up for us the whole structure of the debate by the opinion that he expresses of Rousseau, the proto-Romantic, the dreamer, the revolutionary. The Doctor said, as Boswell reports: 'Rousseau, Sir, is a very bad man' (J. Boswell (1791), 1934, p. 12). When Boswell tried to tempt Johnson 'to argue for the superiour happiness of the savage life, upon the usual fanciful topicks' (ibid., p. 73), Johnson replied 'Sir, there can be nothing more false' (ibid.).

Johnson's scorn for the tenets of primitivism is apparent, and his low opinion of Scotland and the Scottish has been much publicised. These concerns were united by the Ossianic controversy, as Johnson stoutly affirmed the fraudulence both of Macpherson and of his purported Caledonian epics. Johnson's refusal to admit the possibility of the existence of any Gaelic literature can now be regretted as prejudice, but his low opinion of Macpherson's morals turned out to be justified, and he showed a more active concern for the Highlanders and their language than did many who were prepared to speak on Macpherson's behalf. At a time when most authorities in Lowland Scotland would gladly have seen an end of the Gaelic language, Johnson was instrumental in securing the right of the Highlander to a translation into his own vernacular of the Scriptures. He also made a journey, with Boswell, to see the Highlands and Islands for himself, and this at a time when the North of Scotland seemed, from London, to be no less wild and distant than the Americas or the South Seas (see S. Johnson, 1775). Even so, in judging between a largely hypothetical primitive life and his own civilised London, there can be no doubt where his sympathies lay.

Many of those who were most interested in early man were also the most enthusiastic and progressive of agricultural improvers. Henry Home (Lord Kames), for example, who produced his *Sketches of the History of Man* in 1774, and James Burnet (Lord Monboddo), who produced his *Of the Origin and Progress of Language* in 1773, were both 'thoroughly anti-primitivistic in spite of their interest in early man' (D.M. Foerster, 1950, p. 312). Smout says of these two and others like them that they had 'an overpowering interest in improvement. Lord Kames, with an estate in Stirlingshire, was the author of *The Gentleman Farmer*, the most influential of all Scottish handbooks before the 1790s: . . . Lord Monboddo had a model estate in Kincardineshire' (T.C. Smout, 1969, p. 351). Whitney expresses the ideologies of primitivism and progress as follows:

> The primitivistic ideology bade men look for their model of excellence to the first stages of society before man had been corrupted by civilisation; the idea of progress represented a point of view that looked forward to a possible perfection in the future. The primitivistic teaching, again, extolled simplicity; the faith in progress found its ideal in an increasing complexity. The former system of thought, finally, taught an ethics based on the natural affections; the latter system was built on an intellectualist foundation (L. Whitney, 1934, p. 1).

We should note, however, that these two ideologies were not, although they imagined themselves to be, mutually exclusive, but rather two sides of the same coin, contrary expressions of the same concern. Pearce says:

> it is perhaps erroneous to call the Scottish writers primitivists in any full sense of the word. For they were concerned to demonstrate, even when they were dissatisfied with certain aspects of civilised life, that there was no question of preferring savage to civilised life (R.H. Pearce, 1945, p. 203).

Those concerned with these issues were not possessed of any clear or detailed knowledge of the peoples whom they subjected to discussion, whether Highlanders or South Sea Islanders. It is therefore something of a misunderstanding to try to isolate the primitive and the progressive as discrete and internally coherent ideologies. The terms of the argument gathered strength from each other by their very opposition, and the debate was very much within and concerning a particular intellectual world. Foerster says:

> Perhaps it seems odd that critics should shift from one approach to another. But in one sense there was no real shift. If the primitivist was deeply interested in the epic, it was certainly not because it was early or reflected ways of life which he idealised. Fundamentally he did not care when a poem was written: it was simply that in primitive literature he found in abundance the poetic qualities which he happened to like best—passion and enthusiasm, novelty and vividness of expression . . . But he felt too that these admirable qualities were almost if not as common among certain writers of early ages. Hence, the primitivist idealised not merely Homer and Ossian but a rather large group of poets who were almost as exuberant and as picturesque as they: Ariosto, Tasso, Spenser, Shakespeare, Milton, and occasionally, Chaucer (D.M. Foerster, 1950, p. 322).

> [The primitivist] was in open rebellion against a system that appeared to enchain the poetic imagination and to put undue emphasis upon the use of judgement, a system which he found lifeless, calculating, analytical, objective (ibid., p. 315).

Clearly, primitivism could simply be read as a metaphorical criticism of the formalities and conventions of contemporary society. The Romantic movement, which grew out of primitivism, was, indeed, often quite self-consciously radical in a less indirect way than were the primitivists, who located their implied criticism of society elsewhere in time and place. Adam Ferguson, in *An Essay on the History of Civil Society*, published in 1767, after the appearance of Ossian, says:

> Every tribe of barbarians have their passionate or historic rhymes, which contain the superstition, the enthusiasm, and the admiration of glory, with which the breasts of men, in the earliest state of society, are possessed (A. Ferguson, 1767, p. 263).

> The artless song of the savage, the heroic legend of the bard, have sometimes a magnificent beauty, which no change of language can improve, and no refinements of the critic reform (ibid., p. 265).

> He delivers the emotions of the heart, in words suggested by the heart:

> for he knows no other (ibid., p. 266)

The dualities of primitivism are here clearly expressed. Whitney links the knowledge of the heart that is ascribed to the savage to the currently fashionable philosophy, arguing that the 'thesis of the immediacy of moral perception, purely non-rational in its nature, . . . paves the way for primitivistic inferences' (L. Whitney, 1934, p. 93). Ferguson also says of the savage:

> Whether at first obliged by the mere defects of his tongue, and the scantiness of proper expressions, or seduced by a pleasure of the fancy in stating the analogy of its objects, he clothes every conception in image and metaphor (A. Ferguson, 1767, p. 264).

This, deriving as it probably does from an experience of the poems of Ossian, is particularly interesting when we come to consider the peculiar symbolic skills which Renan and Arnold ascribe to the Celt. It could be argued, indeed, that Ferguson was moved to write this by the same sense of philosophical inadequacy that prompted Renan and Arnold almost a century later. Whitney says, 'There seems to have been considerable apprehension on the part of the scientists of the possible materialistic implications of their mechanical hypothesis' (L. Whitney, 1934, p. 140).

Although, when Ferguson was writing, the duality of science and arts was not thus clearly expressed, and although under 'arts' he includes, for example, science and politics, he is clearly concerned with the potential reductive capacity of a rationalist philosophy and a materialist world, expressed by the ominous terms 'industry' and 'manufactures' in the following:

> Many mechanical arts, indeed, require no capacity; they succeed best under a total suppression of sentiment and reason; and ignorance is the mother of industry as well as of superstition . . . Manufactures, accordingly, prosper most, where the mind is least consulted, and where the workshop may, without any great effort of imagination, be considered as an engine, the parts of which are men (A. Ferguson, 1767, p. 280).

Whitney says:

> Ferguson, who might have been led by his interest in the method of science into an attempt similar to that of Godwin and the utilitarians

> to found a moral science that would have the same objective validity as physical science, was diverted from that direction by his sense of the inadequacy of such an ethics (L. Whitney, 1934, p. 148).

These are issues which will be raised again throughout this work, particularly as they concern the image constructed of the Celt. The moral concerns and symbolic attributes considered appropriate to the opposed worlds of the physical sciences and of imagination, art and ethics are formative in the ostensibly ethnological discussions of the nineteenth century wherein the Celt acquired his character.

There are two other features of this proto-Romantic eighteenth century which should be mentioned in connection with the Celts – the cult of sensibility, and the Celt as Druid. The cult of sensibility, perhaps now best remembered for its parody in Jane Austen's *Sense and Sensibility*, found various literary forms, and was not overtly associated with Celts in any way. However, the ascription in the next century of a peculiarly acute sensibility to the Celt can perhaps be understood in its light, particularly when we consider the position of the Celt as a creature of prehistory and ancient customs, and remark that 'the language of sensibility passed very early into the literature of primitivism' (ibid., p. 108).

The second feature concerns the peculiar position of the Celt as a locus for the prehistoric, especially of all pre-Christian religion, in the form of Druids. Stuart Piggott, in his book *The Druids*, shows how an array of archaeological and literary facts and social conjectures were conflated in the construction of the literary Druid. Of particular importance in this context are the works of William Stukeley, the eighteenth-century antiquarian whose works *Stonehenge* (1740) and *Abury* (1743) popularised the now unshakeable and annually commemorated belief that these monuments were Druidical and Celtic. Piggott says that Stukeley's 'advocacy for a Druidic origin for Avebury, Stonehenge and other stone circles long continued to consolidate and reinforce what was now an established piece of national folk-lore' (S. Piggott, 1977, p. 135). It is to the eighteenth century that we owe the association of many prehistoric monuments and rock formations with Druids, which is still a major source of the association of the Celts with mysticism and the more exotic of religious practices. Piggott says, 'Stukeley was eagerly followed, adopted, improved upon and even outdone as English taste moved towards new ideas of romanticism and the idealization of a hypothetical simplicity among primitive peoples' (S. Piggott, 1966, p. 21). The primitive, the Celt and sensibility all came together as 'Archaeology and

Romanticism walked hand in hand, familiar twin figures in the English scene' (S. Piggott, 1937, p. 36).

It was into this world, inclined as it thus was to debate the nature of the primitive, the peasant, the prehistoric and their associated customs and arts that James Macpherson brought the Scottish Gael, by the publication, beginning in 1760, of epic prose poetry, which he claimed to be his translation of the works of Ossian, an ancient Caledonian bard. It will be helpful at this stage to give a short account of the appearance of the Ossianic poems, their rise to popularity, and the controversy that gathered around them. This is well trodden ground, although there is still room for argument. The following summary is drawn from a variety of sources, notably J.S. Smart (1905), D. Thomson (1963), and H. Mackenzie (1805).

James Macpherson was born in 1736 at Ruthven, in Badenoch, the son of a farmer. He attended both Aberdeen and Edinburgh universities, before taking a job as schoolteacher in his native parish. He soon left this to take charge, as tutor, of Thomas Graham (later Lord Lynedoch), son of the Laird of Balgowan. It was in this capacity, in the autumn of 1759, that he met John Home (author of the then famous tragedy *Douglas*) in the spa town of Moffat. Macpherson claimed (quite possibly in good faith) a knowledge of Gaelic poetry, Home expressed an interest, and shortly afterwards Macpherson supplied him with a short tale called *The Death of Oscar*, which Macpherson claimed to be his own translation of a Gaelic original. Thomson says that this meeting 'may justly be regarded as the beginning of the Ossianic industry' (D. Thomson, 1963, p. 7). Macpherson, at Home's request, produced more of these 'translations'. Home, much impressed, showed them to his literary friends the Rev. Dr Alexander Carlyle, and the Rev. Dr Hugh Blair, then Professor of Rhetoric and Belles Lettres in the University of Edinburgh. The reaction was, in Carlyle's words, 'I was perfectly astonished at the poetical genius displayed in them. We agreed that it was a precious discovery, and that as soon as possible it should be published to the world' (cited H. Mackenzie, 1805, Appendix 66). The pieces of Ossianic poetry thus gathered were indeed published, in an anonymous little edition, in 1760, as *Fragments of Ancient Poetry, collected in the Highlands of Scotland, and translated from the Gaelic or Erse Language.* These caused considerable interest, and a second edition was produced within the year to which Blair wrote a preface, where he says:

> The public may depend on these as genuine fragments of ancient Scottish poetry. . . . there is reason to hope that one work of considerable

> length, and which deserves to be styled an heroic poem, might be recovered and translated, if encouragement were given to such an undertaking (H. Blair, 1760, vii).

Encouragement was not slow in arriving. A subscription list was started by the Faculty of Advocates, an important centre of the cultured and influential in eighteenth-century Edinburgh, to provide Macpherson with funds to collect the supposed epic. The subscription list included Hugh Blair, John Home, Adam Ferguson, David Hume and James Boswell. Thus provided, Macpherson set off for the Highlands from Edinburgh in August 1760 and, as Smart puts it, 'journeyed northward to Skye, crossed the sea, and scampered briskly through North Uist, South Uist and Benbecula. He had introductions and was well received' (J.S. Smart, 1905, p. 99). After only two months Macpherson had returned from the Isles to Badenoch, saying in a letter that he had 'gathered all worth notice from that quarter' (H. Mackenzie, 1805, p. 151). At this stage Macpherson's activities became, not for the last time, shadowy, but it is thought that he spent his time in Badenoch in the winter and spring of 1760-1 preparing his epic, probably with the help of two relatives who were better Gaelic scholars than he, Ewan Macpherson, a Badenoch schoolmaster, and Lachlan Macpherson, the Laird of Strathmashie. Macpherson had, in fact, in his travels gathered together an important collection of Gaelic manuscripts which, but for his intervention, might have been entirely lost. Important among these were the early-sixteenth-century work now known as *The Book of the Dean of Lismore*,[4] *An Leabhar Dearg* or *The Red Book*, which Macpherson acquired from Neil MacMhuirich, a member of the famous bardic dynasty, and *An Duanaire Ruadh* or *The Red Rhymer*, from the archives of Clanranald. The subsequent loss of the latter has led Mackintosh to say: 'Its disappearance raises the question of how many others of the Mss. may have gone the same way. Mackenzie and Macpherson were not very conscientious guardians of their treasures according to present day ideas of trusteeship' (D.T. Mackintosh, 1947, p. 15).

It is clear that Macpherson had a considerable amount of genuine Gaelic material, manuscript and orally collected, some at least of which was concerned with the characters with whom Macpherson was already familiar from Highland lore, and on whom he had already based his *Fragments.* Some of the *Fragments* have a basis in the Gaelic oral tradition (see L.C. Stern, 1898), and Thomson argues that:

> It is probably fair to say that at first Macpherson intended no serious

> deception. His 'translations' in the *Fragments* were either very free, or in some cases practically fictitious, but this was not in violent disagreement with the literary ethics of the time (D. Thomson, 1963, p. 12).

However, faced with the intractable orthography of the manuscripts that he had collected, Thomson suggests that 'the bold decision was taken to use imagination where scholarship failed' (ibid.). The relationship of Macpherson's translations to their originals was thus clouded and ambiguous from the beginning. Thomson says, 'The study of Celtic history and Celtic philology was in its infancy, and Macpherson and his close friends apparently judged that their work would not be seriously challenged' (ibid.). Macpherson secured the patronage, with the help of introductions, of Strahan, a London publisher, and of the Earl of Bute, then Prime Minister, to whom the completed epic, *Fingal*, published in London in 1761, was discreetly dedicated. *Fingal*, an epic prose poem, conflating the characters of the Irish Ulster and Ossianic mythological cycles, Roman British history, and borrowings, conscious or otherwise, from English literary sources, was followed in 1763 by *Temora*, another epic. By the time this latter was published, the Ossianic controversy was in full swing.

The controversy is usually considered to be principally concerned with the ambiguous relationship between Macpherson's Ossian and its real or imagined source. The Ossianic controversy concerned itself, however, with much more than the location of the Gaelic originals of Macpherson's 'translations'. The poems of Ossian provided a medium within which all the dominant preoccupations of the age could be aired, as the relative merits of Celt and Anglo-Saxon, modern and ancient, civilised and savage, Scottish and Irish, etc., were endlessly debated. There is not space here to do justice to the history of the controversy, but it is worth noting, when we consider the longevity of the debate, that sound argument against the authenticity of the poems was raised very soon after the publication of *Fingal.* Dr Ferdinando Warner, in his *Remarks on the History of Fingal and Other Poems of Ossian*, 1762, pointed out that as authentic history *Fingal* was glaringly inaccurate, locating Irish heroes in Scotland, and permitting the anachronism of contact between Cuthullin, Finn, Romans and Danish invaders, which characters were known to span a period of at least five hundred years. Macpherson attempted to forestall such criticism in his introduction to the third edition of the Poems of Ossian, saying of Irish poems concerning Ossian that:

> they appear to have been the work of a very modern period. The pious ejaculations they contain, their allusions to the manners of the time, fix them to the fifteenth century . . . The idiom is so corrupted and so many words borrowed from the English (J. Macpherson, 1765, xli).

He speaks of the 'improbable and self-condemned tales of Keating and O'Flaherty. Credulous and puerile to the last degree, they have disgraced the antiquities they meant to establish' (ibid., xvii).[5] This provocation helped to establish one prominent feature of future debate – a struggle for ownership of Ossian between the Gaels of Scotland and Ireland. Macpherson's claim for Scotland as the birthplace of his heroes, and the very question of the authenticity of the poems themselves, became matters of Scottish national pride. Walter Scott, speaking of the question of authenticity, said:

> It has been unnecessarily and improperly made a shibboleth, to distinguish the true Celt from his Saxon or Pictish neighbours; and, of course, it becomes more difficult to attain truth, in proportion as the passions take arms in the controversy (W. Scott, 1805, p. 436).

Flower says:

> The inauthenticity of the translations was made a matter of national honour and every Scotchman who had ever heard a shepherd or a boatman declaim an Ossianic lay persuaded himself that in Macpherson's poems he recognised the very voice of ancient tradition (R. Flower, 1928, p. 6).

Another serious criticism of Macpherson's Ossian was raised in the *Journal des Sçavans* in 1762. Various similarities between *Fingal* and both *Paradise Lost* and the *Book of Isaiah* were pointed to, and the conclusion reached that 'L'honneur d'avoir créé ces Poésies touchantes et sublimes, vaudroit bien l'heureux hazard de les avoir découvertes' (November 1762, p. 64). This accusation of plagiarism was thoroughly taken up by Malcolm Laing in his ironically entitled exegesis *The Poems of Ossian etc. containing the Poetical Works of James Macpherson*, where 'a critical and minute examination was bestowed upon the poems, in the course of which every simile, and almost every poetical image, were traced to their source' (Malcolm Laing, 1805, v). The Highland Society of Scotland, worried by the slur cast on Highland culture and Highland integrity by the controversy, appointed a committee to enquire into the authenticity of Ossian, which published its report in 1805. The committee could not, although they wished to, discover any simple Gaelic original for any of Macpherson's poems, and were reduced to creating an original by borrowing lines and images from a variety of sources. Walter Scott, in a review of this which Smart calls 'one of the most satisfying contributions to the debate' (J.S. Smart, 1905, p. 178), concludes that:

> we believe no well informed person will now pretend that Ossian is to be quoted as historical authority, or that a collection of Gaelic poems does anywhere exist, of which Macpherson's version can be regarded as a faithful, or even a loose translation; . . . But there existed, before the times of Macpherson, a sort of general basis of tradition, on which the poems, whether collected or composed by himself, appear to have been founded (W. Scott, 1805, p. 429).

This balanced conclusion was reinforced by the most scholarly of later works, such as J.F. Campbell's *Leabhar na Féinne* of 1872. This important collection of genuine Scottish Gaelic Ossianic material would probably never have been gathered but for the impetus provided by Macpherson, as Campbell admits, while reluctantly dismissing Macpherson's Ossian as a fake. Ossian, however, remained a force to be reckoned with in the European literary world, creating its own validation and its own authenticity in the revolution of sentiment that accompanied it. It is not in the racial issues, in accusations of plagiarism, in the obscurity of Macpherson's activities, or in concern for the location and nature of the Gaelic originals that we can understand the enduring appeal of Macpherson's Ossian, but rather in a 'study of the romantic temperament which [Macpherson] did so much to form' (R. Flower, 1928, p. 5).

Macpherson's Ossian was largely inauthentic with respect to any genuine Gaelic verse tradition, but it was the very voice of authenticity for the developing sentiments of Romanticism in Europe. The inauthenticity of Ossian was related, in no simple way, to the inauthenticity of the whole Romantic movement in its relation to its imagined source, in human nature, and a natural society freed from conventions, allowed spontaneously to speak its truths. This inauthenticity, however, was not so easily established as was that of Ossian in its relationship to its more specifically defined source, as we can see from the meagre effect that the proof of Macpherson's duplicity had on the eminence of Ossian in the literary world. Ossian, ambiguously located in a contemporary peasantry and an ancient Heroic age, provided a perfect medium for contemporary debate about the nature of art and society. We can get some idea of the self-absorption of the debate from the lack of interest shown in genuine Gaelic traditions except in so far as they were to constitute validation for Macpherson. Stern says, 'While the poems of Macpherson were the object of unprecedented popular laudation, the veritable folk ballads on which they were founded got scarcely any attention, although the latter were of the highest probative value in the controversy' (L.C. Stern, 1898, p. 277). Scott speaks of the difficulties involved in trying to determine the question of authenticity by asking the Highlanders themselves:

> The names of the heroes, and of their more noted adventures, being deeply riveted in the imagination of the Highlanders, it has become difficult for them to understand that it is the fidelity of Macpherson's translations which is in question, and not the existence of traditionary poetry respecting Ossian and Fingal (W. Scott, 1805, p. 435).

This difficulty of understanding on the part of the Highlanders is not, perhaps, as surprising now as it seemed then. If Macpherson had indeed produced his poems from oral rather than manuscript sources (in so far as they had any Gaelic basis), then surely the next step on the part of the critics would be to take an interest in the oral 'literature' rather than to revise totally their opinion of Ossian? The interest stimulated in the Gaelic oral tradition did not, however, bear significant fruit until the middle of the nineteenth century, and the majority of English critics refocused their attentions on Byron rather than turn to the study of folk ballads in a strange and difficult tongue.

Stuart explains the appeal that Ossian had to the eighteenth-century reader:

> To us, there is nothing wildly strange in the spectacle of these gigantic, gloomy, verbose warriors, ranting, battling, and bleeding in an atmosphere of continuous meteorological metaphor and simile; but to a large part of the reading public it was in 1762 (and for long after) a wonder, an enchantment, something to set nerves tingling and hearts throbbing (D.M. Stuart, 1948, p. 16).

Flower argues that 'The success of Macpherson's Ossian is one of the miracles of opportunity. It fell upon an age already infected with the twin passions of Jean Jacques Rousseau for the noble savage and the mountains' (R. Flower, 1928, p. 16). Thomson makes the same point, tying it more specifically to Scottish history, the uprising of 1745 and the Battle of Culloden being recent memories when Ossian was first published:

> For propagandist purposes, and through simple ignorance, the Highlands had long been designated a barbaric area, and its inhabitants were sometimes called savages. This had the natural result of arousing the curiosity of people who had anthropological interests, and the second half of the eighteenth century brought a long succession of intrepid explorers to the Highlands. We may conclude with some confidence that James Macpherson was instinctively aware of the climate of opinion concerning the Highlands, and took some advantage of it (D. Thomson, 1963, p. 15).

Macpherson's work had not only political and ethnological relevance, but also appealed to 'The literary revolt against the correctness, prettiness, and artificiality of Pope's school of poetry' (A. Macbain, 1887, p. 152). Snyder says that:

> there is a general agreement that the poetry of the late neo-classical period suffered from lack of appeal to the imagination, from monotony of subject matter, from failure to describe adequately the grandeur of nature, and from over use of the mythology of Greece and Rome (E.D. Snyder, 1923, p. 195).

Involved in 'a more or less conscious reaction against the banality of the failing conventions of the classical school' (R. Flower, 1928, p. 4), we find that Macpherson 'emphasises the landscape, marks the revolt of the heart over the mind, sentiment over reason, shows the uprightness of primitive man, and sings the pleasures of melancholy' (H. Okun, 1967, p. 329). Flower notes that:

> the characteristic Ossianic vagueness, the mist on the mountains, the wild landscape under the uncertain moon, the undefined longings of the slackly characterised heroes of Fingal . . . had certainly contributed much to the mental habit of the generation . . . And from that day to this they have formed a great part of the meaning which readers and writers and critics who did not know the Celtic languages have attached to the word 'Celtic' (R. Flower, 1928, p. 6).

Macpherson's Ossianic poems were written in a style which has come to be known as 'measured prose'. Okun describes it as follows:

> His prose is rhythmic and flexible. There are no abstract ideas, only images. The sentences are short and simple but the narrative is weighed down and made abstruse by inserting stories within stories, by naming people rather than by describing them, by strange expressions and by innumerable metaphors, elliptical similes, and long apostrophes. As a result, the poetry moves very slowly and seems to be felt through a fog, a presence as intangible as it is real (H. Okun, 1967, p. 328).

The following example of Macpherson's style is the conclusion to *The Songs of Selma*, where Ossian laments, in characteristic tones, an age gone by:

> But age is now on my tongue; my soul has failed! I hear, at times, the ghosts of bards, and learn their pleasant song. But memory fails on my mind. I hear the call of years! They say, as they pass along, why does Ossian sing? Soon shall he lie in the narrow house, and no bard shall raise his fame! Roll on, ye dark-brown years; ye bring no joy on your course! Let the tomb open to Ossian, for his strength has failed. The sons of song are gone to rest. My voice remains, like a blast, that roars, lonely, on a sea-surrounded rock, after the winds are laid. The dark moss whistles there; the distant mariner sees the waving trees! (W. Sharp (ed.), 1896, p. 416).

Thomson calls this 'a style which bears very little resemblance to anything in Gaelic literature' (D.S. Thomson, 1963, p. 14), although it has been argued that 'many of the peculiar features of his poetic prose result from an attempt to imitate the style of the ballads' (R.P. Fitzgerald, 1966, p. 27).

Dr Johnson strongly disapproved of Ossian. Smart argues that: 'All the canons of excellence, as Johnson understood it, were broken in the Caledonian Epics. Clearness, definiteness, distinctness of idea and perfection of form were his first and final tests: to apply them to Ossian was to condemn it at once' (J.S. Smart, 1905, p. 147). David Hume, although enthusiastic about the *Fragments*, became sceptical on hearing of an epic, and in a letter to Blair in 1763 said of Ossian: 'It is vain to say that their beauty will support them, independent of their authenticity' (cited H. Mackenzie, 1805, p. 5). He later wrote a highly critical *Essay on the Authenticity of Ossian's Poems*, which, however, was never published, from 'a kindly feeling to his friend Dr. Blair' (cited J. Hill Burton, 1846, p. 86). Neither Johnson nor Hume could accept that an unlettered peasantry was capable of producing an ordered work of art. Johnson grudgingly credited them with 'some wandering ballads, if any can be found' (S. Johnson, 1775, p. 273). Hume said, after the publication of the *Fragments*, that 'we have endeavoured to put Mr. Macpherson on a way of procuring us more of these wild flowers' (cited J. Hill Burton, 1846, p. 464). At the same time, however, he voiced the reservation that 'if a regular epic poem, or even anything of that kind, nearly regular, should also come from that rough climate, or uncivilised people, it would appear to me a phenomenon altogether unaccountable' (ibid.).

There were many, however, who felt like Blair, and who saw life and truth where Dr Johnson saw only technical and intellectual inadequacy. Blair says, in the *Critical Dissertation on the Poems of Ossian* which he appended to the third edition of Ossian in 1765, and which provides a clear picture of the intellectual preoccupations within which Ossian made his appeal:

> in every period of society, human manners are a curious spectacle; and the most natural pictures of antient manners are exhibited in the antient poems of nations. These present to us . . . the history of human imagination and passion. They make us acquainted with the notions and feelings of our fellow creatures in the most artless ages; . . . before those refinements of society had taken place, which enlarge indeed, and diversify the transactions, but disguise the manners of mankind (H. Blair, 1765, p. 3).

> For many circumstances of those times which we call barbarous, are favourable to the poetical spirit. That state, in which human nature shoots wild and free, though unfit for other improvements, certainly encourages the high exertions of fancy and passion (ibid., p. 4).

> Prone to exaggerate, they describe every thing in the strongest colours; which of course renders their speech picturesque and figurative. Figurative language owes its rise chiefly to two causes; to the want of proper names for objects, and to the influence of imagination and passion over the forms of expression (ibid.).

> As the world advances, the understanding gains ground upon the imagination; the understanding is more exercised; the imagination,

less (ibid., p. 5).

> All the circumstances, indeed, of Ossian's composition, are favourable to the sublime, more perhaps than to any other species of beauty. Accuracy and correctness; artfully connected narration; exact method and proportion of parts, we may look for in polished times. The gay and the beautiful will appear to more advantage in the midst of smiling scenery and pleasurable themes. But amidst the rude scene of nature, amidst rocks and torrents, and whirlwinds and battles, dwells the sublime (ibid., p. 107).

That many agreed with this we can see both from the enthusiasm with which the Romantic movement made use of the dualities that Blair employs, and from the enormous corpus of Ossianic literature that appeared over the one hundred and fifty years succeeding the publication of *Fingal.* Black, in a bibliography compiled in 1926, lists 88 English editions of the poems of Ossian, with various accretions and omissions, and excluding editions of *Fragments* and Gaelic editions. He also lists translations into 'Bohemian', Danish, Dutch, French, German, Hungarian, Italian, Polish, Russian, Spanish and Swedish (see G.F. Black, 1926). Okun describes a minor vogue for Ossianic painting (see H. Okun, 1967) and says:

> *Carthon*, one of the poems, was translated into French as early as 1762 while the collected works followed suit in 1777. Diderot loved them. Voltaire parodied them. Ossianic plays, operas, and mimes were written. They influenced or attracted Mme. de Staël, Chateaubriand, Lamartine, Alfred de Vigny, Victor Hugo, and Alfred de Musset. Napoleon became a fervent admirer after he had read the poems in the Italian translation by Cesarotti (ibid., p. 329).

Smart says, 'The roll of admirers in Germany is a large one. Besides Goethe, Herder, and Klopstock, it includes Lessing, Schiller, Novalis, Bürger and Tieck' (J.S. Smart, 1905, p. 16). Goethe wrote the climax of his novel *Werther* around a tragic reading of the *Songs of Selma.* Bernadotte, under Napoleon's influence, christened his son Oscar after Ossian's son, and the name passed permanently into the Swedish royal house when Bernadotte became king. 'James Fenimore Cooper gave his Indians Ossianic traits and had them speak an Ossianic language. Longfellow, Emerson, Thoreau and Whitman were affected by it' (H. Okun, 1967, p. 329). It was, perhaps, the spirit of the age, a mysterious Ossianic presence, that provided the answer to Blair's innocent question to Hume, in a letter written in 1763:

> is it a thing which any man of sense can suppose, that Macpherson would venture to forge such a body of poetry, and give it to the public as ancient poems and songs, well known at this day through all the Highlands of Scotland, when he could have been refuted and exposed by every one of his own countrymen? Is it credible that he could bring so many thousand people into a conspiracy with him to keep his secret? (cited J. Hill Burton, 1846, p. 468).

The conspiracy was a complicated series of intellectual involutions, where the Celt that the Romantic period imagined became in turn an external validation for the aesthetics of that art. Romance, the Celt and Ossian were read into each other in many different ways, metaphorical and rhetorical, to create a discourse whose autonomy was barely under threat from external disturbance or factual refutation.

A factual settlement persuasive to all parties would in any case have been impossible to provide. Although the issues through which the debate took its form were relatively clear-cut, the possibilities of verification offered were not. Thus none of the protagonists ever said anything that did not have some measure of both plausibility and truth. Both sides gained a veracity from the manifest overstatements and misunderstandings of the other, and forfeited their own veracity in the same way. The vigour of the contest provoked a polarisation such that the poems had to be, for example, either entirely by Macpherson or entirely by Ossian, entirely false or entirely genuine, entirely Scots or entirely Irish, genuine history or a tissue of lies, and so on.

The effete compromises that we can offer today as a solution to these once burning issues would have satisfied no one. We might say, for example, that the Ossianic poems were written largely by Macpherson, whose command of Gaelic was not great; that they did, nevertheless, have a genuine Gaelic basis in both documentary and oral evidence, with which Macpherson was familiar; that the oral tradition, known to Macpherson from his own childhood as well as from his somewhat perfunctory expeditions, was common to both Scottish and Irish Gaelic-speakers, and did indeed speak of genuine historical figures and periods; that the oral tradition nevertheless ran together times, people and places in a manner oblivious to the more literal demands of eighteenth-century historiography, as we now know that an oral tradition, even one concerned with genealogy, is apt to do; that the nature of the process of transmission of an oral tradition meant that to ask questions like 'Who were its composers?' and 'When was it composed?' was to permit of no sensible answer: such solutions would not have been to anybody's taste, and would have been far too complicated for ready accommodation within the self-indulgent dialectics of the nascent aesthetic of Romantic art. The eighteenth-century literary world was exposed to the possibility of an extensive and sophisticated oral tradition, and found itself thoroughly unequipped to deal in any authentic way with such a phenomenon. As the argument proceeded, however, little fuelled as it was by access to hard fact, conjecture became reality, conclusion became evidence, and the Scottish Highlander was often forgotten.

We can get some idea of the impenetrability of the discourse that the Celt and Romantic art conspired to provide, and of the purely internal validations that appeared, from the following:

> whether we regard the Ossianic poems as genuine productions of the Ancient Gael, or fabrications of Macpherson, there cannot be a doubt that in that publication the Gael for the first time put in their claim to be recognised on the field, not only of England's, but of Europe's literature. Henceforth Highland scenery and Celtic feeling entered as a conscious element into the poetry of England and of other nations, and touched them with something of its peculiar sentiment (J.C. Shairp, 1881, p. 260).

The simple tautology whereby the Celt was constructed on the basis of Macpherson's Ossian, and then used to argue their authenticity as a truly Celtic product, can be seen at its simplest in the following, written almost two hundred years after the publication of Ossian, using forms of language that have forgotten their origin:

> Yet when all defects of style and content have been marked, all anomalies and absurdities recognised, all debts acknowledged, there remains in Macpherson's work a curious quality, Celtic and crepuscular, elusive yet pervasive, not to be matched in any antecedent English prose or verse (D.M. Stuart, 1948, p. 17).

Other commentators have had similar judgements to make. Matthew Arnold provided one of the most often-quoted contributions to the debate:

> I am not going to criticise Macpherson's *Ossian* here. Make the part of

> what is forged, modern, tawdry, spurious, in the book, as large as you please; . . . But there will still be left in the book a residue with the very soul of the Celtic genius in it, and which has the proud distinction of having brought this soul of the Celtic genius into contact with the genius of the nations of modern Europe (M. Arnold, 1891, p. 128).

Magnus Maclean says of this passage, 'To recognise the truth of this eulogy, we have only to turn to the poems themselves, and listen to the tender and sublime bard, son of the winged days, as he awakes the voices of the past' (M. Maclean, 1904, p. 86). In any case, Macpherson himself was, for the purposes of later debate, a Celt, and so Blackie says of Ossian:

> it is a genuine Celtic production; if by Macpherson, then the natural outcome of a youth spent in Badenoch, behind the mist-covered caps of the Grampians, and beside the swift-rushing waters of the Spey; if in the main, both in tone and materials, much more ancient (as I believe), and standing on the broad basis of popular tradition, then it possesses all the interest that belongs to every form of popular poetry as an exponent of a certain type of popular life (J.S. Blackie, 1876, p. 233).

Principal Shairp, lecturing in Oxford in the same capacity as Arnold had before him, said:

> there is something which is of the very essence of the Highland glens and mountains, something unexpressed by any modern poet, but which the old Ossianic poetry alone expresses; this, if nothing else, would convince me that the poetry, which conveys this feeling, is no modern fabrication, but is native to the hills, connatural, I had almost said, with the granite mountains, among which it has survived (J. Shairp, 1881, p. 284).

It is not that these commentators fail to take a balanced and informed view of the question of authenticity. It is rather that the language which the poems of Ossian helped to render appropriate for description of the Celt has become entirely divorced from, and of apparently independent origin to, those poems. Consequently even those who are most convinced of the fraudulence of Macpherson's Ossian find no incongruity in employing, to describe genuine Celtic literature, imagery whose origin can only be understood within the context of the Ossianic controversy and the Romantic movement. Macbain, for example, says that 'summed up in a general way, Macpherson is . . . hopelessly astray' (A. Macbain, 1887, p. 149), but he concludes by quoting with approval Arnold's views on Ossian, as to the 'residue with the very soul of the Celtic genius in it' (M. Arnold, 1891, p. 128). Just how problematical a conflict of views this is I attempt to show in Chapter 3, but it is worth quoting here Macbain's views on the Celtic character. He speaks of 'their wonderful quickness of apprehension, their impressibility and great craving for knowledge, . . . generous to a degree; prompt in action but not very capable of sustained effort' (A. Macbain, 1917, p. 56). In Chapter 3, I attempt to show that these characteristics have their roots not in an observable Celtic character, or in misapprehensions by, and over-innocent readings of, Tacitus and Caesar, but rather in the intellectual world whose imagery both brought the poems of Ossian to prominence, and drew strength from them. Nutt's opinion that 'for the student, whether of Celtic myth and saga, of Celtic Archaeology, of Gaelic style and literary form, Macpherson's poems are worthless' (A. Nutt, 1899, p. 2), while it might sound unequivocal enough, cannot unsay what Lovejoy has called:

> a massive historical fact which no one is likely to deny – namely, that in the last quarter of the eighteenth century, especially in the 1780's and 1790's, there were discovered, invented, or revived, chiefly in Germany, a large number of ideas which had been relatively, though not always absolutely, unfamiliar or uninfluential through most of the seventeenth and eighteenth centuries; and that the total impact of what we may call, for short, the new ideas of the 1780's and 1790's (including revivals of old ideas under 'new'), as they developed, ramified, and were diffused during the following decades, profoundly altered the habitual preconceptions, valuations, and ruling catch-words of an increasingly large part of the educated classes in Europe, so that there came into vogue in the course of the nineteenth century and in our own a whole series of intellectual fashions – from styles in poetry and styles in metaphysics to styles in government – which had no parallels in the preceding period (A.O. Lovejoy, 1941, p. 260).

It was into the fabric of this 'massive historical fact' that Macpherson's Ossian brought the Scottish Gael, and it is largely within that fabric that he is still to be found. MacLean says that the Ossianic controversy 'has constituted one of the last outbursts of racial animosity between Celt and Anglo-Saxon, and hence its virulence' (M. MacLean, 1904, p. 83). We can, I think, justifiably turn this judgement on its head, and argue that the controversy was rather the first outburst of racial animosity between Celt and Anglo-Saxon. We must remember that it is an academic assessment from the period since 1760 that makes an argument between Celt and Anglo-Saxon out of, say, Bannockburn, or the 'Forty-five. Piggott has shown that it was not until the eighteenth century that the word that Julius Caesar used to describe a Gaulish people was drawn out of its Classical source to come into common parlance as a word to describe the prehistoric inhabitants of the British Isles, or the modern peoples who speak languages that we now call 'Celtic' (see S. Piggott, 1966). As for 'Anglo-Saxon', MacLauchlan, rather in spite of himself, makes the point well:

> Let it be observed, then, that the very name Anglo-Saxon is a thing of yesterday. In fact, our neighbours do not find it easy to fit themselves with a name. For a long time they were Saxons, a name now well-nigh obsolete, save in the vocabulary of the Celt. Then they became Goths, a name under which Pinkerton fought many a fierce and bloody battle on their behalf. Then they suddenly became Anglo-Saxons, and from that they are passing into Teutons. What they will be before all is over it is hard to say (T. MacLauchlan, 1857, p. 11).

3 ALEXANDER MACDONALD AND DUNCAN MACINTYRE

Before going on to consider the later consequences of the Ossianic controversy, we can profitably turn from Ossian to the genuine Gaelic art, particularly the poetry, that was being produced during the middle and late eighteenth century. To this period belong a group of poets who are considered to represent a period of unusual artistic achievement, comparable, for example, to the roughly contemporary group of English Romantic poets. This particular contemporaneity has been the source of much misunderstanding, as will become clear.

The major poets concerned, who left after them an artistic vacuum that is only recently considered to have been in any way filled, were Alexander Macdonald (*c.* 1700-*c.* 1770), John MacCodrum (*c.* 1710-96), Duncan Macintyre (1724-*c.* 1812), Rob Donn (*c.* 1715-78), Dugald Buchanan (1716-68), William Ross (1762-91), and Ewen MacLachlan (1773-1822). These poets represent a remarkable cross-section of the community, from unlettered gamekeeper (Macintyre) to university academic (MacLachlan), and span a period during which Highland society was undergoing profound change. The failure of the rebellion of 1745 and the subsequent repression of the clans stand as symbols for a century which began with a still largely autonomous Highland world, with vestiges of its ancient institutions, and ended with the first of the Highland Clearances. Thomson illustrates the decline: 'The century had opened with the old age of Niall MacMhuirich, one of the last of the literate bards of the old school. By 1800 the representative of the MacMhuirichs, Lachlann, was not able to read or write' (D. Thomson, 1974, 217). We are told that 'the policy of the Anglicisers was at last showing results, and five hundred years of Gaelic literary history was at an end' (D. Thomson, 1963, p. 19). When we consider the high level of achievement of Gaelic poets in this period, it is instructive to remember Dr Johnson's opinion of Ossian that 'it is too long to be remembered, and the language formerly had nothing written' (S. Johnson, 1775, p. 273). Smout says of these poets that they:

> made no contribution to the culture of the rest of Scotland, where contemporary Highland poetry and music was neither known nor regarded as worth knowing. . . . by the last quarter of the century

> their society was being so rocked by catastrophic social and economic changes as to provide little stable ground even for the further development of Gaelic culture (T.C. Smout, 1975, p. 471).

The eighteenth-century Gaelic poets that I have mentioned did not have immediate access to the formal training of the bardic schools, although Macdonald at least 'may well have known the last two practising poets of the MacMhuirich dynasty' (D. Thomson, 1974, p. 159). He was acquainted with some of their skills, and Thomson suggests (ibid.) that it is his shortcomings in these which he laments in his 'Guidhe no Urnaigh an Ughdair do 'n Cheòlraidh' ('Entreaty or Prayer of the Author to the Muses'), when he says, in the last lines:

> 'S ni gun susbaint ealain gun sgoil
> Air subject mar mhil.
> Gur h-aimhgheur mo pheann, 's neo sgaiteach mo bhil,
> Mo cheann cha mhol;
> Mo phaipeir is m' ink tha iad làn de chron,
> Is uireasbhuidh sin.
> (A. Macdonald and A. Macdonald, 1924, p. 14).

> a thing of no substance is an art that's unschooled,
> though the subject were sweet.
> My pen is blunt, my lips not sharp,
> my brain does not praise,
> my paper and ink are full of defects,
> a sad lack that (trans. D. Thomson, 1974, p. 159).

Besides the bardic tradition, the eighteenth-century poets had non-bardic 'vernacular' poets of the seventeenth century to follow, notably John Macdonald (Iain Lom) of Keppoch, and Mary MacLeod (Mairi Nighean Alasdair Ruaidh) of the MacLeods of Harris and Dunvegan. Thomson says that 'By the end of the 16th century we are justified in speaking of "the survivors of the bardic order", although in fact there were survivors for more than a hundred years after this time' (D. Thomson, 1955, p. 2). The non-bardic seventeenth-century poets had to some extent assimilated the bardic tradition. Watson says of Mary MacLeod and the classical bardic tradition that:

> her times permitted her to have a thorough familiarity with its characteristics and ways of thought. These she absorbed and made her

own; and if, despite the vast discrepancy in diction and technique, there is to be found in modern poetry any affinity with the earlier style, we owe this to Mary MacLeod and her contemporaries (J. Carmichael Watson, 1965, xxvi).

The Gaelic poets of the eighteenth century were heirs to a long literary history. Although the changes in the society around them led them to respond, such that 'Gaelic poetry breathes a new air in the eighteenth century, and shows a new vigour' (D. Thomson, 1974, p. 156), the new influences were assimilated artistically, and purely Gaelic poetic traditions were found to be adequate to their expression. Alexander Macdonald is considered to be the major figure in this synthesis, and his 'innovations have left a deep mark on eighteenth-century Gaelic poetry as a whole' (ibid., p. 157). In order to detail some of the characteristics of this eighteenth-century poetry, I will limit myself to a consideration of the two most celebrated of Highland bards, Alexander Macdonald, otherwise known as Alasdair Mac Mhaighstir Alasdair, or simply Mac Mhaighstir Alasdair, and Duncan Macintyre, otherwise known as Duncan Bàn (Fair Duncan), Donnchadh Bàn Mac an t-Saoir (Duncan Ban Macintyre), and Donnchadh Bàn nan Oran (Fair Duncan of the Songs).

Our information on the lives of both of these poets is scanty. Campbell says that 'the history of Macdonald's life is extraordinarily obscure for one who is generally accepted as the foremost Scottish Gaelic poet' (J.L. Campbell, 1933, p. 33). Our ignorance in this respect is some measure of the isolation and autonomy of the Highland world of their time. What information we have is gathered in the two most recent editions of their works (see A. Macdonald and A. Macdonald, 1924, and A. MacLeod, 1952). It is a reflection of the difficulties facing Gaelic publishing, with its small readership, that there is no good modern edition of the works of Macdonald, and that MacLeod's edition of Macintyre is a scholarly rather than a popular edition. We might, in passing, quote Blackie in his inaugural address to the Gaelic Society of Perth, in 1880:

I have no doubt . . . that Gaelic societies in Scotland, at the present moment, have a distinct and well-marked sphere of legitimate action; and, if they will in very deed buckle themselves to serious action in the practical world, and not content themselves with vapouring about Ossian, whom they never read, and eulogising Duncan Bàn, whom they do not sing, I have no doubt they will do good service (J.S. Blackie, 1880, p. 2).

Macdonald's most recent editors say of him that his 'place as a poet has long been recognised as in the front rank. There is no other that can be compared to him in the whole range of Gaelic literature, as there is indeed none like him' (A. Macdonald and A. Macdonald, 1924, xli). MacLean speaks of his 'unfailing power and boisterous joie-de-vivre' (S. MacLean, 1938, p. 85). Considering this, it is regrettable that his poems are not readily available in the bookshops.[6]

Macdonald was born in the last years of the seventeenth century into the Clanranald branch of Clan Donald, which has been called 'traditionally the backbone of Gaelic culture and Jacobitism in the Highlands' (J.L. Campbell, 1933, p. 33). His father was a non-jurant Episcopalian clergyman, minister of Islandfinnan in Ardnamurchan. Macdonald is known to have attended Glasgow University, but for how long, and whether his studies were designed to fit him for the law or the Church, is not known. His studies are thought to have been cut short by an imprudently early marriage, and he does not emerge into clearly recorded history until 1729, when he appears on the books of the SPCK,[7] employed as schoolteacher and catechist in Islandfinnan.

It is clear that Macdonald did not entirely waste his time at university. We find, for example, frequent use of Classical imagery in his poems. In his 'Aiseirigh na Seann Chànain Albannaich' ('Resurrection of the Old Scottish Tongue') we also find a familiarity with the dominant concerns of eighteenth-century philology, especially the conventions of locating the native language of the writer as close to the Garden of Eden as possible, and deriving all other languages from it.[8] In spite of his education, however, Macdonald was forced to take 'poor employment for one of his attainments and connection' (J.L. Campbell, 1933, p. 33), demonstrating that 'he had evidently not prospered' (A. Macdonald and A. Macdonald, 1924, xxvii). He must have deserted both the Church of his father, and the traditional Catholicism of his clan, in order to take up his employment with the SPCK, which 'argues that for quite a number of years there must have been a serious breach between Mac Mhaighstir Alasdair and his chief, Clanranald' (J.L. Campbell, 1971, p. 75).

The SPCK, in whose employment Macdonald found himself, was at the time committed to the extirpation of Catholicism, Episcopalianism and the Gaelic language in the Highlands. It was, therefore, a strange employer for one who is now best known as the most fervently Jacobite of Highland bards. Macdonald appears in various places as teacher up to 1745. He eventually abandoned a post he found little to his liking, at about the same time that the SPCK were determining that he was little to theirs. Campbell quotes their minutes for a meeting in June 1745 to the effect that 'Alexr. MacDonald Schoolmaster at Ardnamurchan is an offence to all Sober Well inclin'd persons as he wanders thro' the Country composing Galick songs, stuffed with obscene language' (cited J.L. Campbell, 1971, p. 60). In July 1745 the SPCK 'Resolved he be dismist the Society's service and ordered to be left out of next Scheme' (ibid.).

Macdonald became, at this time, a passionate adherent to the cause of Prince Charles Edward Stuart, who landed on the Scottish mainland in July 1745 to begin his ill-fated campaign. Macdonald is thought to have suffered another politically expedient religious conversion to Catholicism, although 'no one has suggested that it was from conviction' (A. Macdonald and A. Macdonald, 1924, xxx). He appears to have campaigned with Prince Charles, there being record of his having received a commission in his army, and he is reputed to have acted as 'poet laureate' to his shifting and short-lived court. Blackie says that 'what the Greek revolt of 1821 was to Lord Byron, that the brilliant adventure of Prince Charlie in 1745 was to the Ardnamurchan bard' (J.S. Blackie, 1876, p. 125). After the collapse of this cause, Macdonald is said, accompanied by his wife and children, to have 'wandered through hills and mountains till the act of indemnity appeared' (R. Forbes, 1895, p. 354). It is said that in the summer of 1749 he:

> received the situation of Baillie of Canna, and he and his family took up their abode in that Island. This estate appointment is difficult to account for. The Clanranald estates, of which Canna formed a part, were at the time under forfeiture, and it is hardly conceivable that Alasdair would hold his appointment by favour of the British Government (A. Macdonald and A. Macdonald, 1924, xxxiv).

He did not hold this appointment for long, and after he leaves it little is known of his later life. 'During the last twenty years of his life he lived in Glenuig, Knoydart, Moror, and Arisaig, never staying long in any one place' (J.L. Campbell, 1933, p. 40), and 'He died about the year 1770 in Sandaig, and is buried at Kilmorie in Arisaig' (ibid.). We know enough, without reading too much into these rather slender biographical details, to realise that Macdonald was a complex and difficult character, and that 'his life was stormy and checkered, like the historic period which also was then coming to a close' (N. MacNeill, 1929, p. 280).

Macdonald was commissioned in 1740 to compile a Gaelic/English vocabulary for the SPCK. This was published in 1741, the first Gaelic/

English vocabulary ever published as a separate work, with a dedication by Macdonald which is one of only three or four pieces of his English prose that we have. It is entitled *Leabhar a Theagasc Ainminnin no A Nuadhfhocloir Gaoidheilg & Beurla*, Le Alastair MacDomhnuill ('Name Teaching Book, or A New Gaelic English Vocabulary, by Alexander Macdonald'). The dedication, to the President and members of the SPCK, contains the following:

> It seems to have been reserved for you, to be the happy instruments of bringing about the reformation of the Highlands and Islands of Scotland, diverse Places of which were remote from the means of obtaining Instruction; and, indeed, when we consider the situation of the inhabitants, their Ignorance, their Inclinations to follow the Customs, Fashions and Superstitions of their Forefathers, the Number of Popish Emissaries in many Places of these Countries; and add to these their Way of Life, the unfrequented Passes, and the Distance of their Houses from one another, together with innumerable other Difficulties, one could not think; but, that an Attempt to reform them, would be a very arduous Task, to be brought about, even by the most probable means (A. Macdonald, 1741, iv).

> I could with Pleasure enlarge on the Flourishing Condition your Schools are now in in many Places, I could they tell the almost miraculous Change made upon the Tempers and Lives of many of the Inhabitants, and could testify how much they are civilised, and happier than formerly (ibid.).

> The Instruction of the Youth in English Language, is thought necessary to promote the charitable Purpose of this Society, and to make these, who can speak only Gaelic, more useful Members in the Commonwealth (ibid., v).

> we your Schoolmasters are not to carry our Scholars Forward in Reading, but as they understand what they read in English, and most reasonable it is (ibid.).

He expresses the hope that his dictionary will further his pupils:

> in their Progress, and also spread the English Language thro' the Country, and make these young Ones more useful the sooner, as Servants at Home, and also when they come Abroad to the Lowlands,

> and be imployed in the Navy, or Army, or in any other service in the Commonwealth (ibid.).

Of the request, from the SPCK, through the Presbytery of Lorne, to prepare the vocabulary, he says:

> I did cordially undertake to give my Assistance therein, in order to introduce the English Language over the whole Highlands and Islands of Scotland (ibid., vi).

> If this Attempt of mine shall contribute to advance your good and pious Design, and if it shall be esteemed useful by your Honourable Body . . . it will be a great Pleasure to me (ibid.).

Even allowing for a conventional deference to an employer, this is a fairly whole-hearted acceptance of a *status quo* against which Macdonald was soon to revolt. In 1751, while on a visit to Edinburgh 'unsuccessfully in quest of a position as a teacher' (J. Kennedy, 1888, p. 265), he published the first book of original Gaelic poems ever to appear. This was entitled *Aiseirigh na seann Chanain Albannaich* (*Resurrection of the Old Scottish Tongue*), and the introductory poem of the same title (with the sub-title 'Moladh an Ughdair do 'n t-seann Chanain Ghaidhealach' – 'The Author's Praise of the Old Gaelic Language') contains the following lines, strange from the pen of the dedicated employee of the SPCK:

1.25 Is ge h-iomadh cànain
O linn Bhàbeil fhuair
An sliochd sin Adhaimh,
Is i Ghàidhlig a thug buaidh.

1.37 Mhair i fòs,
Is cha téid a glòir air chall
Dh'aindeoin gò
Is mìoruin mhóir nan Gall.

Is i labhair Alba
Is gallbhodaich féin,
Ar flaith, ar prionnsaidhe
Is ar diùcanna gun éis.

1.53 Is i labhair Goill is Gàidheil,
Neo-chléirich is cléir,
Gach fear is bean
A ghluaiseadh teanga am beul.

Is i labhair Adhamh
Ann a phàrras féin,
Is bu shiùbhlach Gàidhlig
O bheul àlainn Eubh.

Och tha bhuil ann!
Is uireasbhach gann fo dhìth
Glòir gach teanga
A labhras cainnt seach ì.

(W.J. Watson, 1959, pp. 98, 99).

1.25 Although many languages / came from the age of Babel / with Adam's race / It was Gaelic that won the victory.

1.37 She still survives, / and her glory will not be lost / in spite of the deceit / and great ill-will of the Lowlander. / She is the speech of Scotland, / and of Lowlanders themselves, / of our nobles, princes / and dukes without exception.

1.53 She is the language of Gall and Gael, / layman and churchman, / every man and woman / that would move a tongue in his mouth. She is the speech of Adam / in Paradise itself, / and Gaelic was sweet / from Eve's beautiful mouth. / Och here's an end to it! / Needy, poor, lacking / is the sound of every tongue / that speaks any accent but hers (my translation).

This volume also contained several Jacobite poems in which the House of Hanover is addressed as a family of pigs. For example, the following is from 'Oran Mu Bhliadhna Thearlaich' ('A Song about the Year of Charles'):

O! 'n cullach sin Rìgh Deòrsa,
Mac na cràine Gearmailtich;
'S e chàirdeas ruinn, 's a dhàimh,
Gaol fithich air a' chnàimh;

(A. Macdonald and A. Macdonald, 1924, p. 122).

Oh that boar, King George!
Son of the German sow,
His love for us 'tis known
Is the raven's for the bone;
(trans. A. Macdonald and A. Macdonald, 1924, p. 123).

There are several interesting points to be made about the way in which the slender details of Macdonald that we have have been interpreted, and there is not room here to go into details. Politically, affirming his Jacobitism has held an important place, the editors of the 1924 edition of his poems only mentioning his vocabulary, without exploring the sentiments of its dedication, and saying of Macdonald's part in the 'Forty-five:

> Not even a whisper, either by friend or foe, as to the conduct of our bard during the campaign has reached us. That he took his full share of the fighting like the bold and fearless man he was . . . need not be doubted (A. Macdonald and A. Macdonald, 1924, xxxiii).

We will see when we come to Duncan Bàn that such inference on the strength of no evidence is a double-edged sword. Thomson, himself a Scottish nationalist, says of Macdonald that his poetry flows from:

> a total involvement with the Jacobite cause. The mainspring of this, however, was not a narrow dynastic loyalty to the House of Stuart, but a dream of Gaelic independence. There are signs that his nationalism was a Scottish as well as a Gaelic one (D. Thomson, 1974, p. 158).

It is, however, arguable that the route from Gaelic Jacobitism to modern Scottish nationalism is a doubtful road, and by no means the self-evident expansion of horizons that Thomson makes it. Although modern nationalism purports to speak for a united Scotland rather than simply for the Gaelic Highland world in which Macdonald lived, there are grounds for maintaining that the political world in which Macdonald operated was of broader horizon, although geographically less ambitious, than modern nationalism. This is suggested by the imagery of self-definition employed. Macdonald shows no need to look outside Gaelic life for symbols to express the Gael to himself, and the political and social world of which he speaks thus appears possessed of a normal and unselfconscious autonomy. Modern nationalism, on the other hand, frequently employs for its expression symbols of polarisation which only have meaning as long as Scotland remains a fragment of a larger political unit. This is evident in some of the poems of George Campbell Hay and Derick Thomson, which I quote in Chapter 6. The road from Macdonald to Hay is not a slow growth into an awareness of identity, but a slow retreat into a position where identity is so problematical that it must be both sought and asserted. We might wonder what the Macdonald who wrote the dedication of 1741 to the SPCK would have thought of Jacobitism had his career prospered, and argue that, in espousing the Jacobite cause, he 'had little to lose and much to gain' (A. Macdonald and A. Macdonald, 1924, xxxi). The 'Forty-five rebellion perhaps provided an outlet for a man of great talent to escape from 'the illiterate and factious Highlanders of Ardnamurchan, in a district so remote and impoverished that it entailed a life-long, and to him sordid struggle, to keep the wolf of poverty from the door' (M. Maclean, 1904, p. 24).

Macdonald is, in some of his poetry, explicit about sexual matters in a way that some of his later commentators found unacceptable. I discuss this in more detail later in the chapter. J.L. Campbell has shown how expurgation was achieved by omission from the various editions of his works (see J.L. Campbell, 1971), in order to confirm the truth of Watson's remark that 'The tone of modern Gaelic poetry is clean and virile' (W.J. Watson (1918), 1959, xxv). This is a fascinating study, although a narrow moralism was not of course unique to Gaelic scholars in the nineteenth century. What is more significant for the present purpose is that most of the commentary on eighteenth-century Gaelic poets that we have comes from a tradition that has internalised the language and values of romanticism.

This use of an aesthetic and critical language from outside Gaelic poetry leads not only to significant misinterpretation of the whole Gaelic tradition, but also manipulates the works and biographies of individual authors. Speaking of the Gaelic muse in general, we can take the following as a typical assessment: 'how . . . forcibly must the bold chanting of heroic verse . . . have affected a people like the Gael, imbued with all the fervour of unaffected nature, and who paid ardent devotion at the shrine of freedom' (J. Logan (1841), 1904, iii). This is from the first important published collection of Gaelic poetry, *Sàr-Obair nam Bard Gaelach: or, The Beauties of Gaelic Poetry*, first published in 1841. It is written in full acceptance of the authenticity of Ossian and of a Druidical Celtic past. From a more critical age, but recognisably similar nevertheless, is the following: 'The poets of the new school were born, not made: they sang because they must sing, and they sang of things in which they were keenly interested. Their poetry is spontaneous; it has the notes of freedom, freshness, sincerity' (W.J. Watson, 1959, xix). MacLauchlan says that 'the ancient tongue of the Celt is left to the unlettered but often brilliant muse of the peasant' (T. MacLauchlan, 1857, p. 145), and that:

> The country in which these men lived is one in which the natural objects are marked and prominent: mountains, lakes, waterfalls, glens, and islands abound. There is everything to excite the descriptive muse, and it has been excited among the Highland peasantry to a remarkable extent (ibid., p. 163).

MacNeill speaks of 'The feeling for the romantic universally attributed to the Gael' (N. MacNeill, 1929, p. 568) which will, 'allied with a reconstructed native culture, discover a rejuvenated Gaelic muse' (ibid.). Donald MacLean says of the bard of this period that: 'Impelled by the Celtic spirit that ever seeks after the ideal, the poet pursues the eternal illusion beyond his reach and grasp, but not beyond his thought' (D. MacLean, 1912, p. 47).

Much of this commentary is inseparable from a consideration of the Celtic character which Renan and Arnold did so much to form, and which I discuss in the next chapter. We can see, however, that a Gaelic poet is expected to be peasant, untutored, romantic, simple, sincere, and in pursuit of an eternal illusion. Alexander Macdonald was arguably none of these things, but he has been pruned into shape. It is important to remember that the most famous poems of both Macdonald and Macintyre are concerned with subjects that we would now call 'natural'. For Macdonald, one thinks especially of his 'Oran an t-Samhraidh' ('Song of Summer'), 'Oran a' Gheamhraidh' ('Song of Winter'), 'Oran do Allt an t-Siùcair' ('Song to the Sugar Brook'), 'Moladh Moraig' ('The Praise of Morag'), and 'Birlinn Chlann Raghnaill' ('The Barge of Clanranald'). This evident 'naturalness' was, according to Watson, a conscious innovation of subject-matter by Macdonald into the tradition that he inherited from Mary MacLeod and Iain Lom (see W.J. Watson, 1959, xxiii). Thomson says, however, that 'there was of course much natural description in earlier Gaelic verse, . . . Mac Mhaighstir Alasdair may well have been familiar with this tradition' (D. Thomson, 1974, p. 160). Whatever the influences on Macdonald, it has been easy to speak of him in critical language derived from the romantic tradition. This is, however, both anachronistic and distorting, although its fits Macdonald neatly into the picture of the Celt that the nineteenth century drew.

It is difficult to assess the influence of eighteenth-century English-language poetry and sentiment on the Gaelic world, but it can be said with some confidence that the intellectual traditions and preoccupations which gave rise to Romanticism were simply not felt within Gaeldom, except in very superficial form. Certainly, Macdonald had an education in English, and his acquaintance with English literature is evidenced by his composition of a 'Song of Summer' and a 'Song of Winter', in probable imitation of James Thomson's highly successful 'Seasons', which were published between 1726 and 1730. D. Thomson shows, however, that:

> We can see a difference in method, and a complete independence of thought, in the two poets description . . . Thomson's has some artificiality, and a hint of pompousness: . . . Mac Mhaighstir Alasdair has less Border Twilight in his description, and a more direct and unmixed observation (D. Thomson, 1974, p. 161).

It was probably a fashion set by Macdonald rather than by James Thomson that caused Dugald Buchanan, Rob Donn, Duncan Bàn, William Ross, and Ewen MacLachlan, of those included in *Sàr Obair nam Bard Gaelach*, to compose a song or songs to the seasons. Derick Thomson has suggested that Rob Donn (*c.* 1715-78) 'was influenced at least marginally by the poetry of Alexander Pope, as mediated to him by the Rev. Murdoch Macdonald' (D. Thomson, 1974, p. 194). Later in the century we have the suggestion that the poetry of William Ross (1762-91):

> differs from that of his fellow Gaelic poets of the eighteenth century. His personality seems the most vulnerable, and he either wears his heart on his sleeve or pretends he hasn't got one: two reflexes of the same emotional disturbance. This subjective element, and more especially the conscious manipulation of it, was new in the poetry of the century, though not perhaps entirely original.
>
> We have seen, momentarily, that James Macpherson's writings left a slight mark on Ross's sensibility. No doubt they both responded to the atmosphere of their time, though Macpherson did something to create that atmosphere too (D. Thomson, 1974, p. 216).

Ross, therefore, by the end of the century, was affected by the concerns of Romanticism. Macdonald and Macintyre, however, the second of whom remained unlettered throughout his life, cannot be regarded as occupying any clear place in an English-language literary tradition, least of all a romantic tradition. Important recent commentaries on Macdonald have said that he is 'intolerant of haziness' (W.J. Watson, 1959, xxviii) and has 'a desire for completeness or exhaustiveness' (D. Thomson, 1974, p. 159). Watson says that:

> Gaelic poetry, as a rule, deals with phenomena without seeking to analyse or explain them; it is objective, not introspective; concrete, not abstract. That the Gael appreciated the beauties of nature there is ample evidence, but his appreciation is shown by incidental allusion or by deliberate enumeration, not by reflection on the 'soul' of nature (W.J. Watson, 1959, xxiv).

Thomson speaks of Macdonald's 'hardness and intellectual grasp' (D. Thomson, 1974, p. 171). When we consider the way in which 'nature' was appropriated by the English Romantic poets as a source of and allegory for moral and ethical power, we must consider also Derick Thomson's assessment that:

> Thomson [i.e. James Thomson] had experienced a deep delight in Nature, and . . . felt an urge to relate Nature to man, and to man's ethics. Not so Mac Mhaighstir Alasdair. He seldom or never moves from the particular to the general, nor does he use Nature to illustrate aspects of man (D. Thomson, 1974, p. 160).

Bearing this in mind, and also remembering the conflation of primitivism and romanticism in the Celt, given its definitive form in Ossian, we can look at some comments on Macdonald and his poetry made in the shadow of romanticism. Logan asks:

> Could Macdonald's Iorram be translated so as to carry all its force of expression with it? Language is used to convey ideas and express action and feeling. In a primitive tongue it does so emphatically to a natural mind; when society becomes artificial, language undergoes a similar change (J. Logan (1841), 1904, liv).

Blackie says that:

> Some of the . . . works of this poet exhibit that love for natural scenery, and that delicate descriptive power in which the Celts seem, by a natural instinct, to have excelled before Thomson and Wordsworth made it part of the fashionable currency of the modern muse

> (J.S. Blackie, 1876, p. 130).

MacNeill, while recognising differences between Ossian and Macdonald, says: 'The minds of both were nurtured by the same poetical elements, the same influences and scenic images; . . . Both breathe a spirit that speaks of "the land of the mountain and the flood"' (N. MacNeill, 1873, p. 87). Kennedy tells us: 'All Macdonald's poems are lyric – the spontaneous outburst of a heart overflowing with emotion' (J. Kennedy, 1888, p. 266), and: 'Nature was to him instinct with meaning and delight. In this respect he may well be compared to Wordsworth' (ibid., p. 307). MacLean, expanding on this, argues that Macdonald:

> has the inspiration evoked by the towering mountains, the deep mysterious valleys, and the surging ocean. All his poems are lyric, the spontaneous utterance of a strong emotional nature finding easy expression (M. MacLean, 1904, p. 26).
>
> It is in his descriptive poems and his representations of Nature that Macdonald is seen at his best. As to Wordsworth half a century later, so to him, Nature was instinct with meaning and life, and it was his unfailing delight to hold converse with her (ibid., p. 29).

It is a significant and recurrent mistranslation, deriving from what I have called the symbolic appropriation of the Gael by English-language literary discourse, that gives to Macdonald a place somewhere in the romantic tradition. One outcome of this appropriation is shown in the next chapter, and it is the power of the metaphors there discussed that gives to Macdonald the ability to see 'Nature instinct with meaning'. Before discussing this problem further I will introduce Duncan Macintyre, of whom such judgements are ostensibly more easily made.

Angus MacLeod has gathered the information from various sources about the life of Macintyre (see A. MacLeod, 1952). The following selections are taken from the short biography of the author prefacing the fifth edition of his works, published in 1848:

> Duncan Macintyre . . . was born of poor parents, at Druimliaghart, in Glenorchy, March, 1724, where he spent the earlier part of his life, engaged in fowling and fishing, of which he was very fond. He never enjoyed the benefit of attending school, and never learned to read during his lifetime . . . Although he early displayed a strong love for his native poetry, and exhibited symptoms of having the poetic vein

> himself, he produced nothing worthy of preservation until his twenty-second year (Duncan Bàn Macintyre, 1848, iii).
>
> Duncan was shortly after this period appointed forester or Game-keeper to the Earl of Breadalbane, in Coire-Cheathaich and Beinn-dòrain, and afterwards to the Duke of Argyll in Buachaill-Eite (ibid., v).
>
> Our author afterwards served six years in the Breadalbane Fencibles, in which regiment he held the rank of sergeant; and on its being broken up in 1799, he became one of the city-guard of Edinburgh. . . . he often neglected his duty, by falling into one of his poetic reveries; . . . He died about the 14th of May 1812, aged 88 years (ibid., vi).
>
> He was noted for his convivial and pleasant company; and many anecdotes of his wit and repartee are still on record (ibid., vii).
>
> We have already noticed that our author could not read, and consequently could not write down his poems when composed; but so tenacious was his memory, that he could recite all his own verses, and great part of his native bards. The first edition of his poems, published in 1768, was written by a clergyman from oral recitation (ibid., viii).

MacLeod, in the 1952 edition, adds the information that Macintyre spent a considerable period in the City Guard of Edinburgh before he joined the Breadalbane Fencibles, probably from 1766 until 1793. Macintyre was, therefore, an Edinburgh resident from the age of 42 to the age of 69. The biography in the second edition (1790) of his works simply mentions that he was 'for a considerable time in the City Guard of Edinburgh' (cited A. MacLeod, 1952, xvi). The biography in the third edition (1804), which was 'written to Macintyre's own instructions' (A. MacLeod, 1952, xxviii), and that in the fourth edition (1834), ignore his Edinburgh residence altogether. The fifth edition, cited above, simply mentions the period from 1799 onwards.

It was during his employment as gamekeeper that Macintyre composed his most famous poems, which are, like those of Macdonald, on 'natural' subjects. Particularly famous are his 'Oran Coire a' Cheathaich' ('Song of the Misty Corrie'), and his 'Moladh Beinn Dóbhrain' ('Praise of Ben Dobhrain'). During his stay in Edinburgh he was the successful competitor for the annual prize offered by the Highland Society of London for a poem on 'Gaelic and the Bagpipe', in the years 1781, 1782,

1783, 1784, 1785 and 1789. MacLeod says that 'These six poems might nowadays be regarded as Mòd prize poems' (ibid., p. 512).[9] MacLeod also mentions that Macintyre applied, unsuccessfully, for the post of bard to the Highland and Agricultural Society. We can see that Macintyre who, in his youth, produced poetry that is considered to be among the very finest Gaelic verse, became involved in Edinburgh in the late eighteenth century in a world where Gaeldom and its customs were used to satisfy a taste for exotic ephemera. It was a world where Highland culture was little regarded except as it flattered with its decorative symbols, the clan and the claymore, the kilt and the bagpipe. It was the Edinburgh where Ossian became the talk of every drawing-room, where the disappearance of the ancient Erse was anticipated, and where rationalists and improvers constructed their economies. In Macintyre, composing poems on 'Gaelic and the Bagpipe', we can see the self-conscious parading of a culture which is today such an important feature of the activities of An Comunn Gaidhealach (The Highland Society), particularly in the annual National Mòd, a festival of Gaelic music and song. We can also perhaps see in Macintyre's poems for this purpose the tendency towards inauthenticity, and a kind of sterile conservatism, that such a histrionic celebration of 'culture' risks. MacLeod says, concerning the poems on 'Gaelic and the Bagpipe', that 'Macintyre, with all his resources of vocabulary and metrical variations, finds it difficult to produce new ideas on the same topic, year after year' (ibid., p. 512).

Thomson says of this period that:

> The notion, and ideal, of patriarchal leader, accompanied by a traditional panoply, had been in decline for some three centuries, and had indeed gone far enough to justify some attempts at artificial revival in the mid-eighteenth century and after. Sir James MacDonald of Sleat made John MacCodrum his bard, in a vain romantic attempt to call back an age that had gone (D. Thomson, 1974, p. 156).

When the name of Ossian was on every tongue, Macintyre was:

> but one of many humble Highlanders who migrated to the city to find work. Even among the small circle of people who could understand his songs he was but one of several Gaelic bards, and no one thought at the time that the bard of Glen Orchy was worthy of a biography (A. MacLeod, 1952, xxxv).

There are two obvious features in Macintyre's life that fit him ill for his role as 'pure Highland singer'. These are his long residence in Edinburgh, and his fighting on the Hanoverian side at the battle of Falkirk in 1746. His residence in Edinburgh, in eighteenth-century Scotland a centre of sophistication, is clearly in conflict with a picture of an untutored Highland bard. When we remember that the 1804 edition of Macintyre's poems omits, possibly at the author's request, any mention of his residence in Edinburgh, we can speculate that Macintyre himself had by this time absorbed sufficient of the intellectual atmosphere to feel that his position as a Highland bard was compromised by such an urban life. This is speculation, but the difficulty provoked is still felt, as Thomson expresses it, saying of Macintyre that:

> His output of verse seems to have kept up in Edinburgh, but there is reason to think that his poetry died when he left the countryside that he belonged to . . . when we contrast the poetry of his rural period with that of the later years . . . we realise most clearly that he needed this physical background of Nature to sustain his poetry (D. Thomson, 1974, p. 186).

Although Thomson admits that 'there might well be other, more prosaic explanations of the change of tone and talent' (ibid.), it is interesting that the loss of 'Nature' should be the first that comes to mind.

Of Macintyre and Falkirk, Thomson says 'Donnchadh Bàn made a brief appearance at the Battle of Falkirk in 1746, fighting without enthusiasm on the Hanoverian side, but the rising and politics play little part in his poetry' (ibid., p. 190). MacLeod says of Macintyre: 'Here we have no Jacobite, but the Laureate of the clan that Alexander Macdonald regarded as the most powerful enemy of the Stuart cause in the Highlands' (A. MacLeod, 1952, xl). The government forces were routed at Falkirk, which caused Macintyre to gently deride in verse the Hanoverian army to which he belonged, in his 'Oran do Bhlàr na h-Eaglaise Brice' ('Song to the Battle of Falkirk'). MacLeod assesses his political commitment:

> Macintyre gives no hint that he was reluctant from the first to serve . . . , or that he would have preferred to fight in the Jacobite army. Only afterwards, when he had to make explanations, does he appear to favour the Prince. Indeed, his unstinted praise of the might and valour of the Macdonalds may be a measure of his own discomfiture and an excuse for his own conduct (A. MacLeod, 1952, xxiii).

Campbell, however, has gone so far as to include Macintyre in his *Highland Songs of the 'Forty-Five,* where Highland poetry is taken to be evidence of 'the actual sentiments of the ordinary Highlanders who formed the backbone of the Prince's army' (J.L. Campbell, 1933, xvii). We can fully agree with Campbell that (his emphasis): 'the actions of the Highlanders are to be judged, . . . from what *they believed* was the truth. To set up any other standards for the judgement of their motives or actions is to be guilty of a moral anachronism' (ibid.). We can also agree that 'It is astonishing . . . that any historian should feel himself properly equipped to write the history of his country while remaining in ignorance of the language spoken over half its area' (ibid., xviii). It must nevertheless be admitted that to present Macintyre as a Jacobite bard is a significant suppression of information. To argue that a poet who wrote against the Disclothing Act of 1747, whereby Highland dress was proscribed, was necessarily a Jacobite, is like arguing that one who objects to the slaughter of Jews is necessarily a Zionist. We can take two examples of Macintyre's political verse, the first from 'Oran do 'n Bhriogais' ('Song to the Breeches'):

'S olc an seòl duinn am Prionns' òg
  A bhith fo mhóran duilichinn,
Is Rìgh Deòrsa a bhith chòmhnaidh
  Far 'm bu chòir dha tuineachas;
(A. MacLeod, 1952, p. 8)

Dire is our plight that the young Prince
should be in great adversity,
and that, where he ought to be established,
King George should be the occupant.
(trans. A. MacLeod, 1952, p. 9)

The second is from 'Oran do 'n Rìgh' ('Song to the King'):

Is mór an t-àdh a th'air an òigear,
  An treas Deòrs' a shuidh 'sa' Chathair;
Chan 'eil rìgh anns an Roinn Eòrpa
  Chumas còmhrag ris le claidheamh;
(ibid., p. 26)

'Tis great good fortune doth attend the youth,
The third George to sit upon the throne;

there is not a king in Europe
who can contend with sword against him;
(trans. A. MacLeod, 1952, p. 27)

Which of these we should take as a true expression of Macintyre's sentiments would depend largely on whether we had a political axe to grind.

We have seen that a simple sincerity has been lauded as a Highland characteristic. Duncan Bàn's political equivocations are something of an embarrassment in this respect. Nevertheless, they offer us the opportunity to do justice to the subtleties and uncertainties of a political situation that is too often presented in simple blacks and whites. The events of the 'Forty-five – the coming of Prince Charles, the unfurling of his standard at Glenfinnan, the victory at Prestonpans, the gallant march south, the retreat and disaster at Culloden, and the final breathtaking hunt by the redcoats for the fugitive prince – all these have been wound very closely into the sensibilities of the Scottish nation, and the political context in which they are placed is invariably one wherein the honest and guileless enthusiasm of the Highlander is pitted hopelessly against the subtle and heartless machinations of the Establishment. It is in this retrospectively endowed political context that poets like Macdonald and Macintyre are allowed their voice.

We might argue, however, although it seems vaguely impious to do so, that we should allow to these poets, and to the eighteenth-century Highlander in general, a thoroughly human capacity for subtlety, equivocation and hypocrisy. We must credit them with a capacity to write what they do not mean, and mean what they do not say, and this not just because they were driven to compromise with an unsympathetic political régime, but because, like men before and after them, they were possessed of a normal degree of pragmatism. Whatever concealed pessimisms we choose to read into the somewhat lukewarm reception that Prince Charles Edward Stuart received on his arrival in Scotland, it is at least certain that those that chose to follow him did not do so in order to write themselves into the terminal event of Scottish Gaelic history. They did not know that they were acting out what the future would come to see as the definitive struggle between old and new, and they did not know that they were casting themselves irrevocably in the role of historically fated and gallant losers. Had they been able to read this history in advance they would have stayed at home. We discredit them by thinking otherwise. MacInnes has argued that an 'ambivalent attitude' towards the 'Forty-five was a 'general feeling in the Highlands' (J. Mac-

Innes, 1972, p. 365). Ambivalence is, however, difficult to place within the traditional picture of an enthusiastic and volatile race welcoming with joy the return of their hereditary monarch. It is to the Lowlander, the Gall, that 'guile, or sleekitness, or fawning for place' are normally ascribed (S. MacLean, 1977, p. 172).

Macdonald also finds himself put to the blush, in one context at least, by this requirement for a simple sincerity. He wrote two poems about the same person, in which he expresses violently contrary sentiments towards the object of his attentions. The story is told that he wrote the first – 'Moladh Moraig' ('Praise of Morag') – to please Morag, and that he wrote the second – 'Dimoladh Moraig' ('Dispraise of Morag') – to please his wife Jane after she had heard the first. This evident duplicity, and the sexual obscenities contained in the 'Dispraise', have caused a certain amount of heart-searching among critics that wish Macdonald's moral character to be that of the unflawed, if somewhat unidimensional, 'Highland singer'.

His most recent editors regret his 'filthy rhymes' (A. Macdonald and A. Macdonald, 1924, xxxv), which reveal the 'coarseness and moral degradation of the author' (ibid.), and will 'remain a blot for ever on the memory of our bard' (ibid.). Macdonald is saved from this flaw, however, by the fact that his love songs are only 'an intellectual exercise' (ibid., xlii), in which there is 'a coldness and artificiality which are entirely wanting in his Jacobite songs' (ibid.). In politics, if not in love, Macdonald is a true Highlander.

Watson also regrets Macdonald's weakness in this respect. He says of Gaelic poetry in general that 'there are passages and poems which we could well do without' (W.J. Watson (1918), 1959, xxvi), although 'the great poets, with one exception, never sin in this respect' (ibid.). The one exception is, regrettably

> the greatest of them all, Alexander Macdonald, who, by some strange twist in one or two of his poems, appears to have deliberately aimed at being shocking, in imitation, probably, of certain much older examples. But when all is said, the total amount of Gaelic poetry unfit *virginibus puerisque* is so small that we are left with a strong sense of the clean-mindedness and good taste of its composers (ibid.).

Since the introduction of the Protestant religion into the Highlands, Gaelic scholarship has been very much associated with the Church, and we cannot be surprised that the more racy productions of eighteenth-century Gaelic literature are regretted in such a context. We might note that Watson, keen as he was to stress in print the clean-mindedness of the Gael, must certainly have been aware of the existence of a strong and old tradition of bawdy Gaelic verse. Scholarship, however, sometimes makes ambiguous demands.

Returning to Macintyre's work, this obvious problem of sexual and moral censorship does not arise in the same way. It is still, however, in the assessment of Macintyre as a 'perfect, uncorrupted, unqualified son of the mountains' (J.S. Blackie, 1876, p. 156), that our chief interest lies. Since he was unlettered, he has been easier to fit than Macdonald into the Homeric mould. It was not necessary to say of Macintyre, as MacLean said of Macdonald, that 'His college training did not much influence his poetical compositions. In these he is always the pure Highland singer' (M. MacLean, 1904, p. 27). Logan says of Macintyre that 'unassisted by the slightest education' (J. Logan (1841), 1904, li) he has obtained 'a comparison with Ossian himself' (ibid.). Blackie says of him that:

> Of all the Highland poets this man is the one unquestionably who bears even more distinctly than Ossian, the features of his Celtic origin on his face. He is in all respects as native to the land of the Bens as the purple heather on the braes (J.S. Blackie, 1876, p. 156).

> he had neither school nor college to stimulate the natural vitality of his root or to trim the untutored expansion of his growth. . . . Nature is always right; culture not seldom wrong; dangerous always to a poet, if it either leads him away from the sympathies of general humanity, or, what is worse, teaches him to array his Muse in an incongrous tissue, composed partly of native rustic plaiding, partly of purple patches and curious network of outlandish finery (ibid.).

Shairp says of Macintyre that 'when inborn passion promoted, he sang songs of natural and genuine inspiration' (J.C. Shairp, 1881, p. 287). He goes on:

> Macintyre's poetry eminently disproves – as indeed all Gaelic poetry does – that modern doctrine, that love of nature is necessarily a late growth, the product of refined cultivation. It may be so with the phlegmatic Teuton, not so with the susceptible and impassioned Gael (ibid., p. 311).

MacLean tells us that:

> The love of Nature . . . is recognised as a late growth in English poetry . . .
>
> Yet from the earliest times . . . the Gael seems to have evinced this peculiar intimacy with and regard for the phenomena that we class under the term Nature. For him, as for the later English poets, Nature was instinct with life, full of wonder and delight. . . . So near and intimate was this kinship of the Highland bard with his environment that he conceived of all outward things as suffering with him in his sorrow and rejoicing with him in his day of triumph.
>
> And if ever there was a pure unsophisticated poet of Nature sensitive to the feelings she inspired, Duncan Macintyre was one (M. MacLean, 1904, p. 47).

D. MacLean says of Macintyre's poems 'Coire Cheathaich' and 'Ben Dobhrain' that they:

> reflect idealism as well as that close affinity between man and nature which characterised the youth of the Celtic people. Nature's mystic voice vibrates on sympathetic chords, and the dulcet notes, in perfect harmony of sounds, are lilting to the outer world on waves of choice words without a jarring note (D. MacLean, 1912, p. 47).

The atmosphere has cooled somewhat over the last fifty years, at least in the sphere of literary criticism, although the metaphors that surface in one form in works such as that cited above still retain their power undiminished in other forms. J.L. Campbell says of Macintyre that 'No one could have been less like the gloomy Celt of literary tradition' (J.L. Campbell, 1933, p. 193). MacLeod reaches the balanced conclusion that:

> We must accept him as he was—a peasant who could not read but had a wonderful memory and a wide knowledge of Gaelic poetry; a poet who could compose readily about people and places and objects; one whose thought was not deep but who rose to great heights in descriptive composition (A. MacLeod, 1952, xl).

In agreement with this assessment, Thomson says:

> The poetic gift which Donnchadh Bàn was perhaps best endowed with was that of observation. . . . Nor is there any attempt to philosophise. He does not question the workings of Nature, nor attempt

> to draw from them lessons for Man. . . . The close and detailed observation implies a strong and effective concentration, evidenced again in the transfer of that observation to verse that is tightly constructed metrically. But it may leave us with the impression of an artefact to be admired for the moment, rather than a work of art whose reverberations are unpredictable (D. Thomson, 1974, p. 186).

If we allow, as I think we must, that this assessment is an accurate one, how are we to account for those statements quoted earlier with which it is in part in downright contradiction? We can perhaps approach this misunderstanding, which has led Sorley MacLean to say that 'the Celtic Twilightists achieved the remarkable feat of attributing to Gaelic poetry the very opposite of every quality which it actually has' (S. MacLean, 1938, p. 87), through an examination of a further remark of Magnus MacLean's. He says of Macintyre:

> Even cultured contemporaries of his own, such as Captain Burt and Dr. Johnson, had no eye for the real beauties of Highland scenery. The big bens repelled them, as did also the barren moors covered only with heath and shrouded with frequent mists. But before even Sir Walter Scott threw his magic wand over the land of the mountain and the flood and transfigured it for English eyes, the hunter bard of Glenorchy had already done this service for Highlanders (M. MacLean, 1904, p. 58).

Certainly there is no doubt that Burt and Johnson saw with different eyes than either Macintyre or Walter Scott, but this is not to argue that Macintyre and Walter Scott had the same vision. Dr Johnson says of the effect of the landscape in the Highlands:

> the imaginations excited by the view of an unknown and untravelled wilderness are not such as arise in the artificial solitudes of parks and gardens. . . . The phantoms which haunt a desert are want, and misery, and danger; the evils of dereliction rush upon the thoughts; man is made unwillingly acquainted with his own weakness, and meditation shows him only how little he can sustain, and how little he can perform (S. Johnson, 1775, p. 87).

Of the mountains which produce such a powerfully sentimental response a century later he drily remarks:

> The height of mountains philosophically considered is properly computed from the surface of the next sea; but as it affects the eye or imagination of the passenger, as it makes either a spectacle or an obstruction, it must be reckoned from the place where the rise begins to make a considerable angle with the plain (ibid., p. 82).

This is not the eye of Walter Scott, but we cannot suppose that Highlanders ever saw their landscape in this peculiarly rationalist manner, and it is only in the historical context of rationalism that we can understand the eye of Walter Scott and the other Romantics. Macintyre and Macdonald are simply outside this historical context, although theirs was the last generation of Highland poets of which this could be said. We are not therefore justified in using the capital N for the nature that surrounded Macintyre and of which he writes. 'Nature' in the nineteenth century came to have a host of metaphorical associations, none of which are historically or artistically appropriate to the works of Macdonald or Macintyre. The nature that Macintyre describes is simply the world that he lives in. The Nature which the Romantic poets describe is one metaphorical location in a moral topography. We should not, simply because Macintyre's greatest poems are descriptions of deer and mountains, casually ascribe to him any epithet such as 'nature poet'. Our language is replete with precisely the metaphorical associations which created Romantic poetry and the Romantic Highlands, and which are frankly inappropriate to Macintyre. We run the risk of our metaphors running wild, and our finding, as has been averred, that Macintyre's character is 'natural', his vocabulary 'natural', his subject 'natural', his rhythm 'natural', and his life 'natural'. He was composing highly-wrought poetry within an autonomous culture with a long literary tradition, to which he had at least partial access. Nevertheless Romantic criticism has subsumed him and orientated him to its own purpose. While we might argue that the romantic aesthetic was generative of inauthenticity in a variety of ways, it also had various ways and means of establishing its own validity, and creating its own authenticity, as it shows in its ability to subsume alien traditions, and turn them into its supports.

Sorley MacLean argues the case for the independence of eighteenth-century Gaelic poetry from the Romantic tradition. Criticising this tradition, he argues that:

> the chief reason for this romantic escapism in the poets of England, France, and Germany was the fact that 19th century poetry, a product of the bourgeoisie, found the industrial capitalism created by that

> class so sordid that poets had to eschew contemporaneity by an escape to the past or the exotic (S. MacLean, 1938, p. 86).

While this is in part true, it should be emphasised that there was more coherence to the Romantic aesthetic than simple 'escapism' suggests, as is evidenced, for example, by its organising power in relation to the Celts and Celtic art. It is important, however, to recognise that Romanticism was historically specific, and must be understood as such. One of the features of the period was certainly the rise of industrial capitalism, with all the demographic and social disruption that that entailed.

MacLean recognises that many of the metaphors used to situate Gaelic verse are seriously misleading. The concept of the 'natural' is a good example. As Crichton Smith says, 'nature simply reflects the man who sees it' (I. Crichton Smith, 1961, p. 175). Nature is never simply there, but has to be appropriated by man in order to be used by him, whether figuratively or physically, and as such is always a man-made product, even if, as within Romantic art, its exclusion of man and his arts is one of its categorical requirements. MacLean uses the word 'realism' to deride 'romance, escapism, fantasy, and their concomitants, affectation, fancifulness, far-fetchedness, and falseness' (S. MacLean, 1938, p. 81). He also uses 'realism' to contrast to: 'The special brand of romanticism attributed to the Gael and his poetry [which] is a romanticism of the escapist, other-worldly type, a cloudy mysticism, the type suggested by the famous phrase "Celtic Twilight"' (ibid., p. 86). He argues, perhaps over-optimistically, that 'Macintyre's objective naturalist realism is likely to be considered far more permanently significant than the mixture of sentimentalism, pure illusion and ruminating subjectivity lit up by great flashes, which constitutes Wordsworth's poetry' (ibid., p. 99). He says: 'To the modern Gaelic poet the sea gives spiritual messages; to the older poet the sea gives no messages. It is either a power to be conquered or enjoyed by man or a ruthless force that destroys precious lives' (ibid., p. 99). We can compare MacLean's assessment of the traditional Gaelic poet to whom nature 'gives no messages' with the earlier English poets described in the following: 'Roughly speaking, where earlier poets – like Shakespeare or, say, Chaucer, accept and enjoy, Romantics elegise and idealise. Nature is seen by Romantics to be consoling or morally uplifting' (D. Wright, 1968, xv). Although the Gaelic poets with whom we are concerned here were contemporaries of the English Romantics, it is perhaps with the earlier English poets that they are better compared (if comparisons must be made), in that neither looked to a Romantic Nature for consolation and moral uplift. MacLean says: 'As far as I can see the 18th century Gaelic poet did not dissociate his sensibility from any aspects of life' (S. MacLean, 1938, p. 105), but admits that 'for many reasons 19th century Gaelic poetry is not predominantly realist. Its most characteristic mood is a weak, half romantic nostalgia' (ibid., p. 111). He also tells us that 'real Gaelic poetry seeks extraneous decoration neither from fairy lore, foreign countries, Gothic castles, superstitions nor religiosity, Greek myth nor Celtic twilight' (ibid., p. 84) and that 'the authentic Gael is realist, recording simple human joy or sorrow' (ibid., p. 97).

Certainly, the wheel has turned, but we begin to realise that the equation of realism with Gaeldom is as tautological and as axiomatically irrefutable as is, within the Romantic tradition, the equation of the Gael and twilit mystery. The way in which the structure of this discourse is maintained while permitting a complete change of mind on the part of the protagonists is interestingly close to, and the change of fashion in some ways a simple reversal of, the progress of the primitivist debate in the eighteenth century. Whitney says that:

> there was a transition during the century from a rationalistic primitivism at the beginning, which tended to derive the qualities of goodness and sagacity in the savage from the unobstructed operation of the 'light of reason', to a more emotional, sentimental, and antinomian primitivism which became increasingly the favoured type as the century progressed (L. Whitney, 1934, p. 69).

MacLean argues that 'the fogs of the Celtic twilight' (S. MacLean, 1938, p. 114), are 'a purely foreign non-Celtic development' (ibid.), and that the works of the Celtic twilight 'have soothed the ears of the Anglo-Saxon bourgeoisie' (ibid., p. 87). We can understand MacLean's impatience at the misappropriation of his culture for use by another, but to locate outside the 'Celtic' world all that is considered undesirable is no more realist than the activities of those who, like Arnold and Yeats, set up the Celtic world of their imagination as a location for all their fondest dreams. I would also argue that the use of the racialist rhetoric of Celt and Anglo-Saxon courts a relapse into the discourse which generated the very inauthenticity from which MacLean is trying to escape. To imagine that Gaeldom could be isolated from the rest of the world and left to pursue its authenticity is no more realist than the attempt to restore a timeless Gaelic world by the collection of folklore.

It should also be pointed out that although Gaelic poetry in the eighteenth century did not suffer the 'dissociation of sensibility' that Eliot ascribed to English poetry of the seventeenth century (see T.S. Eliot, 1966, p. 288), neither did the Gaelic world produce the scientific revolution of the post-Newtonian world. If every aspect of the relationship of Gaelic to English culture must be seen as a projection of blame and opprobrium in one direction or another (as sometimes seems to be the case), it might be argued that the Romantic tradition achieved an assimilation of the enormous social and intellectual changes of the eighteenth century that Gaelic art clearly did not. It is only now, after a century or more of following in the trail of Romantic art, that Gaelic poetry is discovering once again what it considers to be its own voice. This failure to respond to change and internalise it creatively was of course in part a result of the social disruption caused by political and economic oppression. At the same time, however, it should be borne in mind that political and economic oppression was not unique to the Highlands. The Highland Clearances, for example, however nasty they were, were only a minor drama within the world of *laissez-faire* industrial capitalism, and are neither demographically nor politically comparable with the sustained economic oppression of the poor in British industrial areas in the early nineteenth century.

MacLean is prepared to grant to the Gaelic poets of the seventeenth century a measure of realism, on the grounds that they believed what they said, or that they are realist in sensuous detail. To assess what is realist or not in the works of a praise-poet of the seventeenth century would involve trying to appreciate that what is often clearly 'untrue', nevertheless has, in its historical context, an authenticity, a 'realism', which it is now difficult to appreciate. As Derick Thomson says of Clan poetry: 'These outworn rivalries and preoccupations may sometimes make it difficult for the modern reader to achieve empathy with the seventeenth-century poet' (D. Thomson, 1974, p. 116). If we are to accord the courtesy of extending to the seventeenth-century poets an attempt at empathy, then we are surely obliged to be as courteous to the poets of the Celtic Twilight. It should not be the first purpose of either literary or political criticism to consign whole historical periods to the dustbin. Furthermore, I am in no doubt that more writing about Gaels by Gaels has been inspired by the themes of Romanticism, and the Celtic Twilight that it engendered, than by an appreciation of the 'realism' which MacLean quite rightly praises. To make an 'alien', 'bourgeois', 'Anglo-Saxon' intervention out of this is neither realist nor honest. I would not agree that MacLean was 'wasting the time of the Gaelic Society of Inverness attacking a phenomenon whose absurdity was plain to any Gaelic speaker' (S. MacLean, 1938, p. 87). Nor would

I agree that the naturalist realism of 'Beinn Dòbhrain' is 'the authentic natural magic that Arnold found in Celtic poetry' (ibid., p. 99). The world which Arnold built around the Celt is, as I show in the next chapter, very much an artefact of Romanticism, and the inauthenticity of that discourse is still maintained in many different ways. Not least of these is in the assumption of the unitary character of Celtic art, defined in opposition to something outside itself, whether that unitary character is argued to be realist or mysterious.

It is a feature of the symbolic appropriation of the Celtic world that it should have become possible to speak of 'Celtic art' as though this were a homogeneous corpus of work. MacLean uses the adjective 'Celtic' in this casual manner just as readily as do those he is criticising. 'Celtic art' declines to be a body of work with its own normal internal variety and structure. Instead it becomes, for rhetorical purposes, an unstructured unity, defined in opposition to all that it excludes. To get some measure of the diminution that this invites we can construct the expressions 'Anglo-Saxon art', 'Gothic art', 'Teutonic art', and discover both how limiting and unlikely they are. It is some measure of the authenticity of the works of Macdonald and Macintyre, and of their near total independence from the ever-encroaching world of the English language and its symbolic manipulations, that the Gaelic world within which they operate is symbolically entirely autonomous. Even where it might be expected (as in, for example, Macintyre's poems on 'Gaelic and the Bagpipe') their poetry shows no attempt or necessity to look outside the world of the Gael for metaphors to express the Gael to himself, in contrast to much twentieth-century Gaelic poetry. The Gall is often present in their poetry, as an enemy or as the location of cowardice or weakness, but he is never the sophisticated, worldly, artificial, scientific, heartless, capitalist, progressive, materialist Anglo-Saxon that he becomes in later poetry. It is to this Anglo-Saxon, and his Celtic *alter ego*, that we will now turn.

4 ERNEST RENAN AND MATTHEW ARNOLD

Two of the most influential works in the history of Celtic studies were supplied, in the middle of the nineteenth century, by two prominent *literati*, Ernest Renan and Matthew Arnold. Although the ideas that they were expressing were not entirely new, they gave to them a respectability and a coherence that had previously been lacking. It is a measure of their influence that it would in many ways be more appropriate to discuss their work before discussing the poets Alexander Macdonald and Duncan Macintyre, since the bulk of commentary on these poets was made under the influence of Renan and Arnold. Consequently much of the commentary discussed in the last chapter is best seen as an attempt to make the eighteenth-century Gael conform to a picture of the Celt painted in the nineteenth century. The appropriation of the Celtic world to serve the symbolic ends of a dominant intellectual discourse, which began with Ossian in the eighteenth century, continued throughout the next. Renan's and Arnold's knowledge of Celtic matters was relatively slight, but they spoke with metaphors that carried their own validity. Their influence on later consideration of the Celt, both serious and frivolous, was enormous. The 'Celtic Renaissance' movement of the late nineteenth century took its 'Form and aims, and ideas . . . from the influence of two men – M. Renan, who may be called the Moses of the proceedings, and Mr. Matthew Arnold, who was the eloquent Aaron' (A. Lang, 1897, p. 181).

Both Renan and Arnold were ostensibly dealing with the different characteristics of the races of Europe, and were primarily concerned with the opposition of Celt and Teuton (Anglo-Saxon, German, etc.). In entering any nineteenth-century discourse concerning race we open the door on a huge arena of discussion within which the learned and the ignorant, the journalist and the scholar, the ponderous and the witty, found it possible to air any view they chose, and it is not possible to do more than graze the surface of such discussion, either in reading it, or in presenting it within a limited format such as this. It is not, however, within the strictly racial issues that the works of Renan and Arnold are best understood. Their ostensibly racial discussions provided, as had Ossian a century before, a medium within which more fundamental intellectual preoccupations could be debated. And just as Ossian had gathered authenticity, rather than lost it, owing to its suitability as a medium for contemporary debate, so the Celt of Renan and Arnold became an established figure by the same route. The issues at stake were, indeed, remarkably unchanged, although the heat of the Ossianic debate had temporarily subsided.

We have seen that the Ossianic controversy promoted a picture of the Celt as natural, emotional, naïve, and a failure in the rough and tumble of the modern world. This Celt soon began to occupy a place in European history. Two prominent precursors of Renan and Arnold in this were Henri Martin and Amédée Thierry. Both these latter wrote, as did Renan and Arnold, under the assumption that modern France was still a predominantly Celtic nation. Thierry described the Ancient Gauls, and their relationship to the Germans, by arguing that they had:

> un esprit franc, impétueux, ouvert à toutes les impressions, éminemment intelligent; mais à côté de cela une mobilité extrême, point de constance, une repugnance marquée aux idées de discipline et d'ordre si puissantes chez les race germaniques, beaucoup d'ostentation, enfin une désunion perpétuelle, fruit de l'excessive vanité (A. Thierry, 1828, v).

This assessment was corroborated by Martin, who wrote of the Gauls that they were:

> à la fois naifs et sagaces, ennemis de tout détour et pénétrant aisement les détours d'autrui, rudes et fins, enthousiastes et moqueurs, imitateurs et spontanés; ils pussent, dans leur discours, d'une brièveté énigmatique et sentencieuse à une éloquence impétueuse et intarissable en figures hardies; leur mobilité singulière en ce qui concerne les personnes et des choses extérieures ne tient pas seulement à la vivacité de leur imagination, mais aussi à leur indomptable personnalité, toujours prête à réagir contre le despotisme du fait (H. Martin, 1855, p. 36).

He called them 'une race où domine le sentiment, le principe essentiel de la femme' (ibid., p. 39). We have, therefore, the qualities that were going to dominate future debate – sentimentality, impressionability, femininity, and, in perhaps the most quoted phrase in the history of Celtic studies, a readiness to 'react against the despotism of fact'.

Renan, in his essay *La Poésie des Races Celtiques*,[10] elaborated this theme and applied it to religious and literary matters. Renan was born, and spent the early part of his life, in Brittany. Consequently his consideration of the Celt cannot be divorced from his personal biography, since he found it appropriate to speak of the Celt in imagery that any intellectual of his period would have found appropriate for describing a fondly remembered childhood. This is a theme that is, as we shall see, multiply compounded by the time we come to the consideration of modern Scottish Gaelic poets. Renan said of his Brittany and the literature that it inspired:

> Je pense à ma belle mer de Bretagne, a mes rochers de Bréhat, et j'ai presque envie de pleurer. Ah! que je conçois bien que ces lieux aient inspiré ces conceptions vagues, tristes, contemplatives, pleines d'espérances pour l'avenir d'au delà (E. Renan, 1947-64, Vol. IX, p. 107).

Renan's mother continued to live in Brittany, and he retained a great fondness for his birth-place. His education however led him away from the domesticity and simple Catholicism of his childhood, to a Jesuitical training, and finally to a crisis of faith that led him to write his *Vie de Jésus* (1863), a work that was construed as one of the most serious of nineteenth-century assaults on religion by the forces of amoral rationalism. His allocation to the Celts of a simple religiosity and an idealism that declined to take note of factuality can in part be understood as a simple nostalgia. At the same time Renan was much influenced by theories of the development of literature in society that can be traced directly to the Ossianic controversy. Galand says that in 1845-6:

> Renan subit l'influence, à la Sorbonne, de trois professeurs, Gérusez, Egger, et Ozanam, dont les vues sur la naissance et l'évolution des littératures sont l'aboutissement de théories qui, commes celles que l'ont vient de décrire, ont surgi au XVIIIe siècle. Dès cette époque, une distinction s'établit entre la poésie naïve et sincère des peuples primitifs, et la poésie froide et artificielle des siècles trop civilisés. Herder est sans doute le champion du primitif en littérature dont les écrits exercèrent l'action la plus forte, sur ces contemporains et sur les générations postérieures (R. Galand, 1959, p. 46).

Herder had been much influenced in his theories by the poems of Ossian (see J.G. Herder, 1964, and J.S. Smart, 1905, Ch. 1), and Renan went back to Ossian to find confirmation of these theories. The circularity of such confirmation was no simple tautology to be removed on careful inspection, but rather the self-confirmation of a creative and autonomous discourse, with a life outspanning the generation of those who found themselves theorising within it. 'De nombreux critiques, dont les plus importants sont, en Allemagne, Les Frères Grimm, et, en France, Fauriel, developpèrent les idées de Herder et s'efforcèrent de préciser les lois qui ont présidé à la formation des littératures primitives' (R. Galand, 1959, p. 47). It is important to note, particularly when we come to Arnold's work, that 'Renan ne fait guère de distinction entre l'émotion esthétique, l'émotion poétique, l'émotion religieuse et l'émotion morale. Il voit en elles toutes la manifestation d'un même instinct. L'aspiration vers l'infini, la soif de l'absolu, le culte de l'idéal' (ibid., p. 48). For Renan, 'la poésie est . . . un état subjectif, un entraînement de la sensibilité, une extase devant le Beau' (ibid.). He argued that

> il y a deux espèces de littératures: l'une toute belle, toute spontanée, naïve expression de tout ce qu'il y a de poétique dans l'humanité: toute vraie, sans retour sur elle-même, ne songeant qu'à exprimer l'idéal qui la possède, exhalation de l'humanité . . . Une autre réfléchie, calculée, qui voit l'effet et y vie, qui veut le beau, qui se sent, qui étudie (E. Renan, 1947-64, Vol. IX, p. 77).

When Renan came to write his study on the poetry of the Celts, we find that the Celt becomes a conflation of the domesticity and femininity of Renan's childhood; of the emotionality that he felt his intellectuality had lost him; of all the supposed characteristics of primitive literature, *naïveté*, spontaneity and simple unaffected truth; and of the aesthetic emotion, the poetic emotion, the religious emotion, and the moral emotion. Renan describes the change in the character of the people as a traveller enters Brittany:

> à la vulgarité normande, à une population grasse et plantureuse, contente de vivre, pleines de ses intérêts, égoiste comme tous ceux dont l'habitude est de jouir, succède une race timide, réservée, vivant toute au dedans, pesante en apparence, mais sentant profondément, et portant dans ses instincts religieux une adorable délicatesse. La même contraste frappe, dit-on, quand on passe de l'Angleterre au pays de Galles, de la basse Ecosse, anglaise de langage et de moeurs, au pays des Gaëls du Nord, et aussi, avec une nuance sensiblement différente, quand on s'enfonce dans les parties de l'Irlande òu la race est restée pure de tout mélange avec l'étranger (E. Renan, 1947-64, Vol. II, p. 252).

The observed reserve and diffidence might easily be ascribed to a mistrust, bred of long political experience, of visitors from outside. However the coherence of this picture of the Celt, as it grows, comes to be largely independent of the Celts themselves. He says that:

> On oublie surtout que ce petit peuple . . . est en possession d'une littérature qui a exercé au moyen âge une immense influence, changé le tour de l'imagination européene et imposé ses motifs poétiques à presque toute le chrétienté. . . . dans le grand concert de l'espèce humaine, aucune famille n'égala celle-ci pour les sons pénétrants qui vont au coeur. Hélas! elle est aussi condamnée a disparaître, cette émeraude des mers du couchant! Arthur ne reviendra pas de son île enchantée, et Saint Patrice avait raison de dire à Ossian: 'Les héros que tu pleures sont morts; peuvent-ils renaître?' (ibid., p. 253).

We must note the great effect on the nineteenth-century imagination of the Arthurian legends, through the translations from the Welsh published as the *Mabinogion* by Lady Charlotte Guest from 1837 to 1849, and later through the works of Tennyson and the Pre-Raphaelites. We also find reference both to Ossian and to the great age and likely disappearance of the Celtic languages, where the gloom of Ossian before St Patrick and the theory of the Indo-European expansion easily and without incongruity become the same wistful metaphor.

Renan says further of the Celtic race that: 'C'est par excellence une race domestique, formée pour la famille, et les joies du foyer . . . Toute l'institution sociale des peuples celtiques n'était à l'origine qu'une extension de la famille' (ibid., p. 255). He concludes from this that:

> Il ne semble pas qu'à aucune époque elle ait eu d'aptitude pour la vie politique: l'esprit de la famille a étouffé chez elle toute tentative d'organisation plus étendue (ibid., p. 257).

> S'il était permis d'assigner un sexe aux nations comme aux individus, il faudrait dire sans hésiter que la race celtique, surtout envisagée dans sa branche kymrique ou bretonne, est une race essentiellement féminine (ibid., p. 258).

From sensibility, delicacy, intuition, he has passed easily into domesticity and femininity. He says of their imagination and their art: 'Comparée à l'imagination classique, l'imagination celtique est vraiment l'infini comparé au fini' (ibid.) and: 'L'élément essentiel de la vie poétique du Celte, c'est l'aventure, c'est-à-dire la poursuite de l'inconnu' (ibid.). Remembering how Ossian brought the Gaels into the centre of the

Romantic movement, we are not surprised to read that 'chaque fois que le vieil esprit celtique apparaît dans notre histoire, on voit renaître avec lui la foi à la nature et à ses magiques influences' (ibid., p. 271). Nor are we surprised to find that there is a 'vivacité toute particulière que les races celtiques ont portée dans le sentiment de la nature. Leur mythologie n'est qu'un naturalisme transparent' (ibid., p. 269). It is also of interest, when we come to consider the easy analogy between this picture of the Celt, and femininity, that 'les Germains ne reçurent le christianisme que tard et malgré eux, par calcul ou par force . . . Il n'en fut pas de même chez les peuples celtiques; cette douce petite race était naturellement chrétienne' (ibid., p. 289). Religiosity was one of the fields of activity within which nineteenth-century middle-class women were permitted to take a full part. The political and religious conservatism that is a marked feature of European womanhood is easily explained as a simple consequence of an isolation, within the home, from the mainstream of thought and political activity. The Celtic fringes have been, for geographical rather than ideological reasons, similarly isolated. Renan remarks of the Breton Celt that:

> La dernière, elle a défendu son indépendence religieuse contre Rome, et elle est devenue le plus ferme appui du catholicisme; la dernière en France, elle a défendu son indépendance politique contre le roi, et elle a donné au monde les derniers royalistes (ibid., p. 256).

Exactly the same case could be made, *mutatis mutandis*, for Scottish Gaels and for French and British women. The equation of Celthood and femininity is thus powerfully confirmed, and the conclusion drawn that they are alike in sentiment and feeling, rather than alike in political subjection and marginality.

We can see that Renan's Celt, while ostensibly the *alter ego* of the German or Classical character, takes much of his shape in opposition to rationality, intellectuality, and a materialist world of scientific and political manipulation. Instead of these the Celt has an artistic capacity beyond the ordinary, a religious instinct of unusual depth, a strength and profundity of thought and feeling but a weakness in the external world of action, a ready emotionality and an easy communion with nature, a strength in domesticity but a weakness in a wider political sphere, and a femininity. Renan explains more fully elsewhere his picture of the relationship of man and woman to scientific activity, and we can get from the following passage a clearer idea of the coherence of the metaphors that he applies to the Celt. This is from the preface to his *Recollections of My Youth*:

> The natural sequence of this book, which is neither more nor less than the sequence in the various periods of my life, brings about a sort of contrast between the anecdotes of Brittany and those of the Seminary, the latter being the details of a darksome struggle, full of reasonings and hard scholasticism, while the recollections of my earlier years are instinct with the impressions of childlike sensitiveness, of candour, of innocence, and of affection. There is nothing surprising about this contrast. Nearly all of us are double. The more a man develops intellectually, the stronger is his attraction to the opposite pole: that is to say, the irrational, to the repose of the mind in absolute ignorance, to the woman who is merely a woman, the instinctive being who acts solely from the impulse of obscure consciousness . . . The superiority of modern science consists in the fact that each step forward it takes is a step further in the order of abstractions. We make chemistry from chemistry, algebra from algebra; the very indefatigability with which we fathom nature moves us further from her. This is as it should be, and let no one fear to prosecute his researches, for out of this merciless dissection comes life. But we need not be surprised at the feverish heat which, after these orgies of dialectics, can only be calmed by the kisses of the artless creature in whom nature lives and smiles. Woman restores us to communication with the eternal spring in which God reflects himself (E. Renan, 1883, xi).

This woman that Renan draws, in opposition to the world of science, is so akin to the picture of the Celt that he draws, that we can profitably look to a scientific world-view to provide a mirror wherein to understand the logic of the qualities ascribed to the Celt. Passion, irrationality, obscure consciousness, sensitiveness, affection and nature are opposed to and thus defined by contrast to intellectuality, reasonings, hard scholasticism, merciless dissection and science. The opposition of the Celt to the qualities ascribed to science is made more explicitly by Arnold, and I will delay discussing Renan's Celt further until I have given Arnold's version of what is essentially the same myth. It will be necessary in doing so, as it has been for a presentation of Renan's work, to quote at considerable length. It is not possible, in summary, to give any adequate idea of either the rhetorical power, the familiarity of the imagery, or the ease with which diverse metaphors glide easily into one another, and derive strength and aptitude from their place in the larger text. Much that would sound banal and unlikely in summary becomes, in these works, powerfully persuasive, as all the dominant intellectual concerns of the nineteenth century polarise about the Celt and the Anglo-Saxon, thus conjuring these racial stereotypes into their most likely and appealing existence.

Arnold gave a series of lectures as Professor of Poetry in Oxford in the winter of 1865 and the spring of 1866, with the subject *On the Study of Celtic Literature.* In these he drew heavily on Martin and Renan. Arnold, like Renan, was much concerned with the place of religion in a modern and self-consciously rational world. Both were concerned to reconcile the obvious material advantages accruing from the pursuit of science and industry with a more sensitive approach to art, the humanities and humanity than was inherent in the often banal and reductive philosophy with which the popular science of the day imagined its validation. Mott argues that we can readily understand the attractiveness of Renan's work for Arnold. Arnold found in Renan's *Essais de Morale et de Critique* that:

> The poetry of life was exalted above the machinery of life. In politics there was no sympathy with the gross and vulgar materialism of the prevailing school, proud of industrial and administrative improvement, which, beneficial though it be, is yet no compensation for spiritual degradation (L. Mott, 1918, p. 67).

Arnold said, in a letter to his sister, that:

> I have read few things for a long time with more pleasure than . . . 'Sur la Poésie des Races Celtiques'. I have long felt that we owed far more, spiritually and artistically, to the Celtic races than the somewhat coarse German intelligence readily perceives, and have been increasingly satisfied at our own semi-Celtic origin, which, as I fancy, gives us the power, if we will use it, of comprehending the nature of both races (cited L. Mott, 1918, p. 66).

When we consider the way in which both Arnold and Renan employ Martin's phrase 'revolt against the tyranny of fact', it is worth remembering that 'fact', as it was often imagined, was indeed a tyranny in the middle of the nineteenth century. This was the great age of 'the entry of institutionalised hyper-formalism into social study, through the work of the Registrar-General's office from its inception in 1837' (P. Kreager, 1977, p. 65). When we come to consider the place which this picture of the Celt has within the larger sociological discourse in the nineteenth century, we should note that 'the broad dispersion of applied and theoretical mathematical discourses in the middle of the last century . . . doubtless has a great deal to do with our notions of fact, evidence, formalism and scientificity' (ibid., p. 77). This is an important point to bear in mind when we later come to consider the contemporary application, to marginal communities like Scottish Gaeldom, of sociological constructs which themselves had their genesis in this period. The confirmation of their logic that such constructs find in gazing on such communities as that of the Celts is, perhaps, mere evidence of their common origin as artefacts of, reactions to, 'institutionalised hyper-formalism'.

The same unease at the power of materialism that caused Arnold to look to the Celt caused Dickens to provide, in *Hard Times*, a parody of utilitarian views. We get a clear idea of the 'tyranny of fact' that such a philosophy was felt to represent. Thomas Gradgrind, the successful mill-owner who conducts his life by statistics, is addressing a school full of children:

> 'You are to be in all things regulated and governed', said the gentleman, 'by fact. We hope to have, before long, a board of fact, composed by commissioners of fact, who will force the people to be a people of fact, and of nothing but fact. You must discard the word Fancy altogether. You have nothing to do with it. You are not to have, in any object of use or ornament, what would be a contradiction in fact. You don't walk upon flowers in fact; you cannot be allowed to walk upon flowers in carpets. You don't find that foreign birds and butterflies come and perch upon your crockery; you cannot be permitted to paint foreign birds and butterflies upon your crockery . . . You must use,' said the gentleman, 'for all these purposes, combinations and modifications (in primary colours) of mathematical figures which are susceptible of proof and demonstration. This is the new discovery. This is fact. This is taste' (C. Dickens (1854), 1974, p. 7).

The polarisation, within popular discourse, of the sentiments and associations appropriate to 'fact' and 'fancy', which still march together in our language, defining one another as opposites, can be understood by briefly considering the relationship of Arnold's work to that of J.S. Mill. Both were concerned to find a compromise between idealism and materialism – 'they were concerned with the growing rift between the humanistic and the scientific streams of Western culture and with the means of closing it' (E. Alexander, 1965, p. 19). Nevertheless, 'contemporaries of Arnold and Mill seem to have thought of them as representatives of opposed schools of thought' (ibid., p. 2). We will see that Arnold's attempt to resolve this philosophical duality by miscegenation, fixing a compromise in the blood of the British people, had as its most conspicuous outcome a literary movement which adopted wholesale the idealist half-view that he attributed to the Celt. Mill found himself similarly misrepresented, in a contrary way. We can get a clear idea of what utilitarianism was thought to be, and of what the moral implications of materialism were, from Mill's own irritated assertion of what utilitarianism was not. He said:

> A passing remark is all that needs be given to the ignorant blunder of supposing that those who stand up for utility as the test of right and wrong, use the term in that restricted and merely colloquial sense in which utility is opposed to pleasure (J.S. Mill, 1968, p. 5).

> Yet the common herd, including the herd of writers, not only in newspapers and periodicals, but in books of weight and pretension, are perpetually falling into this shallow mistake. Having caught up the word utilitarian, while knowing nothing whatever about it but its sound, they habitually express by it the rejection, or the neglect, of pleasure in some of its forms; of beauty, of ornament, or of amusement. Nor is the term thus ignorantly misapplied solely in disparagement, but occasionally in compliment, as though it implied superiority to frivolity and the mere pleasures of the moment. And this perverted use is the only use in which the word is popularly known, and the one from which the new generation are acquiring their sole notion of its meaning (ibid., p. 6).

Mill was perhaps wrong in thinking that a 'mere colloquial sense' could be thus argued away and replaced. The moral overtones of utilitarianism partook inevitably of those appropriate to rationalism and materialism, and could not, in popular usage, be compromised by idealism. The ease with which Arnold built an ethnological construct out of metaphors of mutual exclusion shows how total the polarity was, even though he wished thereby to effect a *rapprochement.*

Arnold begins his study of Celtic literature by telling us how, after attending an Eisteddfod meeting in Llandudno, he came out into the street and met:

> an acquaintance fresh from London and the parliamentary session. In a moment, the spell of the Celtic genius was forgotten, the Philistinism of our Anglo-Saxon nature made itself felt, and my friend and I walked up and down by the roaring waves, talking not of ovates and bards, and triads and englyns, but of the sewage question, and the glories of our local self government, and the mysterious perfections of the Metropolitan Board of Works (M. Arnold, 1891, p. 8).

It is clear that the world of tangible, material affairs, of instrumental activity, is opposed to creativity and the world of ideas, the former being the talent of the Anglo-Saxon, the latter the talent of the Celt. The derisive 'mysterious perfections of the Metropolitan Board of Works' echoes Dickens' ironic 'board of fact, composed of commissioners of fact', and puts us firmly in the age of 'institutionalised hyperformalism'.

In so far as Arnold can be considered a Celtic scholar, one of the most antique features of his work, notwithstanding his use of a now outmoded racialist discourse, is the ruthless logic by which he affirms the spirituality of the Celtic genius. He denies it any place in the practical material world with the uncompromising assertion that 'the sooner the Welsh language disappears as an instrument of the practical, political, social life of Wales, the better' (ibid., p. 10). He says that the Celtic genius 'cannot count appreciably now as a material power; but . . . it may count for a good deal . . . as a spiritual power' (ibid., p. 13). Even the least sentimental of Celtic scholars nowadays would hardly hold the disappearance of a Celtic language as a desirable goal, even if fearing its inevitability. It is some evidence of the encapsulating logic of the metaphors within which Arnold was working that he could, without incongruity, hold such a position, and that others could bitterly resent it, feeling that this was giving far too much away to the Celt. Arnold, in the introduction to the published lectures, quotes a *Times* critic who objected to any championing of the cause of Celtic literature, however slight:

> The Welsh language is the curse of Wales. Its prevalence, and the ignorance of English have excluded, and even now exclude the Welsh people from the civilisation of their neighbours. An Eisteddfod is one of the most mischievous and selfish pieces of sentimentalism which could possibly be perpetrated. It is simply a foolish interference with the natural progress of civilisation and prosperity. If it is desirable that the Welsh should talk English, it is monstrous folly to encourage them in a loving fondness for their old language. Not only

> the energy and power, but the intelligence and music of Europe have come mainly from Teutonic sources, and this glorification of everything Celtic, if it were not pedantry, would be sheer ignorance. The sooner all Welsh specialities disappear from the face of the earth the better (cited M. Arnold, 1891, xii).

Arnold cited this in order to deplore such intellectual parochialism. Nevertheless, he himself insisted, 'For all serious purposes in modern literature (and trifling purposes in it who would care to encourage?) the language of a Welshman is and must be English' (M. Arnold, 1891, p. 11). This would in many circles nowadays be regarded as just another tyranny of the imperialist English language. Bromwich says of Arnold that:

> He argued passionately for the recognition of Celtic as a part of the English cultural heritage, yet he seems to have deliberately ignored the possibility of any post-mediaeval continuance of Celtic literature: he was uncompromising in his attitude to the Celtic tradition as something which was dead and belonged solely to the past (R. Bromwich, 1965, p. 32).

She therefore argues that 'Arnold's expressed admiration of the National Eisteddfod of Wales was thus based on a contradiction' (ibid.). Arnold, however, never suggests that the Celts have disappeared, or that the qualities that they show are outdated. We notice that he asks for the disappearance of the Welsh language as an *instrument* of the *practical*, *political*, social life of Wales, while elsewhere arguing that the words that I have emphasised are inappropriate to the Celtic genius. There is not, within the metaphors that he employs, any contradiction in asking for the disappearance of the Welsh language, since a spiritual influence can exert itself without being materially manifest at all. That Arnold did not worry about the very plain contradiction that Bromwich points out is further justification for treating his lectures as a philosophical allegory, dressed in ethnological clothing. Arnold says that:

> If his rebellion against fact has . . . lamed the Celt even in spiritual work, how much more must it have lamed him in the world of business and politics. The skilful and resolute appliance of means to ends which is needed both to make progress in material civilisation, and also to form powerful states, is just what the Celt has least turn for (M. Arnold, 1891, p. 88).

The world of instrumentality, practicality and politics is thus not in any case a 'Celtic' sphere, and the disappearance of Welsh from these areas is expected, natural and right. We have slightly more difficulty explaining Arnold's insistence that if a Welsh poet has anything to say he should say it in English, since the arts are very much within the ethos that he gathers round the Celt. However even a poem, as an end product, is a materiality, an external presence, and the Celtic spirit can, even without its language, be argued to inspire creativity from within. Arnold showed this by finding the Celtic spirit in Dante, Shakespeare, Milton, Byron and Keats, and others showed it, more enthusiastically, by finding it everywhere they looked, from Homer to Goethe.

Prepared as he was to see the end of the materiality of the Welsh language, Arnold still drew bitter attack for his championing of the Celt. He was working within a discourse which gave his statements an appeal and a coherence independent of any simple argument over the status of the Welsh language. His plea for a British race uniting the best qualities of Celt and Anglo-Saxon, as he pictured them, is, in some ways, suggestive of a healthier and more robust attitude towards the Celtic tradition than is the often excessively protective, nervously assertive attitude that is later so common, and invariably constituted by an uncritical acceptance of precisely those characteristics of the idealist half-world that Arnold built around the Celt.

In contrast to his picture of the Celt, Arnold provides us with a description of the German genius. It is (his emphasis):

> Steadiness with honesty; the danger for a national spirit thus composed is the humdrum . . . The excellence of a national spirit thus composed is freedom from whim, flightiness, perverseness; patient fidelity to Nature,—in a word, *science*—leading it at last, though slowly, and not by the most brilliant road, out of the bondage of the humdrum and common, into the better life. The universal dead-level of plainness and homeliness, the lack of all beauty and distinction in form and feature, the slowness and clumsiness of the language, the eternal beer, sausage and bad tobacco, the blank commonness everywhere, pressing at last like a weight on the spirits of the traveller in Northern Germany, and making him impatient to be gone,—this is the weak side; the industry, the well-doing, the patient steady elaboration of things, the idea of science governing all departments of human activity,—this is the strong side (ibid., p. 82).

To this he opposes an assessment of the Celtic genius (his emphasis):

> *Sentiment* is, however, the word which marks where the Celtic races really touch and are one; sentimental, if the Celtic nature is to be characterised by a single term, is the best term to take. An organisation quick to feel impressions, and feeling them very strongly; a lively personality therefore, keenly sensitive to joy and to sorrow . . . it may be seen in wistful regret, it may be seen in passionate penetrating melancholy; but its essence is to aspire ardently after life, light, and emotion, to be expansive, adventurous, and gay (ibid., p. 84).

He gives us an anatomical metaphor to express the idealist Celt and the materialist Anglo-Saxon:

> The German, say the physiologists, has a larger volume of intestines (and who that has ever seen a German at a table d'hôte will not readily believe this?), the Frenchman has the more developed organs of respiration. That is just the expansive, eager Celtic nature; the head in the air, snuffing and snorting . . . For good and for bad, the Celtic genius is more airy and unsubstantial, goes less near the ground, than the German. The Celt is often called sensual; but it is not so much the vulgar satisfactions of sense that attract him as emotion and excitement; he is truly, as I began by saying, sentimental (ibid., p. 85).

The metaphors by which the respective qualities of idealism and materialism are expressed, the German with over-developed intestines and the Frenchman with large lungs, the one dull and plodding, the other mercurial, provide us with a clear moral picture as well as with an ethnological type-casting that we can still recognise. The defects of idealism are also expressed in a way that is familiar enough in the popular imagery of much social science, that it is 'airy and unsubstantial' and is not, to its detriment, 'near the ground'.

Arnold's Celt is, therefore, constructed in opposition to those qualities which were at the time associated with 'science' in popular discourse. The intellectual origins of these texts by Renan and Arnold can thus be found in the Enlightenment, and the discourse of which they were a part is still very much with us. Arnold himself had expressed doubt that he would be able to interest anybody in so apparently insubstantial a topic as Celtic literature. To tie two such ephemeral topics as poetry and Celts together was, however, asking for controversy. Alexander points out: 'Victorian hostility to poetry drew from many sources.

Benthamites doubted the utility of poetry; Puritans in modern dress suspected its moral intentions or its lack of them; scientists and logicians thought poetry incompatible with knowledge and truth' (E. Alexander, 1965, p. 152). Much of Arnold's work was an attempt to restore to the Anglo-Saxon Philistine the 'sweetness and light' (see M. Arnold, 1969, p. 43) which utilitarianism, materialism, science and Puritanism had robbed him of. In *Culture and Anarchy* he uses the metaphorical duality of Hebraism and Hellenism to much the same effect as he had used the Celt and Anglo-Saxon. He says, 'The idea of perfection as an inward condition of the mind and spirit is at variance with the mechanical and material civilisation in esteem with us, and nowhere, as I have said, so much in esteem as with us' (M. Arnold, 1969, p. 49). He speaks of:

> our preference of doing to thinking . . . energy is our strong point and favourable characteristic rather than intelligence . . . And these two forces we may regard as in some sense rivals,—rivals not by the necessity of their own nature, but as exhibited in man and his history,—and rivals dividing the empire of the world between them. And to give these forces names from the two races of men who have supplied the most signal and splendid manifestations of them, we may call them respectively the forces of Hebraism and Hellenism (ibid., p. 129).

Remembering the Celt and Anglo-Saxon, we can note that: 'The governing idea of Hellenism is spontaneity of consciousness; that of Hebraism, strictness of conscience' (ibid., p. 132). The world of the mind, of ideas and thought, is the world of the Celt and Hellenism. The external world, of facts and action, is the world of the Anglo-Saxon and Hebraism. Within the world of the mind those capacities associated with successful intervention in the external world, rationality and intellect, are Anglo-Saxon preserves, while those capacities that, by opposition, remain uncontrollable and ideal, intuition and emotionality, are the attributes of the Celt.

Finding in Ossian the Gael that Romantic art had engendered, Arnold located in the Celt, as had Renan, a femininity and a feeling for nature. The qualities that Romanticism admired, emotionality, spontaneity and a feeling for nature, were all three readily attached by Renan and Arnold to the Celt. In hoping for a British race that would combine the best of both races, Arnold was attempting to 'arrive at a via media between the precepts of Classicism and Romanticism' (E. Alexander, 1965, p. 153), and reconcile idealism and materialism, poetry and science, and James Macpherson and Dr Johnson, all at once. Although Arnold did not have a fondly recollected Celtic childhood to inform his discussion of the Celt and Anglo-Saxon, he did have extensive experience of the ponderous and devastating expansion of industry in 'Anglo-Saxon' England. Arnold, as HM Inspector of Schools from 1851 until 1886, was well placed to judge the poverty and misery of the industrial areas. This, and his contact with utilitarian educationalists involved with educating working-class children, can be argued to have inspired much of the vehemence of his criticism of the Anglo-Saxon character, its Philistinism, materialism and vulgarity, and inspired by exclusion the characteristics that he ascribed to the Celt. A sensation of the intellectual inadequacy and incompleteness of rationalism and materialism, coupled with an unease at the effects of industrial success, have been argued to have engendered Romantic art, and the Ossianic Celt. It is no accident that Arnold found in the Ossianic Celt a metaphor to solve his intellectual problems, which were the same, only more acute, as those that permitted the rise of Ossian and the demise of the Classical tradition a century before. It is often argued that:

> it was the spiritual and metaphysical implications of the scientific and technological revolution which began in the seventeenth century and which was going at full throttle by the end of the eighteenth, together with the changed and changing view of man's place in the universe, that sparked off the Romantic Movement (D. Wright, 1968, xiv).

Arnold used the symbolism of Romanticism to locate the Celt, with the aim of effecting an intellectual rapport by racial admixture. In locating outside the Anglo-Saxon the qualities of taste, whimsy, sensibility, artistry, Arnold was doing no more than did the Victorian public school, whose product, the English middle class, he so deplored. It is indicative of the organising power of the metaphors that he used that the intellectual result of his intervention was no *rapprochement*, but a glorification of the revolt against the tyranny of fact, in the shape of the Celtic Twilight movement.

Since the images that Renan and Arnold used were so ubiquitous in the nineteenth century, there are many threads that can be followed from their work. Two obvious issues are the racial controversy that they engendered, and the question of their relative accuracy with regard to the Celts and the Celtic literature that they were concerned with. The racial issue was enthusiastically joined, as the relative worth, and the relative prevalence, of Celt and Teuton, were hotly debated. Details of the ethnological issues involved can be found in F. Faverty (1951) and L.P. Curtis (1968). It was a matter of pride among many that the English were Teutonic to the core. Pinkerton had said, in the wake of the Ossianic controversy, that 'Celts anciently were, and are little better at present, . . . incapable of any progress in Society' (J. Pinkerton, 1787, p. 68). He summed up by declaring that 'to say that a writer is a Celt, is to say, that he is a stranger to the truth, modesty, and morality' (ibid.). Two prominent literary figures, Thomas Carlyle and Charles Kingsley, held vigorously to the view that the English were Anglo-Saxon, and vehemently not Roman, or French, or Celtic. Kingsley called the English 'the only real Teutons left in the world' (C. Kingsley, 1901, p. 209). Carlyle called his countrymen 'the Saxon British' (T. Carlyle, 1899, p. 140) and attributed to them 'an ingenuity which is not false; a methodic spirit, of insight, of perseverant well-doing; a rationality and veracity which Nature with her truth does not disown;—withall there is a "Bersekir rage" in the heart of them' (ibid.). To this kind of sentiment Arnold's work was unwelcome. Green argued that the Teutonic conquest of England after Roman withdrawal:

> had been complete. Not a Briton remained as subject or slave on English ground. Sullenly, inch by inch, the beaten men drew back from the land which the conquerors had won; and eastward of the line which the English sword had drawn all was now purely English (J.R. Green, 1877, p. 28).

In agreement with this, Freeman argued that 'Teutonic conquest in Gaul did not involve the displacement of one people by another, while Teutonic conquest in Britain did' (E.A. Freeman, 1888, p. 68). Where there were no Celts, it was presumably not worth looking for a Celtic genius. Grant Allen argued, however, that 'while in language, laws, customs, and government we are preponderantly or entirely English, yet in blood we are preponderantly if not overwhelmingly Kymric and Gaelic' (G. Allen, 1880, p. 473).

The confusion over the racial issue cannot be dissociated from the problem of the relative accuracy of Arnold's assessment of Celtic literature. Arnold said:

> If I were asked where English poetry got . . . its turn for style, its turn for melancholy, and its turn for natural magic, for catching and

> rendering the charm of nature in a wonderfully near and vivid way,– I should answer, with some doubt, that it got much of its turn for style from a Celtic source; with less doubt, that it got much of its melancholy from a Celtic source; with no doubt at all, that from a Celtic source it got nearly all its natural magic (M. Arnold, 1891, p. 113).

Such things are difficult to determine. Those who denied the existence of British Celts did not think the enquiry worth while, and others found style, melancholy and natural magic wherever they wished to find a Celt. Andrew Lang argued that these qualities were not Celtic, but rather a general feature of primitive literature:

> Now Finns are not Celts, yet the features of delicacy, love of nature, love of the supernatural and of magic, and the tone of defeated melancholy, which charm us in Finnish old popular poetry, are precisely the things which charm us in the poetry of the Celt. These beauties come of the loneliness, the contact with nature, the fond dwelling on the past, the living in fantasy, which circumstances have forced on both Celts and Finns (A. Lang, 1897, p. 182).

Even if we accept this general point, however, there is no doubt that the primitive life which Lang imagines is not unlike that which Ossian was presumed to have lived. Alfred Nutt, in a critical introduction to Arnold's Lectures, demolished every main point of his thesis, but nevertheless concluded that:

> In spite of errors due to imperfect knowledge, to incorrect interpretation, Arnold's main thesis is, I believe, well founded. English letters, and the whole complex life out of which letters spring, and whose ethos they manifest, are what they are because historically . . . we are a mixed people, composed partly of varying Celtic strains . . . I hold that to the presence of the Celtic strains are due distinct qualities which have greatly enriched the resulting whole, without which it would lack some of its most precious characteristics, would lack precisely that which entitles it to rank among the supreme manifestations of humanity (A. Nutt, 1910, xxvii).

The problem of Arnold's relative accuracy is fully treated by Bromwich, who says that:

> Arnold's attempts to define the characteristics of the Celtic literary tradition had an influence which increased rather than diminished . . . and in certain important respects this influence is still with us today, since Arnold's pronouncements in these lectures continue to be frequently quoted – sometimes in unexpected places – and by writers whose knowledge of the subject far exceeds that of their original author (R. Bromwich, 1965, p. 1).

It is certainly rare to find a study of Celtic literature which does not make some mention of Arnold. His picture of the Celt was adopted with enthusiasm by people in all fields of study, and became an established fact, a security with which an argument could be begun rather than a conclusion to be reached. The spirituality of the Celt and the materialism of the Anglo-Saxon, and all their other associated qualities, are continually referred to in journals of Scottish and Gaelic studies from the 1880s onwards, and still make regular, if slightly less frequent, appearances.

I do not have much space for examples, which are not in any case difficult to find, and will limit myself here to a few favourites. Angus Robertson, one-time president of An Comunn Gaidhealach (the Highland Association), supplies us with the following rather thrilling self-diagnosis:

> I am made commander of sublime eventualities. I beget my own dynamics. Science limits her geometric authority; but I can with intangible splendour, nay, with infallible accuracy, dogmatise on the embalmed conception of conscious power that sent the first electron hurtling into space! . . . confound these science-and-truth men! (A. Robertson, 1933, p. 9).

> Compression is only released by an irruption into a world of spiritual abandon – the native playground and shock absorber of the Celtic soul (ibid., p. 10).

We note that Robertson can locate the Gael with scientific imagery derived from the new world of Einsteinian relativity. The concerns invoked are, of course, very traditional, as the exciting uncertainties of time and space are opposed to the mundane Anglo-Saxon regularities of Newtonian mechanics.

Calum Macleod provides us with a modern Gaelic version of these ideas:

Faodaidh an Sasunnach a bhi gu math fada 'n a cheann, ach tha e car gearr-sheallach; chan fhaic e am bitheantas na's fhaide roimhe na bàrr a shròine. 'S fheàrr leis daonnan ian 's an làimh na dhà dhiag air iteig. Ach bha na Ceiltich an còmhnuidh ag amharc thar fàire, a' sealltuinn air na nithean faicsinneach a bha mu'n cuairt. Theagaisg an cuan siar sin sin dhaibh. 'S an fheasgar, 's iad ag amharc ris an iar, 's a' ghrian a' falbh bhuapa air iomall a' chuain, gu dé bha thall? Bha 'Tìr nan Òg'. Is beannaichte an sluagh aig a bheil léirsinn dé'n t-seòrsa sin.

. . . bha fios aca gu bheil nithean ann nach ceannaichear le òr no airgiod, agus gur iad sin na nithean a tha dà-rìribh prìseil, is buan-mhaireannach.

Tha an saoghal an diugh ag cur feum air na th'aig na Ceiltich ri theagasg, is ri thabhairt (C. Macleod, 1977, p. 55).

The Saxon may well be clever enough, but he is rather short-sighted; he usually does not see further than the end of his nose. He would always rather have a bird in the hand than a dozen on the wing. But the Celts have always gazed beyond the horizon, while looking on the visible things around them. The Atlantic Ocean has taught them that. In the evening, while they looked to the west, and the sun was going down over the sea, what lay beyond? It was 'Tir nan Og' (the Land of Youth). Fortunate are those with such a vision.

. . . they knew that there are things that are not bought with gold and silver, and that these are the things that are truly valuable, and enduring.

The world today is taking heed of what the Celt has to teach and to say (my translation).

The works of Neil Gunn, one of the most prominent of twentieth-century Scottish novelists, are shot through with ideas relating to the Gael and to the Highlands that are drawn from the metaphorical complex that I have been discussing, and that we can trace back to Arnold. In *The Well at the World's End*, we see two people in the Highlands 'setting out to find the – the something in life that we think isn't there' (N. Gunn, 1951, p. 10). Sitting on the moor, they 'listened to the silence as to a fable, and though it was remote beyond hearing or meaning it was startlingly nearer than the quick of the heart' (ibid., p. 14). Thus enraptured, they mused as follows: 'If you sat here and lost yourself for a little you would have the illusion of the races flowing up and round you and vanishing away' (ibid.).

In *The Green Isle of the Great Deep* Gunn tells a thoroughgoing political parable where Teutonic totalitarianism is happily brought to ruin through the free and untameable spirit of an old Highland man and a little Highland boy. The man and the boy fall into a salmon pool while poaching, and inhabit this unsympathetic political régime only in the brief unconscious between near-drowning and rescue. The totalitarian Utopia in which they find themselves is one where men's minds are taught unquestioning obedience, and where life is governed by a behaviourist, rationalist, mechanistic creed. The régime finds itself, not surprisingly, unable to absorb two Celts into its structure. The rulers of the Utopia puzzle over their Celtic intruders, arguing to themselves that they are so intractable because they come from:

> a complete and familiar community . . . Added to that was the background of what they call Nature. Which means that the subconscious responses had a natural field of action. Which further means that their acts must occasionally have the appearance of a high degree of irrationality (N. Gunn, 1944, p. 181).

The Green Isle of the Great Deep could be quoted in its entirety to demonstrate the enduring fertility, in a new political context, of the ideas that Arnold poured into his ethnology. We can leave Gunn by relating the advice given at the end of the story, at the collapse of the totalitarian régime – advice that comes from a figure who is, quite literally, God. The rulers of the departing tyranny are told that they have:

> divorced knowledge from wisdom, the head from the heart, the intellect from the spirit – for man has many words for these two regions – and because of this divorce, the taste of life has gone bitter and its hope sterile (ibid., p. 242).

I have quoted Bromwich to the effect that Arnold continues 'to be frequently quoted – sometimes in unexpected places' (R. Bromwich, 1965, p. 1). One of the most unlikely examples that I have discovered appears in Hugh Macdiarmid's quarterly *The Voice of Scotland*. This publication, at once nationalist and left-wing, treats the Celtic influences on English literature as an example of imperialistic exploitation: 'English literature, as Stopford Brooke and others have showed, has always drawn its best elements from the "Celtic fringe" and bitten the hand that has fed it' (*Voice of Scotland*, Vol. 1, No. 3, p. 3). Stopford Brooke (1901, p. 1) had merely echoed Arnold's views. Those anxious to develop a political voice for the Celt have nevertheless wished to preserve the self-image of the Celt that Arnold gave to them. Erskine speaks of the 'impressionable and somewhat credulous nature of the Celt' (R. Erskine, 1914a, p. 316). At the same time he argues that 'one of the charges most frequently brought against the Celt is that he has neither aptitude nor capacity for rule' (ibid.), which he calls a 'silly libel of the Saxon' (ibid., p. 317). This desire to run with the idealist hare and hunt with the materialist hounds finds a cunning resolution at Robertson's hands:

> To reach a close understanding of the Celt it is nearly always necessary to equate him in terms of poetic retrospection. Yet he can be modern without being artificial, but only temporarily. For he has a congenital dislike to the worldly-wise, however much he may, without envy, calculate their prosperity. At the same time he finds devolution of sentiment and peregrine mood to be in no way inconsistent with his obligations to those civil environments to which he may casually tune his ambitions, but seldom his soul (A. Robertson, 1933, p. 67).

One could truly say, for Arnold's Celt, as Galand says for Renan's, 'Ce mythe celtique deviendra pour les Celtes eux-mêmes un mirage où ils seront souvent les premiers à se reconnaître' (R. Galand, 1959, p. 153).

The most conspicuous result of this self-recognition was the literary movement at the end of the nineteenth century that is known as the Celtic Twilight movement. There is not space here to do more than mention its leading figures, but it is important to note that this movement only represented in extreme form ideas that were prevalent in many intellectual fields at the time. The most important figure in this movement, in retrospect at least, was W.B. Yeats. Like Lang, he argued that what had appeared Celtic to Arnold was in fact primitive, but the picture that he then draws of primitive life is taken with little modification from Renan and Arnold. He says of their works on Celtic literature, 'How well one knows these sentences' (W.B. Yeats, 1924, p. 214). He argues that:

> When Matthew Arnold wrote it was not easy to know as much as we know now of folk song and folk belief, and I do not think he understood that our 'natural magic' is but the ancient religion of the world, the ancient worship of nature and that troubled ecstasy before her, that certainty of all beautiful places being haunted, which it brought into men's minds (ibid., p. 217).

Remembering the Victorian passion for classification, statistics and measurement, for 'hyperformalism', we can understand Yeats' assertion that:

> Men who lived in a world where anything might flow and change, and become any other thing; and among great gods whose passions were in the flaming sunset, and in the thunder and the thunder-show, had not our thoughts of weight and measure (ibid., p. 219).

He locates the idealist other-world that the Celt had come to inhabit:

> a thirst for unbounded emotion and a wild melancholy are troublesome things in the world, and do not make its life more easy or orderly, but it may be the arts are founded on the life beyond the world, and that they must cry in the ears of our penury until the world has been consumed and become a vision (ibid., p. 227).

Arnold, he says, derived the turn for melancholy and the turn for natural magic in English literature from a Celtic source. In what is hardly a disagreement, he says:

> I will put this differently and say that literature dwindles to a mere chronicle of circumstances, or passionless phantasies, and passionless meditations, unless it is constantly flooded with the passions and beliefs of ancient times, and that of all the fountains of the passions and beliefs of ancient times in Europe, the Slavonic, the Finnish, the Scandinavian, and the Celtic, the Celtic alone has been for centuries close to the main river of European literature (ibid.).

An important member of this 'Celtic' group, William Sharp (alias Fiona MacLeod) says:

> The Celtic writer is the writer the temper of whose mind is more ancient, more primitive, and in a sense more natural than that of his compatriot in whom the Teutonic spirit prevails . . . And as the Celt comes of a people who grew in spiritual outlook as they began what has been revealed to us by history as a ceaseless losing battle, so the Teuton comes of a people who have lost in the spiritual life what they have gained in the moral and the practical (F. MacLeod, 1899, p. 36).

Representative works of artists who modelled themselves on this image, for example George Russell (alias 'A.E.'), W.B. Yeats, Douglas Hyde, Norah Hopper and William Sharp (alias Fiona MacLeod), can be found in the anthology *Lyra Celtica* (1896), edited by 'Fiona MacLeod's' wife, Elizabeth Sharp. We can also find there works by the 'Celtic' poets Emily Brontë and Lord Byron. The work is full of misty idealism and tender grief, in poems of which we might say, as Ford Madox Ford said of Norah Hopper's work: 'one looks in vain – one craves perhaps a little – for the touch of modernity' (F. Madox Ford, 1906, xii).

Dora Jones, reviewing Yeats' early poetry, said of the Celt that:

> He goes on his visionary way, . . . not with the desperate doggedness of one who sees his aim ever defeated and will not accept defeat, but with a wistful yet exquisite renunciation of the tangible for the intangible, the reality for the dream (D. Jones, 1900, p. 61).

The Celts are:

> a people who lived very near to nature's heart, sharing the life of flowers and birds, troubled or cheered by the face of the sky, in a way of which the modern man, the creature of an industrial civilisation, has forgot the secret (ibid., p. 63).

Some had little patience with this. Andrew Lang speaks of 'the Celtic tendency to claim whatever is excellent in a certain way as "Celtic"' (A. Lang, 1897, p. 182).

The question of the authenticity of Ossian, taken up once again into a web of wishful thinking, was again re-decided. William Sharp wrote a very scholarly introduction to the centenary edition of *The Poems of Ossian*, in which obscurantism and erudition lead us subtly to the conclusion that 'of this there can be no question: that the ancient poetry, the antique spirit, breathes throughout this eighteenth-century restoration and gives it enduring life, charm, and all the spell of cosmic imagination' (W. Sharp, 1896, xxiv). Lang was not satisfied with this, quite rightly. He says that 'Mr. Sharp is not very lucid or logical in his introduction' (A. Lang, 1897, p. 187). He goes on: 'the essence of Macpherson's "Ossian" is vagueness, mistiness, obscurity. To imitate this, as some Neo-Celts do, is not to Celticise, but to Macphersonise' (ibid.). He says of the new generation of Celtic writers:

> The young generation is Celtic enough, but that proves nothing. It has read Mr. Arnold, and Mr. Sharp, and Mr. Renan, and Mr. Grant

> Allen, and it says, 'Go to, let us be Celtic'. The Celticism is self-conscious, voulu, of malice prepense (ibid., p. 189).

The Celtic Twilight movement had a great appeal for many, and its renunciation did not remove the more fundamental preoccupations that underlay its appeal, and which lay behind the constructions of Arnold's and Renan's Celt. In order to demonstrate the generality of these preoccupations, I will try to tie this study of the Celt into the wider intellectual field. The congruence that I have already noted of this picture of the Celt and the picture of the ideal woman provides a point of departure. I have already quoted Renan to show the similarity of the metaphorical structures that he used to locate both Celt and Woman. Arnold echoes this, saying:

> the sensibility of the Celtic nature, its nervous exaltation, have something feminine in them, and the Celt is thus peculiarly disposed to feel the spell of the feminine idiosyncrasy; he has an affinity to it; he is not far from its secret (M. Arnold, 1891, p. 90).

Yeats, in *The Celtic Twilight*, says that:

> women come more easily than men to that wisdom which ancient peoples, and all wild peoples even now, think the only wisdom. The self, which is the foundation of our knowledge, is broken in pieces by foolishness, and is forgotten in the sudden emotions of women, and therefore fools get, and women do get of a certainty, glimpses of much that sanctity finds at the end of its painful journey (W.B. Yeats, 1959, p. 115).

It is remarkable how often the Celt is located in some kind of opposition to the modern world, of rationality, economics, bureaucracy and, as an image to stand for all of these, *machinery*, which instantly conjures up an opposition of untroubled nature, free from artifice. We will see that these images have not ceased to be apt for modern writers on Celtic matters. The areas of competence of the Celt, according to Arnold, are religion, the minor arts (he lacks the patience for major works, see M. Arnold, 1891, p. 87), emotionality, sentimentality. These are precisely the areas of competence that Victorian middle-class women lived in and with. To this is opposed the Anglo-Saxon world of politics, business, intervention in the material world, and science – still male preserves. Within the texts that I have quoted, and still within modern discourse, there are many oppositions that do not seem obviously related, but which are capable of sliding easily into one another to form a coherent and satisfying picture. Such oppositions are, for example: intellectual/emotional, rational/intuitive, science/religion, science/arts, externality/internality, instrumentality/creativity, practicality/sentimentality, culture/nature, materialism/idealism, objectivity/subjectivity, artificial/spontaneous, society/family, modern/ancient, male/female, Anglo-Saxon/Celt. The list could go on, and put in this form it seems rather empty and philosophically naïve. It should be made clear that I am not arguing that these dualities all represent, in any sense, the 'same' opposition. Within many texts, however, they are capable of ready association, making a coherent system of imagery that has informed not only the 'Celt', and 'Woman', but also the foundations of modern social science and many of its apparent problems.

It is not easy to begin a discussion of this imagery. There are no obviously secure oppositions with which the meaning of the more ephemeral can be rendered, by analogy, secure. Each duality gains strength and colour from its association with the others, and all could be given prominence without necessarily having more than a fragile status in dependence on the rest. Indeed, the metaphorical density that appears on close inspection in texts that appear innocently 'literal' must lead us to conclude that none of these dualities is properly independent of the rest, or more epistemologically secure.

Social anthropology, particularly since Lévi-Strauss's *La Pensée Sauvage* (1962), has made much of the opposition of 'culture' to 'nature' which is found to be a very general feature of otherwise disparate cosmologies. It is frequently found that women are symbolically related to 'nature' within such systems. Ardener has suggested that this derives from the fact that men, because of their political dominance, are usually more likely to need to come to grips with the problem of bounding their society apart from others. He says that 'ways of bounding society against society, including our own, may have an inherent maleness' (E. Ardener, 1972, p. 142). Men, however, besides being posed the problem of defining 'themselves and their women' in opposition to other societies, also define themselves as a sex in opposition to women. Consequently, 'because their model for *mankind* is based on that for *man*, their opposites *woman* and *non-mankind* (the wild), tend to be ambiguously placed' (ibid., p. 154). Remembering the enthusiasm with which the Celtic Twilightists took up as a self-image the idealist half-world that Arnold offered, we can note Ardener's further remark that 'Women accept the implied symbolic content, by equating womankind with the wild' (ibid.). Speaking of the sexual differentiation as a basis for other imagery, Ardener argues that 'the undoubted anatomical and functional differences become a powerful and convenient metaphor . . . it is no surprise that spatial concepts (inside/outside, village/wild) should be lined up with these pairs' (E. Ardener, 1975, p. 24). Certainly the sexual duality involves certain procreative *differentiae* that appear to supply both spatial and symbolic confirmation of other dualities that can arrange themselves about man and woman. The relative internality and inaccessibility of the capacities and activities of woman at every stage of the reproductive process lends itself readily to an association with the internal and uncontrollable world of the emotions and intuition. The strictly biological creativity of woman becomes a locus for all that is idealist, creative and fanciful. By contrast, the male procreative faculty, external and controllable, becomes intellectuality, rationality, and the conscious manipulation of the external world. Mitchell hopes to find, within psychoanalysis, an explanation of 'the connection of . . . hysteria and femininity, the different role of romantic love in the lives of the two sexes, women's undue share of "intuition" and men's of "rationality"' (J. Mitchell, 1974, xxi). With the example of the Celt to look to, we can explain such things merely as a function of a metaphorical conspiracy between science and Romantic art, between materialism and idealism.

We might, in the light of recent feminist polemic, consider the qualities attributed to the Celt as both expression of and justification for political and economic oppression. This is how many feminist writers have perceived 'femininity', and certainly in the late-eighteenth and nineteenth centuries Celts in both Ireland and Scotland were suffering such oppression. The esteem that Arnold felt for the Celt of his imagination was not shared by everybody, and the moral overtones of the idealist/materialist metaphor are not exhausted by treating the first as 'good' and the second as 'bad'. Idealism and other-worldliness can, without strain, become irrelevance, as the economics of Adam Smith showed to the Highlanders who lost their land to sheep; and Celtic natural spontaneity could easily become animality and incompetence, as became widely accepted in unsympathetic political commentary on the much-vexed Irish problem in the nineteenth century (see L.P. Curtis, 1968, Chapters III to V). Arnold was not primarily concerned to belittle the object of his study, although many of the words that he made appropriate to the Celt – nervous, unsteady, emotional, fanciful, unreliable, moody, and the like – still form a potent vocabulary for female belittlement. Certainly the qualities ascribed to women were used as justification for excluding them from all arenas of political and economic power, and the analogy with the contemporary political oppression of Celts is too strong to be ignored.

Just as the relationship of woman and her place in society to the stereotype of femininity is multidimensional, and self-validatory in many ways, the same is true of the relationship of the Fìor-Ghaidheal (true Gael) to the picture that has been built of him. The difficulty that modern feminists have in finding an identity to assert that is independent of the imagery that has brought about their oppression, their 'feminisation', is a difficulty that they share with those involved in modern Gaelic political commentary, as I attempt to show in Chapter 5. The problems involved in trying to find a voice independent of that which is supplied by a dominant and manipulative external discourse are discussed in S. Ardener (1975) and T. Jenkins (1976). This question is also central to modern Marxist philosophy (see, for example, L. Althusser and E. Balibar, 1970).

I have already remarked on the similar tendencies towards political and religious conservatism that are inherent, albeit for structurally different reasons, in the position of women and the position of the Celt. The infolding of vision and reality in the relation of women and the Celts is given a further twist when we consider that because the division of labour in Celtic areas displayed, at least in the nineteenth century, a familiar British pattern, women were more likely to remain monolingual, and men more likely to take part in activities where English was essential. Consequently, Scottish Gaelic is now in large part restricted in use to those very areas in which Arnold gave the Celt a peculiar competence, the home, the Church, the minor arts, and familial and friendly relationships. Gaelic is widely considered to be a very suitable medium for these activities, and its suitability for scientific or business use is a matter for doubt, not surprisingly since it has been attenuated by disuse in the very areas of vocabulary which it would require. It is often said of the Celts that myth and history, myth and reality, become entwined in their lives. We can see that there are some fairly prosaic reasons why this should be so. This is neatly summed up by the appearance of a book which by its want of critical insight into the operation and automatisms of a discursive field, ironically provides us with a statement of general applicability to such problems, while at the same time bringing together Celt and Woman, and making fully contemporary the myth that Renan and Arnold invoked. Markale says, in *Women of the Celts*, that:

> In the Celtic sphere, history is the myth; that is to say, a knowledge of history is already to be found on a mythical level, and at this point the thought provoked by myth takes on an active power because it

influences real life (J. Markale, 1975, p. 17).

We can take this not as a racialist mysticism, which it is, but as an accurate assessment of the metaphorical involutions and elisions, the creative potentialities, of everyday discourse – the everyday discourse which, in the abundance of its imagery, demanded the appearance of the mythical Celt of which Markale is writing.

I have already briefly alluded to the fact that Arnold's Celt was built out of a concern for the same intellectual problems that the nascent sociology of the nineteenth century was concerned with. This topic will recur in later chapters, and I will conclude here by giving some idea of the imagery employed, and the problems thereby invoked, by two of the founding fathers of modern sociology, Max Weber and Ferdinand Tönnies. Weber was concerned, in *The Protestant Ethic and the Spirit of Capitalism*, to show how rationalist materialism had come to replace, via ascetic Protestantism, an old order where religion, magic and belief had their place. He says, 'Since asceticism undertook to remodel the world and to work out its ideals in the world, material goods have gained an increasing and finally an inexorable power over the lives of men as at no previous period in history' (M. Weber, 1948, p. 181). He speaks of materialism and the bureaucratic division of labour as an 'iron cage' in which modern men must live.

> No one knows who will live in this cage in the future, or whether at the end of this tremendous development entirely new prophets will arise, or there will be a great rebirth of old ideas and ideals, or, if neither, mechanized petrifaction, embellished with a sort of conclusive self-importance. For of the last stage of this cultural development, it might well be truly said: 'Specialists without spirit, sensualists without heart; this nullity imagines that it has attained a level of civilisation never before achieved' (ibid., p. 182).

Certainly Arnold's Celt, with his enduring spirituality, could do much to calm this nightmare, where sinister mechanical imagery, to which the Celt is invariably opposed, renders the world meaningless.

The Celt is often described, as we will see in later chapters, as a creature of the 'community', of the 'folk'. It might give us cause for some concern over the source of the appropriateness of this imagery, when we consider the writings of Tönnies in *Gemeinschaft und Gesellschaft* (*Community and Society*), one of the most influential works in the academic consideration of small-scale societies, first published in 1887.

Tönnies contrasts two forms of social life:

> Gemeinschaft (community) . . . is the lasting and genuine form of living together. In contrast to Gemeinschaft, Gesellschaft (society) is transitory and superficial. Accordingly, Gemeinschaft (community) should be understood as a living organism, Gesellschaft (society) as a mechanical aggregate and artifact (F. Tönnies, 1955, p. 39).

Modern European man is, however, to his loss, compelled to live in this *Gesellschaft.* Remembering all the imagery that Renan and Arnold used to locate the Celt, we can look at Tönnies' account of the relationship of the sexes to the two types of society that he is discussing:

> It is an old truth . . . that women are usually led by feelings, men more by intellect. Men are more clever. They alone are capable of calculation, of calm (abstract) thinking, of consideration, combination, and logic (ibid., p. 174).

> . . . all expressions and outbursts of emotions and sentiments, conscience and inspired thoughts are the specific truthfulness, naiveté, directness, and passionateness of the woman, who is in every respect the more natural being. And upon these qualities is based the creativeness of mind and imagination which develops into artistic creativeness through a feeling for and delicacy of choice, or of 'taste'.
>
> Although the performance of great works has usually required masculine strength and cleverness and often also the egotistic motives which spur the man on, the best part, the core of genius, nevertheless, is usually a maternal heritage. And the most general artistic mind of the common people, which expresses itself in trinket, song, and story, is carried by the girlish mind, mother love, female memory, superstition, and premonition. Thus the man of genius is in many respects of a feminine nature: naive and frank, soft, sensitive, lively, changeable in emotions and moods, gay or melancholy, dreamy and enthusiastic, as if living in constant intoxication with a trustful belief in and surrender to objects and persons, thus planless, often blind and foolish in important or unimportant things (ibid., p. 177).

If we desire to present the contrasting dichotomies previously outlined in connection with our theory, they receive their dominant form and expression as:

	the temperament	
of the woman		of the man
through sentiment		through intention
	the character	
of the woman		of the man
through mind		through calculation
	intellectual attitude	
of the woman		of the man
through conscience		through conscious behaviour

(ibid., p. 178).

Tönnies then contrasts youth and old age, and the common people and the educated classes, in much the same way. 'Children are naive, harmless; they live in the present' (ibid., p. 179). 'Belief is a characteristic of the common folks; disbelief, of the scientific and educated classes' (ibid., p. 186).

> For all this discussion the manner in which natural will carries the conditions for Gemeinschaft and rational will develops for Gesellschaft becomes evident. Consequently, the realm of life and work in Gemeinschaft is particularly befitting to women (ibid.).

> Among the arts those connected with speech belong more to the realm of women than do the plastic arts . . . They also learn meaningless gentle things as well as meaningful strange things easily. They have a good memory for forms, ritual, old melodies, proverbs, for conundrums and magic, for tragic and comic stories. They have inclinations to imitate, delight in make-believe, a fondness for play, the charming, and the simple. Also they lean toward the moods of melancholy, sincerity, pious fear, and prayer, and, as has already been said, toward dreaming, pondering, and poetry (ibid., p. 187).

> All art belongs, according to its nature, just as in the case of all rural and domestic pursuits, to the realm of the warm and soft labour. It belongs to organic-living, feminine-natural labour and Gemeinschaft-like labour (ibid., p. 189).

I have quoted at this length in the hope that the points I wish to make will make themselves. It should be clear that the treatment of Scottish Gaeldom as a 'community' rich in 'folklore', which I discuss in the next chapter, derives its genesis from the same preoccupations, the same system of imagery, that allowed Arnold to construct his Celt. And looking to that Celt, and to the *Gemeinschaft* that Tönnies describes, we can get some idea of the intellectual origins of a statement like the following: 'the Gaels are, and were, a profoundly emotional people, and not an intellectual people' (D. Thomson, 1954, p. 3).

5 FOLKLORE AND FOLKLORISTS

At the level of popular academic discourse, the second half of the nineteenth century saw no great upheaval in approaches to the analysis of society and culture, or in approaches to an understanding of their history. Max Müller was sufficiently confident of this to say, in an address to the Anthropological Section of the British Association in 1891:

> When looking once more through the debates carried on in our Section in 1847 I was very much surprised when I saw how very like the questions which occupy us today are to those which we discussed in 1847 . . . ; there has been no cataclysm, no deluge, no break in the advancement of our science, and nothing seems to me to prove its healthy growth more clearly than this uninterrupted continuity which unites the past with the present, and which will, I hope, unite the present with the future (F.M. Müller, 1891, p. 1).

Müller was in some ways among the more *avant-garde* of theorists of the social (for an assessment of his importance see M. Crick, 1976), but his work was, like that of most of his contemporaries, concerned with a search for survivals and origins. Under the tremendous impact of Darwin's biological evolutionism, interest in the more physical aspects of race grew at the expense of philological considerations, but this reinforced rather than subverted the confident claim to historicity that both anthropology and linguistics made. Henson, in a concise account of the intellectual preoccupations of this period and their development through later anthropology, speaks of the dominant concern of late-nineteenth-century linguistics and anthropology as 'classifying according to genetic principles' (H. Henson, 1974, p. 8). In opposition to this unity of commitment, there were, towards the end of the century, immanent renunciations of this kind of historicism.

Within social science, for example, the work of the school of *L'Annee Sociologique* had as one of its obvious offspring the anhistoricist structural-functionalism of Radcliffe-Brown. Within linguistics the work of the Neogrammarians led to the work of de Saussure in the early twentieth century, which is now commonly held to have paved the way for the development of structural linguistics. These two trends, Durkheimian sociology and Saussurean semiology, were united in the 1940s in the structuralism of Lévi-Strauss, which remains to the present day one of the major influences within social anthropology (see E. Ardener, 1971). In spite, however, of this development immanent in the late nineteenth century, the cracks in the evolutionist edifice were perceived only by the few, and the solidity of racial and cultural historicism was relatively undisturbed. The majority of commentators in the 1890s could, as Müller observed, quote theoretical speculations of the 1840s without any sense of anachronism. The conflation of race, language and culture as permanently bound and mutually representative phenomena was still, in spite of denunciation by major figures such as Müller and Lang, a powerful intellectual deceit for many. Theorists of society, drawn as they were from the wealthier and more educated classes of industrial society, saw their own society, either with pride or regret, as pre-eminently utilitarian, pragmatic, scientific, and entirely lacking in symbolic mystery. In accord with this, they marshalled other societies that they saw around them into evolutionary schemata where science and rationality marked the point to which all growth and change were directed. The activities and habits of mind of other peoples which appeared to flout the empiricism of this world-view were classified in terms which made them mere faltering steps on the way to rationality. The 'superstitions' of peasants and the working class, the fancies of children, the mythologies of antiquity, and the beliefs and rituals of savages were all conflated in this epistemological reduction. Models of mental development, like Frazer's compelling 'magic to religion to science' (see J. Frazer, 1949, Chapter IV), carried the appeal of such theories well into the twentieth century. The potency and clarity of this kind of historicism is demonstrated by the way in which it has become the substance of popular (that is, non-academic) sociological discourse, largely defying and ignoring the subsequent revolutions in academic sociological thought.

At the same time, however, as such evolutionary schemata were being constructed, we often find expressed a sense of loss, a sense that material well-being was being pursued at the expense of something less easy to define but none the less valuable. This was the same *malaise* that had prompted Arnold to look for some beauty behind the gross materialism of the industrial society in which he lived. Such an intellectual unease can be variously explained. It can be argued to have sprung from the simple observation of the misery and squalor of industrial areas, coupled with the growing awareness that industrialisation brought about not only social and demographic disruption but also the loss of old habits and customs, as the societies which had supported these were destroyed and replaced by a transient, cosmopolitan, shifting and impermanent society where wage labour moved whenever and wherever it must. This empiricist explanation of the emergence of a new valuation of the 'folk' can be set next to the related philosophical problem that the contemporary theorisation of science seemed to require that all human endeavour be subsumed by rationalism. Such a development suggested, to many, a reduction in the colour and variety of mental activity that was scarcely acceptable. This is the same force that we have argued to be effective in Arnold's work, the related apprehensions of industrial squalor and philosophical inadequacy. Theorists of primitive society later in the century operated with the same metaphorical dualities as had Arnold, as they opposed the apparent literality of their knowledge, their 'common-sense' empiricism, to the systems of knowledge they found among other peoples. Since the knowledges of other peoples were found to be shot through, even in their most obviously pragmatic and instrumental aspects, with apparently 'irrational' and 'non-utilitarian' practices, these knowledges could only be treated as in some sense infirm and inadequate, awaiting a proper appreciation of cause and effect. Science thus became a replacement for and inimical to all that a Victorian observer saw in other societies to be expressive or symbolic, all that offended his sense of the literal.

It was within this intellectual climate that the study of folklore began its elevation into an institutionally autonomous discipline with, for example, the founding of the Folklore Society in 1878.

Sidney Hartland, writing as President of the Society in 1899, demonstrated the mutual exclusivity of explanations from folklore and from science, and located them in discrete strata of society:

> The portion of anthropology with which folklore deals is the mental and spiritual side of humanity. It is now well established that the most civilised races have all fought their way slowly upwards from a condition of savagery.
>
> When the real reason for a given fact is unknown or forgotten, in certain stages of culture a story arises (this is the law) attributing to it a supernatural origin (E.S. Hartland, 1899, p. 2).

The confidence of 'this is the law' leaves us in no doubt as to who has a grasp of 'real reason', as opposed to supernaturality and folklore. Andrew Lang said of folklore that it represented 'survivals of the savage fancy' (A. Lang, 1879, vi). We have seen how, for Yeats, the 'Celtic

Twilight' and an enthusiasm for folklore and folk beliefs were inseparable, both appealing to a distant and untroubled past. Certainly the imagery by which folklore was constituted was remarkably like that that Arnold had employed.

The two major folklorists connected with the Highlands in the second half of the nineteenth century were J.F. Campbell of Islay, and Andrew Carmichael.[11] Both have published monumental works which are uniquely valuable sources for the study of Highland folklore. Campbell set new standards in the presentation and appreciation of 'folk' material by the publication, in 1860, of the first two volumes of his *Popular Tales of the West Highlands.* In the introduction to this, he elaborates the theory by which he explains the superabundance, on the shores of the western sea, of these 'popular tales':

> It is supposed that the races known as Indo-European came from Central Asia at some very early period, and passed over Europe, separating and settling down as nations; retaining words of their original language, and leaving the traces of their religion and history everywhere as popular tales; and that they found the land occupied. Each wave, it is said, 'pushed onwards those who went before', but, as it seems to me, each in turn must have stopped as it arrived at the great sea, and there the waves of this stream must have mingled and stagnated. . . . Brittany, Scandinavia, Ireland, and the west of Scotland, from their geographical positions, should contain more of this light mental debris than Central Europe; for the same reason that more of the floating rubbish of American rivers is found on the shores of Europe than anywhere on the great ocean (J.F. Campbell, 1860, xvi).

Despite his respect and interest we find that the theories of society and knowledge with which Campbell operated reduce the imagery of his people to 'floating rubbish' and 'mental debris'. It is interesting to consider how fortuitously apt Scottish Gaelic society is to be considered by such theories of social development. Campbell was speaking of the relationship between two contemporary societies, Scottish Gaelic society and the cosmopolitan European society of which he was himself a part. At his hands the difference between these, however that is historically derived, becomes the difference between pre-history and modernity. The theory of the Indo-European expansion provides a metaphor that expresses on an evolutionary time scale the fact that the economy of the Highlands is depressed, and fashions different to those in London, even though the time scales within which these apparently congruent phenomena can be understood are different by several orders of magnitude. Within such theories of development the octogenarian Gael sitting in his croft on the west coast of Lewis can be felt to have the weight of 5,000 years of inexorable history pressing him out of existence, or away westwards to Tìr nan Òg. He is going to die because he is old, and his children have left because (say) there is no work, but his fate becomes, within such historicism, a much more grandiose affair than such superficial factualities could, by themselves, imply.

Campbell's interests were both antiquarian and scientific, as we discover from his apologetic plea that 'the stories would be rubbish indeed if they were not genuine traditions' (ibid., xii). His work he calls 'a museum of curious rubbish about to perish' (ibid., xi). He quotes one of his collectors, Hector MacLean, an Islay schoolmaster, who attributed the disappearance of the folk tales 'partly to reading, which in a manner supplies a substitute for them, partly to bigoted religious ideas, and partly to narrow utilitarian views' (ibid., xiv). Modernity, sophistication, rationality and puritanism are driving away the shy old ideas. 'Railways, roads, newspapers, and tourists, are slowly but surely doing their accustomed work. They are driving out romance' (ibid., xxiv). Campbell admits the marginal status of his collection within the larger intellectual world of Victorian Britain: 'Many despise these as frivolities; they are practical moderns, and answer to practical men in other ranks of society' (ibid., xlix).

Before discussing this further I will give some of Alexander Carmichael's ideas on the same subject. Carmichael, a younger colleague of Campbell, published in 1900 the first two volumes of his *Carmina Gadelica*. This contains spells, incantations, hymns, prayers and the like that Carmichael collected, mainly in Barra and South Uist. In the introduction to this work he explains to us the beauty of the life that was lived there, and which his folklore collection represents:

> The people of the Outer Isles, like the people of the Highlands and Islands generally, are simple and law-abiding, common crime being rare and serious crime unknown among them. They are good to the poor, kind to the stranger, and courteous to all (A. Carmichael, 1928, xxi).

His regret for the disappearance of this life is coupled with an acceptance of its inevitability. He says 'Gaelic oral literature has been disappearing during the last three centuries. It is now becoming meagre in quantity, inferior in quality and greatly isolated' (ibid., xxv). Once upon a time, however:

> Gaelic oral literature was widely diffused, greatly abundant, and excellent in quality (ibid., xxii).

> Several causes have contributed towards this decadence – principally the Reformation, the Risings, the evictions, the Disruption, the schools, and the spirit of the age (ibid., xxv).

He asks that 'an attempt be made even yet to preserve these memories ere they disappear for ever' (ibid., xxxiv). Of those from whom he gathered his material he says 'They are almost all dead now, leaving no successors. With reverent hand and grateful heart I place this stone upon the cairn of those who composed and of those who transmitted their work' (ibid., xxxvi).

We can see, therefore, in the works of the two most prominent Highland folklorists, the dominant features that were to define the field of folklore – it was disappearing before science, rationality, and modernity; it was indeed, both are agreed, although writing forty years apart, already all but gone.

In one of the early publications of the folklore society, Henderson argues that unless the collection of folklore be speedily done: 'many a singular usage and tradition will pass away from the land unnoted and unremembered. It would be very desirable if a scheme could be organised, for systematically collecting and classifying the remnants of our folklore' (W. Henderson, 1879, p. 8). Ralston agreed that:

> It would greatly facilitate researches of this kind if some general system of classification of popular tales could be agreed upon . . . Some tales are manifestly capable of being reduced to order . . . But there are others which are not to be so simply denoted, and which seem to require more elaborate formulas for their identification, perhaps resembling those used in chemistry (W.R.S. Ralston, 1878, p. 76).

At the institutionalisation of folklore we find, as we would expect at this period, the desire to found a science, whose primary theoretical practice will be classification. Chemistry is invoked as an ideal to aspire to. At the same time, however, the enthusiasm for the 'folk' derived from its opposition to the science-orientated, 'rational' society that held the enthusiasm. Remembering the imagery that Renan and Arnold used to locate the Celt, we can recognise Henderson's statement that: 'My heart as well as my imagination is too closely bound up with the sayings and doings which gave zest to the life of my forefathers' (W. Henderson, 1879, vii). Thus we have juxtaposed in the 1870s a nostalgia for a lost past where simple songs, stories and magic still held people enthralled, and a commitment in a new undertaking to precisely that hyperformal rationalism that was argued to have destroyed that lost past. Classification, enumeration, entabulation and the like were thus early partners of the enthusiasm for folklore, and these two aspects of life, so often defined by their mutual opposition, retain to the present day this fascinatingly ambivalent partnership.

It is appropriate, therefore, that the Celt should have received much attention as a repository of folklore, since the literary 'Celt' had been constructed from the same imagery that was used to articulate and express the growing interest in folklore. It was, indeed, to be expected that everything Celtic would become, in some sense, 'folk' either of lore or life, and this has indeed come to be true. Alfred Nutt gives us an explicit account of why the imaginative and artistic elements of Gaelic life are of greater importance than its more infrastructural features. He says:

> I have argued . . . *a priori* for the intrinsic inferiority of the political to the artistic element in the history of Gaelic culture (A. Nutt, 1904, p. 50).
>
> . . . the chronicle, the record, the document which alone as a rule is designated historical, is, as far as the Gael is concerned, of secondary importance . . .
>
> It is otherwise with the document which, instead of recording what the Gael did, and how he organised his social life, reveals to us how he imagined the contact of man with man, or of man with Nature, which sets forth his outlook on life and death, which depicts his dream of an unreal, or his denunciation of a real world (ibid., p. 49).

Politically, socially, economically, therefore, Gaelic life may 'without disadvantage, perish almost utterly' (ibid., p. 50). It is only valuable in its possession of the 'archaic emotion or fancy, as preserved to us by archaic artistry' (ibid.). The folk tales of this people who are economically and politically thus reduced to irrelevance owe their supernatural tendencies to 'the influence of pagan superstition on the imagination in an age when there was profound ignorance of science and the laws of causality' (D. MacInnes, 1890, xviii). The tales are 'fragmentary remains of what was once a veritable unwritten library of the memories and poetry of a nation' (W.J. Watson in J.G. MacKay, 1940, xxx). This unwritten library, this whole system of knowledge, of entertainment, and of expression, has its worth in that here:

> we have records that are very close to a much lower civilisation. Herein lies their virtue, the quality that gives them value in the eyes of science. They are a revelation of a much earlier period, a revelation handed down to us by the method which primitive man himself had inaugurated (J.G. MacKay, 1940, xiii).

We learn that 'Folklore . . . is essentially the property of the unlearned and least advanced portion of the community' (G.L. Gomme in D. MacInnes, 1890, p. 3 appendix). We learn that folklore stems from a 'body of individuals entirely ignorant of the results of science and philosophy to which the advanced portion of the community have attained' (ibid.). It is a product of 'traditional sanctity and pre-scientific mental activity' (ibid.). Bearing all this in mind we can imagine that it is not an entirely unambiguous compliment to say that: 'the Gaelic-speaking Outer Hebrides are the richest storehouse of oral traditions, particularly of traditional folk-song, in Great Britain, if not in Western Europe, today' (J.L. Campbell and F. Collinson, 1969, ix).

Modern consideration of folklore operates within a theoretical framework (and a system of imagery) very like that which we find in late-nineteenth-century writings. The School of Scottish Studies, in Edinburgh University, was founded in 1950, and in its first corporate publication we are told that:

> One of the chief activities of the School of Scottish Studies has been and is the study of folk culture . . . The folklore studies pursued by the School might be said to be 'the recording and investigation of the oral and material traditions of rural communities in Scotland, with special emphasis on the traditions of the pre-industrial age' (S.F. Sanderson, 1957, p. 5).

Within this work of folklore studies, we find that:

> Of first importance is the *oral tradition* of the Gaelic-speaking parts

> of Scotland – a part of the world of importance quite out of proportion to the number of its inhabitants. For here we have an ancient culture comparatively unmodified by the influence of twentieth-century 'civilisation': a culture containing many strange blends of things from the past (ibid., p. 7).

Tocher, the journal in which selections from the School's very large and valuable collections are published, says that the Archives of the School are 'a national repository for Scottish traditions and memories of former days and ways' (*Tocher*, Vol. 1, 1971, p. 1). Folklore is thus still defined in opposition to the twentieth century, and is valuable in so far as it is ancient, a memory of former days and ways. Within Scotland it is primarily located, not unexpectedly, in the Gaelic-speaking areas.

Thompson, writing in 1966, says, in an attempt to define folklore:

> My own interpretation is that folklore is the survival of the thought and ways of life of former times. This folklore is knowledge, mostly preserved by oral communication and, generally, divorced effectively from the rationally-based knowledge of educated classes of people (F.G. Thompson, 1966, p. 226).

> Folklore is regarded as the knowledge of former ways preserved by the inhabitants of the less-advanced countries of the world, and by the less-educated classes in industrialised countries (ibid.).

Folklore is still, therefore, to be found in the non-industrial, the less educated, the non-scientific, and the non-rational areas of society or of thought. Perhaps the most significant change that we find from the late-nineteenth-century theorisation lies in statements like the following: 'Every age, of course, has its folklore: it is axiomatic that the "folk" are not simple-minded rustics in Caithness or Kintyre, living in a cloud of bygones and survivals' (S.F. Sanderson, 1957, p. 4).

We might wish to argue that this was simply untrue. The categorical requirements of folklore are, as we have seen, that it be survival, bygone, and simple-minded (or, to put these another way, pre-rational memories of former days and ways). This is what is 'axiomatic'. Sanderson wishes to avoid the implied sneer that the category folklore, by the imagery of its expression, provokes from the modern sophisticate. It should be clear, however, that were it not for the possibility of that sneer there would be no possibility of bounding the field of knowledge covered by the term 'folklore'. The folk that are in possession of the kind of knowledge that an academic might choose to call 'folklore' have not (or at least did not once have) any idea that within somebody else's discourse their knowledge is so peculiarly marked. For them it is a relatively humdrum and everyday affair, and certainly not the pre-rational racial memory that those whose vocabulary contains the word 'folklore' will make of it. We must conclude from this that any attempt to restore to 'folklore' an epistemological status equal to the knowledge that, say, a folklorist has, will be impossible, however good the intention. The categorical requirements of folklore are such that if it becomes, say, 'rational', it will not then be 'rational folklore', but will have become merely ordinary, no longer something to occupy the interest of a university department. C. MacLean struggles with this paradox, saying of the scorn that many express for the superstitious:

> Such a state of affairs is unfortunate indeed, for it renders the collection of material for the study of custom and belief rather difficult. But it is only to be hoped that traditional beliefs and customs will, by some means or other, become respectable (C. MacLean, 1959a, p. 199).

He elaborates his impatience with those scornful of superstition:

> In the early years of the century it was commonly believed that with the advance of knowledge and education most traditional beliefs and customs would eventually disappear, that they would be dispelled by the light of science and rationalism. If beliefs and customs have decayed, it is due to social rather than intellectual reasons. Ignorance and superstition have to a great extent become coterminous, and because of reasons of social prestige, people with any measure of pretentiousness will disclaim any knowledge of or adherence to popular beliefs and customs (ibid.).

The problems before an attempt to restore respectability to the object of study are clear enough. Ignorance and superstition have become coterminous – but this is not a merely fortuitous and unlucky occurrence: it is built into the conditions of the possibility of existence of an academic discourse concerned with folklore. 'Reasons of social prestige' themselves are not mere adventitious worries, but are a part of the twentieth-century intellectual context within which we all must operate, and within which all academic institutions concerned with folklore must exist.

The equation of ignorance and superstition, however regrettable and however caused, has had a particularly vigorous history in Protestant Europe since the Reformation. The 'light of science and rationalism' is the very substance of the solid claim of a particular section of the population to an easy access to obvious truth; it is also the condition of existence of an interest in traditional ways and folk matters. It is interesting that MacLean does not consider it to be a matter for interest that a large number of people have, so to speak, an irrational prejudice against the irrational. This is not a 'traditional' attitude in that it causes the disappearance of the traditional, and so, far from being a folk-belief, is felt to be something like its opposite – a regrettable pretension. While there are undoubtedly class correlates to the direction in which the epithet 'superstitious' is hurled, since there are class correlates to the management of education and the appropriation of knowledge, it is surely not without interest to the folklorist that the people to whom he has traditionally looked for his 'lore', the 'peasants' and the 'uneducated', are becoming those most likely to dismiss such things as worthless nonsense; at the same time, there is a growing body of educated middle-class people who take a certain coy pride in being thought 'superstitious', and who take an interest in, among other things, 'folklore'.

Folklore studies, for all their claim to scientificity, are built upon a desire to save something of a former way of life, and this desire in turn is based upon a misapprehension of the potential of 'rationality', as it is popularly defined, to extend or be extended to all spheres of human activity. Because folklore has been defined as that which is on the retreat before the rational, the scientific, or the utilitarian, those engaged in folklore studies have been continually afraid, and motivated to activity by this fear, that their field of study would shortly disappear. Eighteenth-century commentators on Ossian confidently voiced the belief that the poems had been rescued in the nick of time, since the way of life from which they sprang was doomed to disappear with the march of progress. J.F. Campbell called the stories that he collected 'curious rubbish about to perish' (J.F. Campbell, 1860, xi). Alexander Carmichael said of his informants 'they are almost all dead now, leaving no successors' (A. Carmichael, 1900, xxxvi). J.L. Campbell says that:

> there has always floated in the memory of the Gaelic-speaking people a vast oral tradition going back to the times of the Norse invasions. This offers a very interesting field for research, for it has been only imperfectly explored; but the time is short. In another ten years most

> of this material will have perished forever (J.L. Campbell, 1950, p. 42).

By contrast, however, we find that when the Irish Folklore Commission extended its work on Gaelic folklore to Scotland in 1946, Calum MacLean could, within four years, have 'assembled, in Barra, South Uist and Benbecula, the largest collection of folk-tales yet made in Scotland' (B.R.S.M., 1959, p. 123). The School of Scottish Studies had, by 1957, 'more than six-hundred hours of solid recording' (S.F. Sanderson, 1957, p. 10), and could say that:

> an almost unsuspected wealth of material has been discovered. The collecting has far outstripped the work of indexing and cataloguing, to say nothing of interpretation. The material is so plentiful and the opportunities for fruitful research so numerous, that more workers both in the field and in the archives are needed (J. Orr, 1957, p. 2).

The folklore that is being collected is changing, and the old classifications are somewhat offended by this:

> Students of the folk-tale will, of course, realise that it is becoming increasingly difficult to find the type of material listed in the Aarne-Thompson Register of folk-tale types in current tradition now; and in some countries it is no longer possible to do so (*Scottish Studies*, Vol. 1, p. 14).

There is evidently no shortage of material, in spite of its failure to live up to its institutional and academic requirements. We can compare the way in which folklore is continually disappearing and at the same time continually being rediscovered with the way in which, as Condry has shown, the economic problem of the Scottish Highlands is continually being solved but never disappearing (see E. Condry, 1976). The definitional problems that constitute these paradoxes are remarkably similar.

As long as folklore is defined as that which is in defiance of the overtly rational, it will continue to show resilience, longevity, and unexpected abundance, since 'rationality' is not capable, although it might be imagined to be, of thoroughly invading the field of human activity. This is a question whose consideration owes much to the work of Lévy-Bruhl (see L. Lévy-Bruhl, 1923). The debate over the question of the rationality of 'primitive' thought systems (or, as they are there called, 'non-Western' thought systems) is thoroughly aired by R. Horton and R. Finnegan

(1973). The inconclusivity of this debate is some evidence that the structures of the argument are the source of continuing problems, and as such can be 'solved' not by argument but only by abandonment. As Dresch says: 'The definitive status of particular worlds for those who live in them is hardly in question unless we wish to return to the sterile "rationality" debates of the early sixties' (P. Dresch, 1976, p. 64). It should be emphasised that the status of 'particular worlds' here is not that of, say, environmental facticity, but rather that of reality-defining ideology.

Most of the features which define folklore, apart from its ancient traditionality, suggest that it is best seen as a category of expressive activity, or of symbolic activity. Since the coherence of a symbolic system, and its mode of generation of meaning, are questions entirely outside the limited thematic of rationality/non-rationality, and since man is, as has often been said, a symbolic animal, there is potentially no end to the human activity that will arise to fill the space which folklore claims as its own. There is, therefore, in this sense, no more room for grief that a facet of humanity is disappearing than there is for a celebratory denial of this loss, such as Thompson provides:

> What people have failed to realise is that not only has past folklore survived in different guises to this very day, this very hour, but that new folklore is growing new branches, new twigs, on very old stock . . . Folklore is indeed as old as Eden and as young as the unborn tomorrow (F.G. Thompson, 1966, p. 227).

Just so. The symbolism which Thompson uses to express the nature of this survival of folklore is interesting: 'Nowadays we tend to approach most situations which we meet with a rationalistic cast of mind. But this veneer can crack from side to side whenever we are faced with times of emotion or uncertainty' (ibid.). It is in the depths, the emotions, that folklore is to be found, beneath the veneer of rationalism and intellectuality. Remembering the imagery that Arnold and Renan employed, it is not surprising that folklore and the sentimental Gael should have such an easy symbolic affinity. We are led to ask, however, whether a people whose whole system of knowledge is classified as 'folklore' is consequently devoid of rationality and intellect. Such a suggestion is not, of course, to be entertained. The metaphors used to express the nature of folklore and the nature of the Gael allow, however, such a question to be asked and such a suggestion made. We could only solve this problem by looking to the validity of the original imagery and asking whether, for example, dualities like intellectuality/emotionality are suitably analytical, suitably clear, to bear the theoretical weight which is put upon them. Unless we are seriously to admit that the Gael lives a life entirely of emotions and intuition (which has, of course, been often enough maintained within the Celtic Twilight), then we must confess that such dualities are, indeed, not adequate to the task that they are asked to perform, and that there would be much to be gained from a serious re-examination of the discourse within which 'folklore' can be constituted as a discrete entity, a discrete type of knowledge.

In this context it is of interest to study Carmichael's admiring description of the old Highland way of life. He says:

> Perhaps no people had a fuller ritual of song and story, of secular rite and religious ceremony, than the Highlands. Mirth and music, song and dance, tale and poem, pervaded their lives, as electricity pervades the air. Religion, pagan or Christian, or both combined, permeated everything – blending and shading into one another like the iridiscent colours of the rainbow. The people were sympathetic and synthetic, unable to see and careless to know where the secular began and the religious ended – an admirable union of elements in life for those who have lived it so truly and intensely as the Celtic races everywhere have done, and none more truly or more intensely than the ill understood and so-called illiterate Highlanders of Scotland (A. Carmichael, 1928, xxxii).

Carmichael draws particular attention to the fact that the Highlanders failed to recognise the distinction between the sacred and the secular. We can understand his surprise when we remember that this distinction was one of the cornerstones of European intellectual discourse. The early theorists of primitive religion, like Robertson-Smith and Emile Durkheim (see W. Robertson-Smith, 1907, and E. Durkheim, 1957) built their theoretical edifices from this duality. If features that appeared to the educated mind to be 'religious' appeared in the ordinary life of the Gael, this was not dealt with by abandoning the distinction as inappropriate, but by arguing that the Gael was peculiarly religious; since it was not just a small and discrete part of his activity that was religious but, apparently, all of his activity. Thus he becomes wholly religious, just as he had been wholly emotional, wholly 'folk'. We often see in writings of this period the opinion that religion is the highest development of other symbolic activities like myth-making, ritual and magic. It is not surprising that Carmichael interpreted everything that seemed to him to be expressive, or symbolic, that is everything that was not obviously utilitarian, as in some sense religious. The supposition that symbolism is a religious phenomenon is one made by both puritan religious philosophy and positivist social science, which latter expected, as does much academic consideration of the folk, that symbolism is something that a rational and 'secular' society would lack.

Carmichael's assessment of Gaelic religious activity cannot avoid subjecting the Gael to manipulation within the dominant intellectual dualities of English language discourse. In attempting to deny the relevance of the distinction between the religious and the secular for the Highlander, he finds himself attributing to them a peculiar religiosity, which in turn denies them a simple rationality. We have again the problem of asking whether this is a reasonable conclusion to draw from the observation that the Gaels of the time interlaced their everyday affairs with activities that we, and Carmichael, would assess as non-utilitarian. Religiosity for us is a very special state, confined to certain people, places and times. Can we imagine that religiosity could retain this meaning if it were asked to extend over twenty-four hours of every day? The more the distinction between the secular and the religious, the instrumental and the expressive, the literal and the symbolic, are subjected to scrutiny, the more they appear themselves like 'folk' categories rather than symbolically neutral and well established tools for analysis. We have cause to question the status of such statements, deriving from Carmichael, as the following: 'it is always necessary to be prepared, to condition one's mind to the fact that Nature and natural events had an overpowering influence on the Gael' (F.G. Thompson, 1966, p. 231). Speaking of the place of religion in the Gael's life, Thompson says: 'It was . . . something real, alive, which pervaded his whole life and work from childbirth to death' (ibid., p. 232).

Crick has offered a persuasively argued dissolution of the 'analytical' dualities which underpin the majority of statements about the nature of folklore, and its epistemological status. In a consideration of the nature of the symbolism of alchemy he says that:

> Alchemy . . . was a ritual not a chemical experiment; whatever the source of the signs, they worded a landscape which was not scientific. The literalist view of alchemy as an erroneous science strongly resembles the way in which nineteenth-century ethnologists interpreted primitive magic as something mistaken by its practitioners as efficacious. Like them, those who fail to see alchemy as symbolic statement presume that it is a technique. But once we see both magic

> and alchemy as 'languages', it is clear that neither need be viewed as instances of childish and misguided science (M. Crick, 1976, p. 146).

It is not, however, that we must simply suspend 'scientific' criteria when we examine symbolic systems such as alchemy (or 'folklore'). It is rather:

> not only that one misinterprets if one chooses wrongly between likening a set of statements to religion or science, but that one misunderstands if one thinks of the choice in these terms at all. Thus . . . reminding us that some of the terms we have used to frame our analytical discussion have been highly culture-bound. 'Religion' itself must certainly be included among these. Other cultures (even Hindu and Islamic) do not have concepts at all equivalent to our term 'religion', so it is extremely doubtful that using a general opposition science/religion will be of any great use.
>
> We can generalise this feeling, for it may well be that ethnography will not decide between the literalist/symbolist rivals but rather will suggest that the very oppositions of technique/art, explanation/expressiveness, and so on, must be dispensed with (ibid., p. 159).

Deriving these dualities from a philosophical tradition, he argues that 'Most of what is important to us is spoken about in discourse which mixes inextricably the analytical oppositions which logical positivism offered' (ibid.). That philosophical tradition itself, in the standards of relevance that it applied, was not an independent creation, but was derived very much from a consciousness of the symbolism surrounding such dualities as religion and science. As I have said elsewhere, 'the analytical oppositions of logical positivism are themselves only one recension of a symbolism of enormous scope on which we continually draw' (M. Chapman, 1977, p. 94). The apparently analytical dualities within which most discussion of folklore is couched have, as I have tried in various ways to show, a rich and effective symbolic history.

Whatever reverence is felt for 'folklore' and the 'folk' who are its bearers, it remains an unavoidable fact that the word 'folklore' suggests, in both popular speech and academic argument, the outmoded, the quaint, the non-rational, and the like. It is worth remarking that the most obviously 'folklorish' features of the life of the educated middle class, say, for example, Santa Claus and fairies, represent beliefs that are ascribed exclusively to children. For a young child to express disbelief in Santa Claus is evidence of a kind of indecent precocity, and adults indulgently and patronisingly encourage children to believe things that they do not believe themselves. I remember, as a child, being well aware that I was expected to believe in Santa Claus, and obligingly maintaining, in the presence of adults, that I did. The passage from an implicit belief in the world of fairies to a more informed scepticism is invariably represented, in children's literature, as the first whisper of human mutability, the first step towards the adult world and mundane reality, the departure from Eden. Can we suppose that those living in the Hebrides whom we wish to continue expressing a belief in fairies are unaware of this?

Bearing this in mind it seems possible that a concentration of effort in a particular area to collect folklore will not necessarily have the beneficent effect of making people more interested in their 'lore'. It might be argued that it would be equally likely to rouse suspicion among them that they were being investigated for traces of the 'savage fancy'. Most Gaels, who are, after all, more literate in English than they are in Gaelic (wherever the fault for that lies), cannot fail to be aware that their country and speech is credited with a peculiarly rich and beautiful folklore, and cannot fail to be aware of the peculiar status that folklore, as a type of knowledge, has. This might be increasingly an area to look to for reasons to explain the vehemence of the use of the epithet 'superstitious' which Calum MacLean obviously encountered, and to provide an explanation beyond the religious of the reluctance of people to admit to knowing 'folklore'.

The dangers of treating Gaelic culture as a collapsing museum are voiced by Whitaker:

> A culture is much more than an assemblage of quaint artefacts, and the traditional Gaelic society was much more than a few backward old men and women, sitting by the open hearths of primitive mud hovels, spinning with outmoded distaff and spindle and mumbling their primeval runes. It was a way of life with its own code of values, its own purpose, its own ethical system (I. Whitaker, 1959, p. 175).

It should no longer be necessary, at least within the social sciences, to labour such a point. Nevertheless the very division of the society into the traditional and modern, categories defined by their mutual opposition, permits the maintenance of the discourse within which Gaelic culture is 'folklorised', and permits the entry into that discourse of metaphors and imagery which, by various subtle means, supply a steady intellectual belittlement. That this belittlement is unintentional is beside the point. Whitaker says, of traditional Hebridean farming techniques: 'I do not imply that these technically less efficient practices should be retained – the Hebrides are not a living museum of aboriginal folkways' (ibid.).

Unfortunately, a large number of tourists see them as precisely that. We cannot wish away the everyday meanings and associations of the words that we employ, and we will often find that our language is ahead of us, and resistant to our attempts to change it. Could it be imagined that anybody would ever speak of 'rational, progressive folklore'? Would the tourists still come if it were decided that the Hebrides were an urban industrial area? Whitaker himself, in appealing for photographs of traditional Scottish folklife says that 'often it is the ordinary everyday activities that are forgotten by photographers until it is too late. The scope of this category of photograph is endless' (I. Whitaker, 1958, p. 212). Every aspect of Gaelic life is thus reduced to the status of folklife, just as the Gaels had become wholly religious, wholly traditional, wholly emotional. It seems *a priori* probable that this kind of theorisation will have a damaging effect on those traditions that it wishes to elevate and maintain. It should not be forgotten that academic folklore studies are as much a product of that rational, materialist society that daily assaults Gaelic society as are oil-related industrial development or profit margins. With this in mind, we can look at Whitaker's assessment of Gaelic life:

> It was a way of life with its own code of values, it own purpose, its own ethical system. Once you modify the one by the introduction of a money economy . . . the collapse of the rest was bound to follow (I. Whitaker, 1959, p. 175).

We could argue that the substitution of 'folklore studies' for 'money economy' would not substantially alter the argument. We might, indeed, wonder which was the more serious, an assault upon, say, a people's traditional forms of property inheritance, or an assault upon their rationality. This kind of argument does not only have interest as a minor semantic skirmish, but has serious consequences for the perception of Highland life, and for the perception of the place of the Gaelic language within that life. Nisbet says of the relationship of the Gaelic language and formal education in the Gaelic-speaking areas:

> Though the school system may have little direct influence on society, it can work to create or weaken the attitudes of mind which determine the growth and development of society. In the language of advertising research, we must examine the 'public image' of the Gaelic language. Is it regarded with affection and respect by the people who speak it,

> and especially by the young people with whom its future rests? Or is it associated in their minds with ideas of a bleak unadventurous way of life, as having inferior status, as being stuffy, old-fashioned and out of touch with modern developments? Such attitudes are important, and may be conveyed in subtle ways. The practice of teaching reading in English before Gaelic, the use of bright modern texts for English and old tattered copies for Gaelic, formal methods of teaching Gaelic and preoccupation with the intricacies of spelling – these are all effective means of forming the attitude that the language is second-rate, parochial and obsolescent. There are other ways of killing off a language than by forbidding its use (J. Nisbet, 1963, p. 49).

We have seen that Scottish folklore is located, *par excellence*, within the Gaelic language. We have seen how Gaelic culture has been subjected to literary manipulation such that it is, relative to English, associated with folk-life, the non-rational, the parochial and the spiritual. I have tried to show that this is not mere accident, but the result of a literary and institutional conspiracy (not, of course, in any simple purposive sense of the word) of great generality. It has come to be accepted that Gaelic is a suitable language for such topics. When Gaelic began to appear as a teaching medium in Highland education in recent years it was, and is, used primarily to teach subjects such as nature study, local history and traditional Gaelic lore and music. Although there are now a small number of primary schools in the Outer Hebrides where Gaelic is used, experimentally, as the dominant teaching medium, most Gaels have been through an education which would prepare them to find no incongruity in the 'folklorisation' of their tongue. The 'Scottish' interests, and more particularly the 'Celtic' interests, that are represented on the shelves of bookshops throughout Scotland are predominantly antiquarian and 'folk'. Modern short stories rub shoulders with tales of fairies, clan histories, folksongs and dictionaries of Hebridean flora. The bookshop where I do most of my shopping shelves Celtic books within prehistory, two floors away from modern languages, so that Ian Crichton Smith's contemporary Gaelic prose, realist, sexually explicit, and iconoclastic as it is, stands only inches away from stone circles, druids and speculations on the exact location of Atlantis. Attitudes to language may indeed be conveyed in subtle ways.

I have used the term 'symbolic appropriation' to describe the way in which Gaelic culture, language and life have become the focus of sentiments and associations not intrinsic to an autonomous Gaelic life, but required by the external discourse of the English language, its metaphorical requirements, and the structure of its imagery. This 'symbolic appropriation' has many depths and dimensions, and has, by the possibility that it offers of easy acquiescence to its imagery, often persuaded Gaelic culture that it belongs in that metaphorical half-world which is ascribed to it. The idea of 'appropriation' is, however, given a more materialist sense by the activities of those whom Sorley MacLean describes:

> I will be called the 'true' Gael/according to the extent of my large endowment/with the holy talents I collected/and procured in this country:/I will promenade in Edinburgh/in the belted, kilted plaid;/ I will shine at every 'ceilidh'/ (S. MacLean, 1943, p. 103).

A spectacular example of the way in which reputations could be built by the academic appropriation of a quaint and alien symbolism is provided by the career of Miss Ada Goodrich Freer (see J.L. Campbell and Trevor H. Hall, 1968). It is not surprising, when we remember what has been said about the mystical and other-worldly qualities of the Celts, that the Society for Psychical Research should have turned its attention to the Scottish Highlands and Islands. Miss Freer conducted their enquiry into second sight in the Hebrides in 1894 and 1895 with the financial backing of the Marquess of Bute, and established a considerable reputation. Campbell and Hall show that the principal source for her work was material collected by Fr. Allan Macdonald of Eriskay, which she published, unacknowledged (see A. Goodrich Freer, 1902). J.L. Campbell has since done much to establish the reputation of Fr. Allan Macdonald as an outstanding collector of oral tradition (see J.L. Campbell, 1954 and 1968). The glory, however, was Miss Freer's, and the interest aroused by a Victorian taste for supernatural titillation did not extend to more than a vague sympathy with the distant Celt, and fond imaginings of 'racial memory' in London bosoms.

There can be little doubt, from the evidence of the collections of Carmichael, Fr. Allan Macdonald, J.L. Campbell and Calum MacLean, to name only a few prominent figures in the area, that the islands of the Outer Hebrides have possessed, and still do possess, particularly in the south, a rich oral tradition. Campbell quite rightly tells us that:

> Communities where an oral tradition predominates are so much out of the experience of the modern Western world that it is extremely difficult for anyone without first-hand knowledge to imagine how a language can be cultivated without being written to any extent, or

> what an oral literature is like, or how it is propagated from generation to generation (J.L. Campbell, 1968, p. 6).

We have few ways of expressing the nature of an oral literature adequately, and those ways that we have are symbolically manipulative in ways that I have tried to demonstrate. Campbell demonstrates both the inadequacy of the imagery that we have with respect to any fidelity to the overt object of discussion, and at the same time the symbolically totalitarian way in which that object is subsumed for the purposes of a larger discourse:

> The consciousness of the Gaelic mind may be described as possessing historic continuity and religious sense; it may be said to exist in a vertical plane. The consciousness of the Western world, on the other hand, may be said to exist in a horizontal plane, possessing breadth and extent, dominated by scientific materialism and a concern with purely contemporary happenings. There is a profound difference between the two mental attitudes, which represent the different spirits of different ages, and are very much in conflict (ibid., p. 7).

We get some idea of the tacit moralism that stands behind such assessments of the two different types of community, in the following:

> It is always extraordinarily difficult to convey the feeling and atmosphere of a community where oral tradition and the religious sense are still very much alive to people who have only known the atmosphere of the modern ephemeral, rapidly changing world of industrial civilisation. On the one hand there is a community of independent personalities whose memories of men and events are often amazingly long (in the Gaelic-speaking Outer Hebrides they go back to Viking times a thousand years ago), and where there is an ever-present sense of the reality and existence of the other world of spiritual and psychic experience; on the other hand there is a standardised world where people live in a mental jumble of newspaper headlines and B.B.C. news bulletins, forgetting yesterday's as they read or hear today's, worrying themselves constantly about far-away events which they cannot possibly control, where memories are so short that men often do not know the names of their grandparents, and where the only real world seems to be the everyday material one (J.L. Campbell, 1960, p. 24).

We find again a tacit equation of spirituality with symbolism, and of materialism with plain literality. However we may feel about the virtues of 'Western society', we see opposed those living in a community with an ever-present sense of the spiritual world, and those in a standardised material world, worrying about trivial externalities. I have tried to give some idea of the source of this symbolism, and some of the dangers inherent in its use. Gaelic-speaking children in the late twentieth century may not know much about what it is like to exist in a vertical plane with an ever-present sense of the reality and existence of the other world of psychic and spiritual experience, but they will know a newspaper headline, a BBC news bulletin, or a contemporary happening when they see one. Again, attitudes to language are formed in subtle ways, and the Gaelic language, in the hands of some of its scholars, seems bent on defining itself out of existence.

It must again be emphasised that the imagery that Campbell is using derives from an English language discourse, which can itself be related both to the development of Romanticism in the eighteenth century, and to the rationalist philosophy of the Enlightenment that engendered this. We have, in one sense, almost no testimony from monoglot Gaels of the eighteenth century that has not been processed, in one way or another, by the ideas of the English language. There is certainly no evidence that the Gaels saw themselves in the peculiarly mellow and beautiful light that Campbell throws on them. In the context of folklore, it is of interest in establishing the crucial period of the formation of such sentiments that the earliest collections of Highland folklore show none of the symbolism of the *Gemeinschaft* and *Gesellschaft* type and none of the eloquent sentiments of later works. This can be seen, for example, in the collection made by the Rev. James Kirkwood in the late seventeenth century (see J.L. Campbell, 1975), and Robert Kirk's *Secret Commonwealth* of 1691 (see R. Kirk, 1976). In the latter Kirk shows an unselfconscious mixture of scepticism and credulity towards the beliefs that he is discussing that bears no relation to the lofty dualities of scholarship and peasanthood within which later commentaries construct their theories of knowledge, of society, of mental development, and the like. Whatever validity Campbell's judgements of the relative merits of the two societies that he is discussing may have, it should be clear that his imagery owes its first debt to that discourse within which we have placed Renan, Arnold, Tönnies and others. His observation of Highland society is no innocent gaze, but a perception structured by the metaphors available for its expression. Evans-Wentz says:

> Unlike the natural mind of the uncorrupted Celt, Arunta, or American Red Man, which is ever open to unusual psychical impressions, the mind of the business man in our great cities tends to be obsessed with business affairs both during his waking and during his dream states, the politician's with politics similarly, the society-leader's with society; and the unwholesome excitement felt by day in the city is apt to be heightened at night through a satisfying of the feeling which it morbidly creates for relaxation and change of stimuli. In the slums, humanity is divorced from Nature under even worse conditions, and becomes wholly decadent . . .
>
> Are city-dwellers like these, Nature's unnatural children, who grind out their lives in an unceasing struggle for wealth and power, social position, and even for bread, fit to judge Nature's natural children who believe in fairies? (W.Y. Evans-Wentz, 1911, xxvii).

The distance between Robert Kirk, seventeenth-century minister of the Highland parish of Aberfoyle, and Evans-Wentz, twentieth-century folklorist, is not a simple growth of scientific objectivity from humble beginnings to maturity, but rather charts a radical recreation of imagery appropriate to the assessment of other societies. Although intensive anthropological field-work in the twentieth century has done much to dispel the ideas that the Celtic Twilight, for example, engendered about the incessant spirituality and beauty of primitive life, the metaphors that Evans-Wentz used are still very much the currency of everyday speech, and capable of ordering our world about us whether we will them to or no.

My approach in this chapter might sometimes have seemed irreverent, and my reluctance to take sides in the debates as they are traditionally structured might seem from either side of the argument to represent equivocation, or even hostility. My position, for example, within the structure wherein 'scientific knowledge' and 'folklore' are opposed might be variously misinterpreted. If I refuse to credit science with the capacity to occupy the symbolic field in which 'folklore' exists, it might seem that I advocate a misty and self-indulgent subjectivism. If, on the other hand, I question the conventional pieties of folklore studies it might seem that I am espousing a dismissive rationalism, and attacking the object of study itself—the 'folklore'. What I have tried to do, however, is examine the structure of the arguments in order to demonstrate the larger coherence that exists, and at the same time to show how this larger coherence contains a *categorical* derision of 'folklore'. It is, therefore, only by taking the traditional arguments apart that we can hope to restore to the knowledge of the 'folk' a rationality and a contemporary credibility untainted with an essentially derogatory archaism and sentimentality. My provisional refusal to credit either 'folklore' or 'science' with any substantive reality arises, therefore, from an attempt to show that these two facets of knowledge are, as it were, mutually defining. As Austin said of a rather similar system of dualities, they 'live by taking in each other's washing—what is spurious is not one term of the pair, but the antithesis itself' (J.L. Austin, 1964, p. 4).

I have not discussed the Gaelic folklore itself. Although this was in a sense what I set out to do, I think that there is much undergrowth to be cleared away before the 'lore' itself becomes visible. In any case, others are far better qualified than myself to undertake the study of the folklore, in whatever way might seem appropriate. I hope that I have made it clear that I am not dismissing 'folklore' as a system of knowledge, and that I am not dismissing out of hand the activities of folklorists. It seems to be the case, however, that the majority of folklorists do not much reflect upon their effect on and relationship to the societies in which they conduct their enquiries, and I think that there is much to be gained from such reflection. Conventionally, this topic often appears to be exhausted by the mere voicing of the expectation that the old ideas will continue to wither before the reductive rationality of newspapers, intellectuals and recording machines.

One explanation of this lack of reflection can be found, I think, in the formulation of the folkloric enterprise as one of simple collection. Many folklorists see themselves as mere agents, securing the preservation of phenomena that would otherwise be lost in the erosions of time. This might, indeed, seem like a simple empirical task, demanding no more of an engagement with the object of study than that faced by, say, the geologist or the botanist. To draw a parallel at the simplest level, however, we might note that a bucket of gravel would be of little value to the geologist, or a barn of hay to the botanist. The folklorist, like any other scholar, must ask himself what kind of data he wants, and why he considers that particular kind of data to be worthy of collection.

I must, therefore, admit to a certain ambivalence in my attitude towards the enterprise of the collection of folklore. If this collection is seen to represent a preservation of dying ways, such that they will be available for use by eclectic nationalists, or by those that might someday wish to effect a resurgence of the 'folk', then I can find little value in it. We risk finding ourselves with huge archives of material that has no living context outside the academic journal; that has nothing to rescue it from being merely quaint and, ultimately, dull. It might be argued that avid nationalists might well be expected, on the basis of past performance, to make use of such material, and that that would be a living context, if anything was. I would personally be inclined to argue in reply to this that nationalist iconography was not difficult to come by, particularly in Scotland, and that we have no business dragging the 'folk', mute and unsuspecting, into such affairs.

Even if we are to grant that 'folklore' can in some sense represent a preservation of a lost plenitude, we are still obliged to ask questions like: 'How much folklore is enough folklore?' How will we decide that our collection has reached a size such that it can adequately represent the former days and ways? The Irish Folklore Commission, some years ago, conducted a scheme for collecting folklore in Irish schools, and found themselves, in the end, with 'thirty tons of folklore . . . Who would ever go through them God only knows, but in any case they are there for preservation and later use' (S. O'Suilleabhain, 1953, p. 12). The 'God only knows' bespeaks a certain embarrassment, and it is not difficult to feel that this is prudence and acquisitiveness gone mad. We might suspect that this material, rather like the enormous quantity of anthropometric statistics once gathered by eager anthropologists, will merely gather dust. I am not saying that such material is essentially valueless, but that it is valueless if it is merely stored in a box, or treated independently of the context in which it arose.

Sanderson, in setting the Edinburgh School of Scottish Studies its task, said:

> the tooth of time has made savage attacks on the old Scotland, and it is strange to think of teddy boys in the douce streets of Edinburgh. But a new Scotland is being shaped, with new industries, hydro-electric schemes, forestry and agriculture. The stronger the spiritual roots of that Scotland, the more splendidly will she flourish. There is work for all in the task of preserving and bequeathing our national heritage (S.F. Sanderson, 1957, p. 13).

Folklore is to be collected, therefore, in order to provide Scotland with its spiritual roots. What are we to make of the folklore project conceived in such terms? It arouses, in a sense, instant sympathy. At the same time we must realistically and seriously ask in what sense a folktale, stored in an archive, or published in a journal with at best a very select and limited circulation, can contribute to the strength of a nation's spiritual roots. A folktale stored in an archive is not the same as a folktale on the lips of a story-teller, and never can be. We might indeed be preserving what would otherwise be entirely lost. At the same time, it is difficult to imagine anyone coming to the archive in order to learn stories to tell, in any but the most inauthentic and determinedly dramatic context. What is lost is, in that sense, lost, and whatever value we might find as scholars in our now mute folktale, we certainly do not have the spiritual substance of a nation, stored for transfusion when times are hard, or when the 'teddy boys' start to run amok in the 'douce streets'.

It might indeed give us cause to reflect on the nature of the folklorist's enterprise when we consider that were a 'teddy boy' to appear now in the 'douce streets' he would appear as out of his time as Fionn mac Cumhail. There are doubtless fathers telling tales to their children of their teddy boy youth with all the wistful regret of Ossian lamenting to St Patrick the passing of the heroic age.

There are other facets to the problem. Even if our collected folktale lives on in oral tradition, it is, in important ways, a different folktale once it has been collected – once the oral tradition is conscious of its collection. It is basic to the science of semiology, the science of symbolic systems, that the value of one element in the system depends upon its relation to all the other elements in the system. A Gaelic folktale now exists in a system which includes all its collected versions, and which is, so to speak, informed by a contextual grammar consisting of the awareness of collection, of standardisation, of the possibility of error, of the high moral status attached to the simple folklife, and so on. It is not the same folktale, even if words and delivery have remained constant since the days "nuair a bha Gàidhlig aig a h-uile creutair' (when every creature spoke Gaelic). We can lament this as a lost purity, or we can rejoice in the ever-changing, but we cannot ignore it.

6 MODERN GAELIC POETRY

This chapter is concerned with discussion of some features of modern Gaelic literature which are relevant to the concerns of previous chapters. This will involve consideration of the works of the most intellectual of Gaels and is, in an obvious sense, far away from 'folk-culture'. However, the awareness of the status of the Gaelic-speaking areas as a locus of 'folk' activity, and the problems of assessment and problems of identity that this raises, are clearly raised in some modern literature, and can help us to an understanding of the enduring metaphors by which the 'folk' are constituted.

Poetry has long been considered to be a literary medium to which Gaelic is peculiarly suited, and great Gaelic literature is 'pre-eminently in poetry' (I. Crichton Smith, 1961, p. 172). 'The strength of Gaelic literature does not lie in its prose' (ibid., p. 173). It is with the modern poetry that I will be chiefly concerned here. There has been a revival in both Scottish and Scottish Gaelic literature since the 1930s, and the poets discussed in this chapter have both added to and drawn life from this revival.

Gaelic literature of the nineteenth century existed in a society rocked by the Highland Clearances, and shot through with religious currents that were in many ways inimical to the development of a robust literature. The nineteenth century was:

> the bitter century of the Clearances, when the chaos that the break-up of any traditional society produces was intensified beyond endurance in the bewilderment of a people attacked by their own natural leaders. This broken community eagerly accepted the demands of a passionate and uncompromising faith . . . Predictably, the Evangelical Revival is bound up with social protest, but since the religion was other-worldly, essentially recluse although practised in open society, it could scarcely yield an adequate strategy from the full range of human experience. And so Gaelic poetry in the 19th and early 20th centuries is a strange amalgam: the unsettled complex of a transitional age (J. MacInnes, 1976, p. 61).

Several interesting figures appear from this period, but we cannot be surprised that many, with both the Celtic Twilight and an other-worldly evangelism to retreat into, declined any real engagement with the problems of their time. As a notable exception to this, we should perhaps mention the Skye poetess Màiri Mhór nan Òran (Big Mary of the Songs), otherwise known as Mary Macpherson and Màiri Nighean Iain Bhàin (Mary the daughter of fair Ian). Màiri Mhór was prominent as the voice of the land agitations of the 1880s that led to the Crofters' Act of 1886, which granted to the crofter a security of tenure and ended the possibility of the worst excesses of landlord rapacity.

An important contemporary of Màiri Mhór was Neil Macleod, 'a fine, if limited, craftsman whose work almost always tended toward the pretty and sentimental' (ibid., p. 62) (see, for example, N. Macleod, 1902). Màiri Mhór was no such dreamer, however:

> Bha bàird mar Niall MacLeòid a' dèanamh dealbh dhaibh fhéin air có ris a bha a' Ghàidhealtachd coltach anns na seann làithean, 's air suidheachadh an ám fhéin. Ach bha Màiri ri dhlùth air an fheadhainn a bha thall 's a chunnaic gus sin a thachairt. Bha i cuideachd a' cumail sùil gheur air na pàipearan-naigheachd (D.E. Meek (ed.), 1977, p. 20).

> Poets like Neil MacLeod were painting pictures for themselves of how the Gaidhealtachd was in the old days, and of how it was in their own time. Màiri, however, was interested in what was coming and looking for it to happen. She also kept a sharp eye on the newspapers (my translation).

To many self-styled Celtic poets of the late nineteenth century the very mention of so vulgar a thing as a newspaper would have provoked a refined and sensitive distaste. Màiri Mhór, however, was politically engaged, and it has been one of the dominant desires of the twentieth-century Gaelic poets to escape from the sentimentalities of the nineteenth century and to effect a similar radical engagement, with authentic intellectual foundations. It is not surprising therefore that Sorley MacLean, the major figure in twentieth-century Gaelic (and, probably, Macdiarmid excepted, Scottish) poetry, should look to Màiri Mhór for his immediate intellectual ancestry (see S. MacLean, 1939).

The poets whose work I discuss in this chapter are all concerned to give their literature and language a contemporary realism, a future that both uses and transcends its past. This is no easy task. MacLean said, in 1938, that '19th century [Gaelic] poetry, as compared with 18th century poetry, has a weakness and flabbiness of rhythm' (S. MacLean, 1938, p. 113). Of his own period he said that 'such Gaelic verse as is now being produced I consider very insignificant' (ibid., p. 114). Macaulay, however, writing in 1976, can say that 'the last forty years have seen a remarkable flowering of Gaelic poetry, especially in the modern idiom' (D. Macaulay (ed.), 1976, p. 11). Crichton Smith held the opinion in 1961 that there are 'three writers of importance in this century . . . Sorley MacLean, George Campbell Hay, and Derick Thomson' (I. Crichton Smith, 1961, p. 173). These three, and the two commentators quoted, Macaulay and Crichton Smith, have since been established as the five major modern Gaelic poets, and this estimation concretised by the publication of an important bilingual anthology of their works (see D. Macaulay (ed.), 1976).

The five poets with whom we are chiefly concerned are all prominent intellectually in other fields. At least it cannot be said of any of them that he is a 'simple, unaffected child of nature'. Sorley MacLean (born in Raasay, 1911), an Edinburgh graduate and later headmaster of Plockton school, is now retired and living in Skye, where he is associated with the activities of Sabhal Mór Ostaig; George Campbell Hay (born in Argyll, 1915), an Oxford graduate, earns his living as a translator in Edinburgh; Derick Thomson (born in Lewis, 1921), a graduate of Aberdeen and Cambridge, is now professor of Celtic at Glasgow University; Ian Crichton Smith (born in Lewis, 1928), an Aberdeen graduate, has published a considerable number of volumes of short stories and poems in both English and Gaelic, and is now a schoolmaster in Oban; Donald Macaulay (born in Bernera, 1930), an Aberdeen and Cambridge graduate, is now head of the Celtic department in the University of Aberdeen. Macaulay says of their poetry that it has been:

> written by people who have been transplanted out of their native communities into the ubiquitous outside world. . . . They were all processed out in the course of their education, there being often no secondary school in their community, and certainly no university. Their move into the outside world and their contact with their contemporaries especially at their universities has given them a broader vision of life and a greater experience of exotic literary tastes – a new context in which to see their community and its art. At the same time it has created in them a conviction that they have lost a great deal in exchange for what they have gained. They are strongly dependent emotionally on the communities which were the source of their formative experience and, of course, of their language, but their outside experience has bred an intellectual independence. As Thomson clearly expresses it,

The heart tied to a tethering-post, . . .
and the mind free.
I bought its freedom dearly.

They have become bicultural and it is this situation, a notoriously uneasy one, which creates the tension from which a great deal of their poetry derives (D. Macaulay (ed.), 1976, p. 47).

We have seen that a variety of metaphorical devices has been used to express the relationship of Gaelic culture to the majority society. These poets, who have been 'transplanted out of their native communities into the ubiquitous outside world' in the course of their education, can easily find in their personal biographies a confirmation of much of the imagery that has been employed. The association of Gaelic with childhood becomes its association with innocence and simplicity, with domesticity, family sentiment, and closeness to home. This is made all the more plain by the necessities of education, whereby the development of the 'intellect' becomes associated with English, distance from home, urban life, adult responsibility, sophistication and materialism. Thus the imagery by which a monolingual English speaker would express the attributes of childhood, the relationship of the rural to the urban, or of business life to home life, comes to confirm, for the bilingual Gael, a picture of the relationship of Gaelic to English culture. We have argued the same for Renan's perception of the Celt. Renan's testimony has, however, now had a century of literary independence in which to render itself an external and intellectual confirmation of this assessment by the modern Gael, rather than simply another statement of the same order.

Furthermore, since in the Gaidhealtachd there has been a 'long-standing Gaelic-English diglossia in which English predominated in High Culture . . . and Gaelic in home-neighbourhood domains' (D.J. MacLeod, 1976, p. 24), the biography of a Gaelic-speaking intellectual tends to confirm, over time, the facts of differential language use in the Gaelic-speaking areas at any one time. Gaelic is used in precisely those areas which education ignores and which the world of economic rationality excludes – the home, religion, close personal relationships, and the like. At the same time, the relative social positions of Gaelic- and non-Gaelic-speaking members of the community (with monolingual English-speakers tending to occupy economically important but socially peripheral spaces) confirm the relative significance of the areas of usage of Gaelic that a bilingual person will apply from day to day. These various tendencies towards symbolic congruence are, of course, causally interrelated, and to say that they provoke a conflation of imagery is not to deny the sometimes depressing reality of the situation. It does, however, mean that a Gael can express his own biography in the same imagery that can be used to express the last two hundred years of Gaelic history. With every intellectual advance the forces of rationality and economic materialism, in the shape of the English language, assault the old order, and the battle of Culloden is fought again and again at the boundaries of differential language use. An encroaching modernity and a retreating antiquity, defined by opposition and incapable of compromise, struggle to the death. There will be no compromise between the Gaelic and English languages, no mutually agreed and equal merger, and no collapse of emotionality and intellectuality, of antiquity and modernity, can be either expected or given expression.

I have tried to show that many Gaelic scholars have tended to accept and promote a picture of Gaeldom that derived from the internal coherence of English-language metaphorical and symbolic structures, and that this picture is not, however much it might be imagined to be, a product of innocent observation. Insofar as the poets that I am discussing here are concerned with biculturality and problems of identity, the imagery that is readily available for their use is an imagery which subsumes Gaelic culture within a larger discourse. Problems of dual identity, when one of the identities involved is that of a (linguistically, economically, morally) beleagured minority, invite the tendency to define the two cultures in opposition, thus potentially robbing both of a full claim to containment of the dualities wherewith the two cultures are opposed. This will have little effect on the self-image of the majority, or the more powerful, culture, since it will have its own enormous reserves of confident, unselfconscious, unstated self-definition. There is a real danger for the minority, however, that it will become, in its own eyes, a symbolic half-world, unfit to stand alone. We have seen that there is ample precedent for this kind of diminution of things 'Celtic'.

Macaulay puts the problem as follows:

> Members of a cultural minority have many things to guard against. These things, it would appear, are not always obvious. They may, on the one hand, give up and allow themselves to be taken over. On the other hand they may institutionalise and become assertive in their parochialism, seeing this as their only defence against the continual pressure exerted by the majority and failing to recognise that this

> alternative is itself culturally destructive and constitutes one of the pressures they must resist (D. Macaulay, 1966, p. 136).

Concern with a problem of identity is a very general twentieth-century preoccupation, and does not necessarily constitute an assertiveness in parochiality, but it does tend to preserve, within the Gaelic context, the discourse within which 'symbolic appropriation' is permitted to occur. The systems of metaphor that created the Gael of folklore and sentiment have had over two hundred years to render themselves apt, and have over two hundred years of the inertia of casual usage to render them unwilling tools for any but their accustomed task. They are not, although they have all the appearance of being, innocently apt. It is worth mentioning again here the equation of woman and the Celt that I discussed in Chapter 4. The problem that modern feminism has in deciding exactly what to assert as an identity is one that Gaels share. To assert the accepted image is merely a confirmation of political and economic marginality–at the same time no other identity is offered, and the imagery of the old is virtually impossible to escape from, finding self-confirmation everywhere it looks.

It is not in any obvious feature of content or form that some of the works of these poets are conservative. Indeed, the major work of Sorley MacLean, *Dàin do Eimhir*, marked an entirely new beginning, a literary event of importance for both Gaelic and English poetry, and was largely unexpected. Macaulay argues that MacLean has absorbed and fruitfully used influences both from the Gaelic poetical heritage and from the major movements in European poetry, and has achieved what has been so conspicuously lacking within Gaelic culture over the last two hundred years–'an easy commerce of the old and the new'.

Macaulay places the new developments in their historical context. He says of the eighteenth-century poetic tradition that it was:

> closely tied in with a particular form of social structure. As this social structure disintegrated and was gradually eroded and replaced during the nineteenth and twentieth centuries, and as new life-styles were introduced at a time of rapidly increasing contact with the outside world, the poetry gradually became attenuated. This attenuation can be seen in many ways. The repertoire of the poets narrowed and became stereotyped. The intellectual content of the poetry diminished. An excessive parochialism developed, and with it a sentimentality and a lack of realism, especially in the poetry of the city-based exiles. This attenuation is also to be seen in the fabric of the poetry itself; in the decay of rhetorical power; in the lack of inventiveness and over-

> reliance on formulae; in the mixed metaphor; and in the replacement of rhythmic subtleties with dead regularities (D. Macaulay (ed.), 1976, p. 47).

He goes on to say:

> One dimension of modern verse is a reaction against this decay in culture and poetry. There had of course been traditional reactions to change. These generally took forms such as looking at the past as a golden age in which objects and motives were unsullied, and the weather was good (heroes and milkmaids in a sunny pastoral landscape); suspicion of the new (comic poems about monster trains and esoteric indulgences like tea drinking); and, probably the most telling of all, a rhetorical self-acclamation. The reaction in modern verse is very different. It looks at the process with a much colder eye and at the same time uses less general, more personal, more concrete, and more passionate language (ibid.).

We might note that such a revolution of realism over sentimentality was a general feature of European literature in the early twentieth century, and argue that its genesis cannot be tied to any internal change in Gaelic society. Insofar, however, as the image of Gaelic society has been constituted by sentimentality as, *par excellence*, its own location, we might expect a peculiarly vigorous and interesting 'realist' response.

The revival of Gaelic poetry in the twentieth century cannot be divorced from attempts to develop a specifically Scottish political consciousness. Two figures loom large in this context, Hugh Macdiarmid and Ruaraidh Erskine of Marr. There is not room here to discuss their ideas and activities fully, but some idea of the animating issues is necessary. Erskine, early in this century, attempted to make Gaelic serve as a nationalist political medium, with only limited success. In an attempt to achieve this he promoted several ventures in bilingual journalism, among them the quarterly *Guth na Bliadhna* (*The Voice of the Year*), which appeared from 1904 until 1925. This journal was 'dedicated to the freedom of Scotland and the discussion of all cognate questions' (F.G. Thompson, 1970, p. 83). Erskine's ambitions were large in that he 'was not a Highland separatist. Rather his object was to Celticise the whole of Scotland' (ibid.). Macdiarmid expressed a similar hope, appealing for an end to 'the false Highland–Lowland distinction which has been the main obstacle to Scottish unity' (cited F.G. Thompson, 1970, p. 88).

It is of interest that Scottish Gaelic never came to occupy the position in Scottish nationalist endeavour that the Celtic languages have in Ireland and Wales. Thompson laments that 'not enough capital was made out of the political potential which Gaelic had at the turn of the century' (ibid., p. 81), and that that political capacity was 'not well received in the Scottish Lowlands' (ibid., p. 83). Considering the facts of the political relationship of the Highlands and Lowlands over the last three hundred years, this is hardly surprising. The political oppression of the Highlands, and the use of imagery to describe the Gael that requires of him a political impotence (in much the same way that 'femininity' is used to render women a negligible political force) come neatly together when we consider what happened to this attempt to politicise the Gaelic revival. Thompson says that:

> the Gaelic revival took the emasculated form of reviving the language, its literature, and reviving an interest in the history of the Celtic peoples, in Celtic music, art, dress and sports. An Comunn Gaidhealach [the Highland Society] was formed expressly for the purpose of promoting what might be called the aestheticiana of Gaelic, leaving the more urgent needs of the Highland people, such as socio-economic development, to other bodies (ibid., p. 81).

This is exactly what might have been predicted from a prophetic reading of Arnold's *Celtic Literature*, and we cannot be surprised that 'Gaelic . . . plays little part in politics in the Highlands of the present day' (ibid., p. 93). Blair, writing in *Guth na Bliadhna*, struggles to compromise the traditional picture of the Celt with a political adequacy. He says that:

> No one who has the slightest acquaintance with Celtic history will refuse to admit that Celtic political schemes and projects have too often been characterised by a certain nebulousness and dimness of outline. They may abound in detail of a vague and shadowy sort, but it is true to say that they do not stand on firm clear-cut foundations, and that they are mere shadowy fragments in comparison with the solid and substantial edifices in which less imaginative peoples are wont to lodge their political aspirations. We cannot say that this flaw in the Celt arises from any innate incapacity to rule existent in our race. Some, it is true, have asserted that the Celt is incapable of rule, but those who have ventilated this opinion have been suspected, with good reason, of race prejudice . . . I think we should be justified in regarding his many failures to reduce his political schemes to the

> dimensions of practical politics to his, in this respect, too lively, fertile, and undisciplined imagination. He is too much the sport of his own luxuriant fancy (A.M. Blair, 1915, p. 415).

This is a fascinating expression of a problem that minority and marginal politics seem bound to face. At one level, we can bring Blair's ambitions to ruin within the all-embracing logic of the metaphors that he invokes. We have seen, for example, that a people or a sex are only allowed luxuriant fancy if they renounce political effectivity, and vice versa. To ask for both is to attempt to controvert metaphorical structures of great effectivity and generality of application. It is only entirely outside such rhetoric that the Highlander will be able to grant himself a political competence.

At another level, however, we must ask how we can link this rhetoric with the political conditions that create the 'nebulousness and dimness of outline' of the political aspirations of the Gael. We might, for example, treat this metaphorical rhetoric as an 'expression' of a real political situation (of, say, oppression), and look for a political explanation outside and independent of this literary expression. To do so would, however, introduce a bipolarity in our enquiry that would prevent us from seeing the very real congruence that the 'political' and the 'literary' expressions have.

The rhetoric that Blair employs is one in which the position that the Gael occupies is incomplete. I have tried in previous chapters to show that the rationality of this imagery can only be understood as a coherent system that embraces Gael and Gall, Celt and Anglo-Saxon, and so on. The imagery that Blair invokes is centred, has the source of its rationality, elsewhere than in his writing. This subsuming rationality is not, however, merely literary. The political world that the Gael occupies is one that subsumes him and manipulates him. It is, quite literally, centred elsewhere (in Edinburgh, say, or London), and has been so at least since the eclipse of the Lordship of the Isles in the fifteenth century.

Consequently events that might appear to be purely internal to Gaelic politics can often only be understood in a wider context. The rationality of Gaelic politics is not to be found internally, but in a larger system. The Massacre of Glencoe stands as a good and obvious example of the necessity of seeing the larger context in order to explain an event ostensibly internal to Highland society. We can argue that this is not simply a phenomenon that occurs whenever the dominant external society chooses to 'interfere', but is rather a very general feature of the relationship of a minority to a dominant majority. If the rationality of

Gaelic politics is centred outside the strictly Gaelic sphere, then it is not difficult to see why, from within the Gaelic world, Gaelic politics would indeed seem to lack 'clear-cut foundations', and to consist of 'mere shadowy fragments'. Blair's attempt to find the autonomous and hitherto concealed Gaelic polity within these shadowy fragments is, therefore, doomed to failure.

If we re-insert the merely literary imagery into this evidence, and remember the ascription by the majority to the minority of an imaginative, wild and unreliable incompetence, then it is clear that we are within a fabric of many dimensions, with a multifold capacity for self-validation and reality-definition, wherever in the web we choose to stand. It is also clear that any too simple division between 'literature' or 'mere imagery' on the one hand, and 'history' or the 'simple facts' on the other, will not assist us.

It is of interest that those who are most often concerned to draw the Celtic blanket over the whole of Scotland, and we can take Erskine and Macdiarmid as examples here, are not native Highlanders. Just as there is only one major north/south political division between Caithness and Kent, so there is only one major north/south language division, and it is often easy and appropriate to pretend that these represent the same duality. I have remarked that the institutions that define Scotland in the international imagination are Highland institutions. It is perhaps not surprising, therefore, in an urban and cosmopolitan world, that one of the most readily available means of measuring the political distance between Scotland and England is to draw Scotland away from the Anglo-Saxon, and expand the Highland Celt to fill the entire Scottish political space. This at least is an appropriate strategy for Lowland nationalists. From the Highlands the picture looks rather different, of course. In my experience at least, the Highlanders are reluctant to accept the Lowlanders into any brotherhood of the Celt, and dismissive of the Gaelic pretensions of the urban Scot, however enthusiastic.

Macdiarmid might want an end to the 'false Highland/Lowland distinction' which has been an obstacle to Scottish unity, but at what level of historical thinking beyond the purely wishful this distinction can be said to be 'false' is problematical. His plea obscures the fact that this false distinction has been the very substance of Scottish disunity, and the dominant political dividing line in Scotland since the time of Malcolm Canmore.

The use of both Scots and Gaelic as media for the expression of modern ideas, as opposed to their use for the expression of bucolic and backward-looking sentiments, is a feature of Scottish art very much associated with C.M. Grieve (alias Hugh Macdiarmid), and Grieve's particular brand of socialist nationalism has clearly had an effect, in different ways, on the ideas of Hay, MacLean and Thomson. What has come to be called 'the Scottish renaissance' involves, through Grieve, a belief in the 'value of the Doric' which 'lies in the extent to which it contains lapsed or unrealised qualities which correspond to "unconscious" elements of distinctively Scottish psychology' (C.M. Grieve, 1922, p. 62). Thus, although there is a determination to be 'relevant', there is also a familiar atavism that looks for an unspoken essence of Scottishness, for 'lapsed elements of psychology'. This is imagery that is much used to justify the literary use of Gaelic and to establish its continued relevance, and it is no surprise that a Gaelic movement would find such a sentiment towards the Doric equally applicable to Gaelic.

At the same time as searching for a distinctively Scottish psychology, Macdiarmid is also 'a champion of any and every cause which he believes will facilitate the creation of a society which allows the free and full development of the human personality' (D. Glen, 1964, p. 81). We can pause here to consider how similar this is to Matthew Arnold's ambition. I have tried to show that Arnold's work was pivotal in the intellectual formation within which the Celtic Twilight movement could exist. Macdiarmid has not failed to recognise the self-indulgence and essential inauthenticity of this movement. At the same time he has been reluctant to lose so famous a champion as Arnold. Macdiarmid's determination to find the quality of great art lacking in all English productions (see, for example, H. Macdiarmid, 1970, pp. 77ff) is inspired by an ethnological committment very similar to Arnold's, with the difference that Arnold wished to establish rapport, and Macdiarmid to establish polarisation. Arnold's comments have, of course, the added virtue that they come from within the tradition that they criticised.

As an Englishman Arnold might not, by the very metaphors that he invoked, be credited with any ability to recognise taste and natural magic when he saw it. Macdiarmid, however, rescues Arnold's statements from any suspicion of dubious racial provenance, and thus secures his best-established ratification of the excellence of the Celt, by saying of Arnold that he was 'himself half a Celt – his mother was a Cornish woman' (H. Macdiarmid, 1968, p. 301).

The common ambition of Arnold and Macdiarmid, to restore to man his integrity and wholeness, is of course an ambition shared by many of the great figures of early social science. Social theorists like Tönnies and Weber were much concerned by the restrictions imposed upon the human personality by the modern world, at the same time as they were architects of theories where the folk and the civilised, the traditional and the modern, were arranged in opposition, with the more full and spontaneous realisation of humanity located with the first of the pair of both dualities mentioned. Weber says that 'the great question thus is . . . what we can set against this mechanisation to preserve a certain section of humanity from this fragmentation of the soul, this complete ascendancy of the bureaucratic ideal of life?' (M. Weber, 1924, cited A. Giddens, 1971, p. 236). Since Gaelic culture has been consistently located within the *Gemeinschaft*, it is clear that such an appeal as Macdiarmid's for a full realisation of humanity would be readily received as appropriate to the Gaels and thereby to a greater Scotland. Hay's poetry is particularly influenced by these ideas. His verse is filled with celebration of the Scottish land and the strength to be derived from it. Many of his poems are an assertion of nationalism through naturalism, that despises the concealments and diminutions of civility and civilisation. In his 'Ceithir Gaothan na h-Albann' ('The Four Winds of Scotland') we find:

line 5. Duilleach an t-Samhraidh, tuil an Dàmhair,
    na cuithean 's an àrdghaoth Earraich i;
dùrd na coille, bùirich eas, ùire 'n t-sneachda's
    an fhaloisg i;
tlàths is binneas, àrdan, misneach, fàs is sileadh
    nam frasan i;
anail mo chuirp, àrach mo thuigse,
    mo làmhan, m' uilt is m' anam i;
fad na bliadhna, ré gach ràidhe,
    gach là 's gach ciaradh feasgair dhomh,
is i Alba nan Gall 's nan Gàidheal
    is gàire, is blàths, is beatha dhomh.

(G. Campbell Hay, 1947, p. 33).

The leaves of Summer, the spate of Autumn, the snowdrifts and the high spring wind is she;/the sough of the woodland, the roaring of waterfalls, the freshness of the snow and the heather ablaze is she;/ mild pleasantness and melody, angry pride and courage, growth and the pouring of the showers is she;/ breath of my body, nurture of my understanding, my hands, my joints and my soul is she./ All year long, each season through, each day and each fall of dusk for me,/ it is Scotland, Highland and Lowland, that is laughter and warmth and life for me.

(ibid.).

Those that are required to live in this country are described in 'Dleasnas nan Airdean' ('The Duty of the Heights'):

v. 3 A òigridh mo dhùthcha,
an e ciùine nan réidhlean,
fois is clos nan gleann ìosal,
air an dìon o'n gharbh shéideadh?
Biodh bhur ceum air a' mhullach,
is bhur n-uchd ris na speuran.
Dhuibh srac-ghaoth nam bidean
mu'n tig sgrios 'na bheum-sléibh oirnn.

(G. Campbell Hay, 1947, p. 32).

Youth of my country,/ is it to be the tranquility of the plains, then?/ The peace and slumber of low valleys,/ sheltered from the rough blast?/ Let your step be on the summit,/ and your breast exposed to the sky./ For you the tearing wind of the pinnacles,/ lest destruction come on us as a landslide.

(ibid.).

These have, politically, a rather antique ring. They might be compared to a poem by Carlyle, who loved the Teuton and despised the Celt, and who wrote this 'Ode to the East Wind':

'Tis the hard grey weather
Breeds hard English men.
What's the soft South-wester?
'Tis the ladies' breeze,
Bringing home their true-loves
Out of all the seas.
But the black North-easter,
Through the snowstorm hurled,
Drives our English hearts of oak
Seaward round the world.
Come as came our fathers,
Heralded by thee,
Conquering from the eastward,

Lords by land and sea.
Come, and strong within us
Stir the Viking's blood;
Bracing brain and sinew;
Blow thou wind of God.
(cited F. Faverty, 1951, p. 17).

This and the two last cited poems by Hay, while intended to establish somewhat contrary ethnological propositions, clearly have strong affinities. We might question the authenticity of such symbolism, remembering Macaulay's strictures on 'rhetorical self-acclamation', and MacLean's claim that 'Gaelic poetry is not less but more realistic than most European poetry' (S. MacLean, 1938, p. 83). The naturality of a Scotland ready to burst into its full unconstrained expression, emotionally unfettered, free from convention and the habitual, is required in Hay's 'Priosan da Fhéin an Duine?' ('Man his own Prison?') (G. Campbell Hay, 1947, p. 38).

This plea for complete and spontaneous expression, following the dictates of the heart, as a quality and a necessity for the Scottish people, locates Hay in a strong twentieth-century tradition. It can also, however, in so far as it is tied to Scotland, be easily derived from Celticist Romanticism, and is another recension of symbols that Arnold used and to which Ossian appealed. The ready emotionality of the Scot that Hay admires is clearly shown in his 'Meftah Bâbkum es-sabar' ('Patience the key to our door' – Arabic proverb):

line 34. Beachdan gnàthach, laghach, cinnteach,
òraid dhàicheil à ceann slìogte,
nòsan àbhaisteach no mìnead,

line 40. na iarraibh – tha sinn beò da-rìribh,
agus 'is fuar a' ghaoth thar Ile
gheibhear aca ann Cinntìre.'
Iarraibh gaìre, gean is mìghean,
càirdeas, nàimhdeas, tlachd is mìothlachd.
Iarraibh faileas fìor ar n-inntinn.

line 50. Blàr-cath' ar toile, leac ar teine,
an raon a dhùisgeas ar seisreach,
stéidh togail ar làmhan 's ar dealais;
an talla a fhuair sinn gun cheilear,
is far an cluinnear moch is feasgar

ceòl ar sinnsre is gàir ar seinne;
an leabhar far an sgrìobhar leinne
bàrdachd ùr fo'n rann mu dheireadh
a chuireadh leis na bàird o shean ann –
b'e sin ar tìr. No, mur an gleachdar,
rud suarach ann an cùil 'ga cheiltinn,
a thraogh 's a dhìochuimhnich sluagh eile.
(D. Macaulay (ed.), 1976, p. 135).

line 34. Nice, conventional, certain opinions,/ a plausible oration from a sleek head,/ customary ways or smoothness;/

line 40. do not ask for them – we are alive in earnest,/ and 'Cold is the wind over Islay / that blows on them in Kintyre'./ Ask for laughter and cheerful and angry moods,/ friendship, enmity, pleasure and displeasure./ Ask for the true reflexion of our mind./

line 50. The battlefield of our will,/ the hearthstone we kindle our fire upon,/ the field our ploughteam will awaken,/ the foundation for the building of our hands and zeal;/ the hall we found without melody,/ and where will be heard, early and evening,/ the music of our forebears and the clamour of our singing;/ the book where we will write / new poetry below the last verse / put in by the poets of old – / such will be our land. Or, if there be no struggle,/ a mean thing of no account, hidden away in a corner,/ which another people drained dry and forgot.
(ibid., p. 134).

We notice that Hay, to a readership predominantly urban in the middle twentieth century, talks of building a hall with hands, awakening zeal with a plough-team, and kindling a fire on the hearthstone, in order to sweep away the plausible, customary and conventional, and awaken the Gael of music and song. Looking back to Arnold and Renan, we might well consider that a Scot dealing intimately with natural phenomena in order to invoke spontaneous art was not the obviously authentic phenomenon that it imagined itself to be. Hay says of his birthplace, in 'Cinntìre' ('Kintyre'):

v. 7 Is daor a cheannaich mi mo bheòshlàint'

ma's e mo stòras fanachd uait,
crom gach là os cionn mo leabhair
gun amharc ort, mo ghoirtein uain'.
(G. Campbell Hay, 1947, p. 15).

Dearly have I bought my livelihood
If my wealth is to stay away from you,
bent every day over my book
without looking on you, my green little garden.
(ibid., p. 16).

We see the familiar oppositions of book learning to naturality, materialist alienation to domestic integration. Renan, had he been a poet and written of his Brittany, might have penned such sentiments.

Derick Thomson is, like Hay, a committed Scottish nationalist. Like Hay, he uses in his poetry symbols that locate the two societies with which he is concerned in opposed and mutually defining worlds. In 'Bùrn is Mòine 's Coirc'' ('Water and Peat and Oats') he divides his personality between the Hebrides and the town:

An cridhe ri bacan, car ma char aig an fheist
's i fàs goirid,
's an inntinn saor.
Is daor a cheannaich mi a saorsa.
(D. Macaulay (ed.), 1976, p. 163).

The heart tied to a tethering-post, round upon round of the rope,
till it grows short,
and the mind free.
I bought its freedom dearly.
(ibid., p. 162).

In 'Cisteachan-Laighe' ('Coffins') he tells us how that free mind was formed, by an education where:

cha do dh'aithnich mi 'm bréid Beurla,
an lìomḥ Gallda bha dol air an fhiodh,
cha do leugh mi na facail air a' phràis,
cha do thuig mi gu robh mo chinneadh a' dol bàs.
(D. Macaulay (ed.), 1976, p. 157).

I did not recognise the English braid,
The Lowland varnish being applied to the wood,
I did not read the words on the brass,
I did not understand that my race was dying.
(ibid., p. 156).

We can see that English sophistication and Lowland artifice are killing a race which retains only its unspoilt and untutored heart. In 'Cotriona Mhór', Thomson expresses some of the unease involved in watching a culture being appropriated as a museum of folklore, while at the same time locating it with precisely the images that have allowed and required that appropriation:

Tha do dhealbh ann an cùl m' inntinn
gun sgleò air,
daingeann, suidhichte
a-measg nan ìomhaighean briste,
a-measg a luasgain,
gun aois a' laigh air ach an aois a bhà thu,
clàr mór an aodainn mar chloc air stad
air madainn Earraich,
gam chur ri uair a' bhaile
leis a' ghliocas sin
nach robh an eisimeil leabhraichean,
leis an àbhachdas, leis a' ghearradh-cainnt
a bha a' leum á chridhe a' chinnidh
mus deach a chéiseadh,
mus deach a valve ùr ann
a chumadh ag obair e anns an t-saoghal ùr.
Sud iuchair mo mhuseum,
an clàr air an cluich mi mo bhial-aithris,
an spaid-bheag leis an dùisg mi fonn
na linne a tha nise seachad,
an ìomhaigh tha cumail smachd
air na h-ìomhaighean-bréige.
(D. Macaulay (ed.), 1976, p. 167).

Your picture is at the back of my mind/ undimmed,/ steady, set/ among the broken images,/ amid the movements,/ untouched by age except the age you were,/ the great round of the face where the clock stopped/ on a Spring morning,/ keeping me to the village time/

> with that wisdom/ that flourished without books,/ with the fun, the cleverness with words/ that leapt from the heart of the race/ before it was encased,/ before it had the new valve in it/ to keep it going in the new world./ That is the key to my museum,/ the record on which I play my folklore,/ the trowel with which I turn the ground/ of the age that is now gone,/ the image that keeps control/ over false images. (ibid., p. 166).

We can see that, even in some of its most intimate and thoughtful self-assessments, Gaelic culture becomes that of a race which has wisdom without books, where fun and cleverness leap from the heart. Hugh Blair imagined such a race in 1760, and Arnold gave it enduring literary form in 1865. For Thomson, as for Blair, the force that muzzled this spontaneity was convention, and the modern, always inimical to the Gaelic world, expressed by the shocking borrowing of the mechanical 'valve ùr' (new valve). At what point these images cease to be innocently appropriate and begin to assume the appearance of a continued creation of the world of the Gael according to the demands of a purely external discourse is not a question that can be simply answered. However, since it is the inability, or reluctance, however caused, of the Gaelic world to respond with a fruitful synthesis to external influence that has produced the situation in which the 'death of a race' can be lamented, it is a consolidation of this weakness to celebrate the old entirely at the expense of the new, to find no good in change, and, at root, to be over-concerned with a simple 'dual-identity' metaphorical complex at all. Crichton Smith says:

> It is important to notice in Thomson's poems his primary aim, which appears to be the contrast between two orders, the changing order of the Western Isles (specifically) with the advancing order of a technological civilisation (I. Crichton Smith, 1953, p. 205).
>
> The conversational movement of his poetry is suited to the nature of his theme – decay. (ibid., p. 206).

It is perhaps worth pointing out that a monolingual English speaker who has neither the opportunity nor the materials for the indulgence of locating his *persona* within the dialectics of a culture clash can still appreciate the metaphors that Thomson uses, and can still imagine that he has both head and heart, without feeling the need to make different worlds of these, and to localise these worlds both temporally and spatially. The duality of language difference, and the associated if imaginary dualities of racial difference, supply a ready over-determination of what are, by the conditions of their continued maintenance of meaning, metaphorical unities.

Sorley MacLean, the leading figure both chronologically and, according to accepted opinion, artistically, in this group, is less inclined than the other four to dwell on problems of dual identity. Macaulay says of him:

> The search for . . . a unifying focus has led to different solutions for different people. For MacLean, aware from traditional sources of the traumatic experiences of his people at the hands of exploiters and brought up on the heady dialectics of the 1930's, the answer was socialism. This provided him with an ideal goal, and with a political framework, which added a significant element of coherence to his early poetry and which continues to inform his later work (D. Macaulay (ed.), 1976, p. 50).

Socialism is, in my opinion at least, a far more sensible and historically valid reaction to 'traumatic experiences . . . at the hands of exploiters' than is nationalism. It is, perhaps, some evidence of authenticity that Maclean's political poetry has a symbolic autonomy within a socialist view of the world – the same autonomy (although for different reasons) that Alexander Macdonald had, and that modern nationalism, within the polarisation of sentiment that it frequently feels bound to assert, often loses. MacLean denies the symbolic appropriation of his world by English language discourse not by vigorously rejecting it, which only leads to another form of acceptance, but by ignoring it without apparent difficulty. Crichton Smith says of him: 'For better or worse MacLean leaves a final impression of being set securely in a cosmopolitan city of images' (I. Crichton Smith, 1953, p. 202). We can get some idea of this cosmopolitanism from MacLean's 'Cornford':

v. 4 Dé dhuinne ìmpireachd na Gearmailt
no ìmpireachd Bhreatainn,
no ìmpireachd na Frainge,
's a h-uile té dhiubh sgreataidh!
ach 's ann duinne tha am bròn
ann am breòiteachd a' chinne:
Lorca, Julian Bell is Cornford,
na d'fhan ri glòir nam filidh.

(S. MacLean, 1977, p. 81).

What to us the empire of Germany / or the empire of Britain / or the empire of France / and every one of them loathsome? / But the grief is ours / in the sore frailty of mankind, / Lorca, Julian Bell, and Cornford, / who did not wait for the fame of poets.

(ibid., p. 80).

Next to Hay's Scotland where 'gràin no gruaim cha tig 'na còir-se' ('hate and gloom come not near her') (G. Campbell Hay, 1947, p. 15), we can put the following from MacLean's 'Gaoir na h-Eòrpa' ('The Cry of Europe'):

v. 3 An tugadh corp geal is clàr gréine
bhuam-sa cealgaireachd dhubh na bréine,
nimh bhùirdeasach is puinnsean créide
is dìblidheachd ar n-Albann éitigh?

(S. MacLean, 1977, p. 13).

Would white body and forehead's sun take / from me the foul black treachery, / spite of the bourgeois and poison of their creed / and the feebleness of our dismal Scotland?

(ibid., p. 12).

One of MacLean's few characterisations of the Gael and the Gall using rhetoric derived from the metaphors that I am discussing occurs in his lament for his brother, Calum MacLean. Calum MacLean, a noted folklorist whose work I discuss elsewhere in this book, was much given to the use of such imagery, so that it is perhaps not inappropriate here, in 'Cumha Chaluim Iain MhicGill-Eain' ('Lament for Calum MacLean'):

1.87. On bha t' ùidh anns an duine
'S nach b'aithne dhut an fhoill,
No sliomaireachd no sodal stàite,
Rinn thu Gàidheil dhe na Goill.

(S. MacLean, 1977, p. 173).

Since you cared for the man / and did not know guile / or sleekitness or fawning for place / you made Gaels of the Galls.

(ibid., p. 172).

This is not typical of his imagery, however. Nor is anything that I have quoted, since his most celebrated poems do not lend themselves to my argument, which is, perhaps, to their credit. Crichton Smith says that 'some of his more virulent political poems should never have been written, . . . they are too one-sided to be true at a poet's level of perception' (I. Crichton Smith, 1953, p. 201).

One of the interesting features of the work of these poets is the way in which the symbolic appropriation of Gaelic culture is treated. In the attempt to achieve a clear-eyed realism the most obviously inauthentic aspects of this appropriation are often regretted. Occasionally, however, particularly in the poems of Crichton Smith, there is a suggestion of the ambiguous way in which such inauthenticity can come to generate its own reality.

MacLean, like Thomson, Crichton Smith and Macaulay, has written with distaste of the way in which his culture has been adopted by another, as its ornament. He says, in 'Road to the Isles':

Théid mi thun nan Eileanan
is ataidh mi le m' bhaothalachd
mu bhruthan sìth an Canaidh 's Eige,
mu ghusgul ròn an Eirisgeidh,
mu chlàrsaichean 's mu Eilean Bharraidh,
mu Fhir Ghorma 's mu Chaitligich,
mu thighean dubha 's tràighean geala,
mu Thìr Nan Og 's mu'n Iùbhraich Bhallaich:
cuiridh mi iad ann mo phòcaid
air son snaoisean mo shròine,
air son boillsgeadh mo shùilean,
air son gealaich mo rùintean,
air son braisealachd goil coire,
a thaobh bréige is goileim,
Ghabhar dhiom am fìor Ghàidheal
a réir meud mo mhór phàighidh
leis na tàlantan diadhaidh
a thruis 's a sholair mi 'na chrìochaibh:
gabhar sràid leam an Dùn-Eideann
an crios 's am breacan an fhéilibh;
boillsgear follais aig gach céilidh:
carnar leam tùis mar dh'fheumar
air altairean Khennedy-Fraser,
seinnear duanagan . . .

(S. MacLean, 1943, p. 95).

I will go to the Isles / and inflate with my vapidity / about fairy mounds in Canna and Eigg, / about the wailing of seals in Eriskay, / about 'clarsachs' and the Isle of Barra, / about Blue Men and Catholics, / about 'black' houses and white strands, / about Tir Nan Og and the speckled barge: / I will put them in my pocket / as snuff for my nose, / as a light to my eyes, / a moon to my desires, / to make my kettle boil the quicker, / for lies and chatter. / I will be called the 'true' Gael / according to the extent of my large endowment / with the holy talents I collected / and procured in this country: / I will promenade in Edinburgh / in the belted, kilted plaid; / I will shine at every 'ceilidh', / heap incense, as is fitting, / on the altars of Kennedy-Fraser. / I'll sing ditties . . .

(ibid., p. 103).

Thomson has also expressed this disquiet, less encyclopaedically, in his 'Cotriona Mhór', cited above (p. 155), where he speaks of 'an clàr air an cluich mi mo bhial-aithris' ('the record on which I play my folklore'). Such criticism as MacLean's can easily degenerate into yet another attempt to establish the 'Fìor Ghàidheal' ('true Gael'), by jeering at those who can only pretend. William Neill, of whom Tom Scott said in 1970 that he 'is now about to become a teacher of Gaelic, to which, as a Lowlander, he has experienced an almost religious conversion' (T. Scott, 1970, p. 9) writes, in 'Hip! hip! for the Highland Ball':

In journals of society chat
whenever my photograph appears
with the Master of This and the Laird of That . . .
It brings me very near to tears
to think that in my line I lack
a single qualifying Mac.

(ibid., p. 62).

It is not, however, impossible to do justice to the subtleties and difficulties of this situation. Crichton Smith, in his 'An t-Oban' ('Oban') takes the histrionic aspects of symbolic appropriation and uses them, not to answer, but to act within. He says:

v. 3. Tha am muir an nochd mar shanas-reice,
leabhar an déidh leabhair a' deàlradh.
Tha m' fhaileas a' ruith sìos do'n chuan.
Tha mo chraiceann dearg is uaine.

Có sgrìobh mi? Có tha dèanamh bàrdachd
shanas-reice de mo chnàmhan?
Togaidh mi mo dhòrn gorm riutha:
'Gàidheal calma le a chànan'.

(D. Macaulay (ed.), 1976, p. 179).

Tonight the sea is like an advertisement, / book after
book shining. / My shadow is running down to the sea. /
My skin is red and green.

Who wrote me? Who is making a poetry / of advertisements
from my bones?/ I will raise my blue fist to them: /
'A stout Highlander with his language'.

(ibid., p. 178).

The question 'Có sgrìobh mi?' ('Who wrote me?'), which could have been a subtitle for this book, is not easily answered. For a poet to find his way between what he considers genuine in his culture and what he considers to be imposed fiction is extremely difficult. The appropriation of Gaelic culture has had such manifold effects upon the relationship between Gael and Gall over the last two hundred years that to sort out a simple truth or an unambiguous stance is perhaps impossible. Thomson speaks of 'an ìomhaigh tha cumail smachd air na h-ìomhaighean bréige' ('the image that keeps control over false images' – see 'Cotriona Mhór', cited above, p. 155). It must be admitted, however, that the relationship between these, between the fact and the fiction, the authentic and the inauthentic, the controlling image and the false image, is, from the very first, dialectical. Somewhere within this long running literary conspiracy stands 'Gàidheal calma le a chànan' ('a stout Highlander with his language'), ever elusive, and ever recreating himself from the tenacious immutability that another world ascribes to him.

Thomson gives expression to a sense of the intensity of the imagery that waits on those who would cross and recross the water between Hebrides and mainland, and attempt to live the life of Gael and Gall. The following is from 'Bùrn is Mòine 's Coirc'', ('Water and Peat and Oats'):

1.5. Boile! An cridhe gòrach
a' falpanaich mu na seann stallachan ud
mar nach robh slighe-cuain ann
ach ì.

(D. Macaulay (ed.), 1976, 163).

1.5 Madness! The foolish heart / lapping along these ancient rocks / as though there were no sea-journey in the world / but that one.

(ibid., p. 162).

Crichton Smith expresses the ambivalence of biculturality, but at the same time expresses the ambivalence and doubtful authenticity of the symbolism used to describe that state. In his 'A' Dol Dhachaidh' ('Going Home') he says:

v.1 Am màireach théid mi dhachaidh do m' eilean
a' fiachainn ri saoghal a chur an dìochuimhn'.
Togaidh mi dòrn de fhearann 'nam làmhan
no suidhidh mi air tulach inntinn
a' coimhead "a' bhuachaill aig an spréidh".

v.2 Dìridh (tha mi smaointinn) smeòrach.
Eiridh camhanaich no dhà.

(D. Macaulay (ed.), 1976, p. 175).

v.1 Tomorrow I shall go home to my island
trying to put a world into forgetfulness.
I will lift a fistful of its earth in my hands
or I will sit on a hillock of the mind
watching 'the shepherd at his sheep'.

v.2 There will arise (I presume) a thrush.
A dawn or two will break.

(ibid., p. 174).

As Macaulay says, here are 'repeated qualifications of a traditional interpretation of home-coming' (D. Macaulay, 1976, p. 48).

We have seen that MacLean, in 1938, felt the need to say that 'Gaelic poetry is not less but more realistic than most European poetry' (S. MacLean, 1938, p. 83). Crichton Smith has written: 'I believe that a romantic attitude will no longer be sufficient' (I. Crichton Smith, 1961, p. 176). He looks back to an age that is gone: 'I believe that our earlier poetry shows a greater realism . . . than our later, and it is to this lucid unsentimental starkness that we must return' (ibid., p. 177). Crichton Smith does not, however, invoke the past in order to retreat into it, which is a common Scottish literary device. Indeed, he dissociates himself from those 'whose sympathies are not with the future but rather with the past' (I. Crichton Smith, 1977, p. 31). His desire to escape from past sentimentalities is so vehement, indeed, that as the sentimental Celt is shed, so a voice that could be Thomas Gradgrind's is heard – 'description for its own sake will be pointless. The swallows as swallows have nothing to do with us' (ibid.). Crichton Smith is fully prepared to face up to the present: 'The images of the past are there: images of the present are breaking against them. Out of that clash can not a creative, vigorous literature be created?' (ibid., p. 178). Macaulay expresses this clash as a personal experience: 'The problem which poets operating within a fragmented culture face is that it is difficult for them consistently to recognise what their community is and to disentangle their different relationships with their different communities' (D. Macaulay, 1966, p. 136). This is a problem on both a social and an intellectual level, which cannot be thought away. The only solution is to 'simply rely on the writer's tact' (I. Crichton Smith, 1961, p. 180), and admit that an 'interior synthesis of diverse cultural and language experience seems . . . the only viable poetic solution to the problem' (D. Macaulay, 1966, p. 142).

Macaulay, however, in his poem 'Penny for the Guy, Mister . . . ', says:

Thachair balach beag rium;
thuirt e
"Sgillin dhan a' bhodach, 'ille"
is chum e a mheur ri pasgan
a bha e a' slaodadh air clàr
tràthach an sean chòta
sop 'na cheann air
is ad.

Thachair fear rium a' cluiche
air cluiche a' bhalaich bhig:
"Tasdan" ars esan, "–siuthad;
chan eil tasdan mór–
air son ar cànan, eil fhios agad –
air son a' 'chause'" . . . (sin éibhinn)

Tha
fhios agamsa:
gu feum ar cànan saothair

dha-rìribh;
is,
mur tuig sinn
nach eil fiar-ghràdh is fìor-ghràdh
mar thionntadh an t-sìoda,
gu bheil sinn aig ìre dìol-déirce.

Mur bì ar cùis againn
coimhlionta 'nar facail;
mur bì facail againn
a ghabhas brìgh ar cùise,
cha tuig sinn i:

cha tog sinn dàn a bhuineas dhuinn.
(D. Macaulay, 1967, p. 16).

I met a little boy; / he said, / "a penny for the guy, mister" – / and he pointed at a bundle dragged behind him on a board: / hay stuffed in an old coat; / a tuft for a head – / and a hat.

I met a man playing / at the little boy's game: / "A shilling," he said,– "go on; / a shilling's not much / for our language, you know, / for the 'cause'" . . . (a joke)

I do / know this: / that our language requires / serious effort / and / that if we cannot understand / that false and genuine love / are not facets of the same thing / we are in a beggarly state;

that unless we have our condition / clearly depicted in words, / unless we have the words / to state the meaning of our condition / we will not apprehend it:

we will not build a poem that concerns us.
(ibid., p. 88).

This poses to the poet, and to the 'activist' Gael who wishes to take steps to prevent the disappearance of his language, the task of clearly depicting in words the difference between the genuine and the false. As I have tried to show, this imaginary opposition has never been clear-cut, and there is no simple unprejudiced factuality by which to determine the issue. I have attempted, in various ways, to give some idea of the structures within which the Gael is to be found; structures that, though they have their own mode of specification of the factual and the fictional, the trenchant and the ephemeral, are not to be penetrated simply through the analytical employment of these dualities. Macaulay's desire for authenticity, for realism, is certainly necessary and welcome after the literary treatment of the Gael in the nineteenth century, but it must always be borne in mind, and brought to consciousness, that that treatment is now very much part of the 'reality' that is available for the artist to use. Furthermore, the status of that literary treatment as a facet of 'reality' is not merely that of erroneous commentary, fleeting and insubstantial; on the contrary, the literature has a creative capacity to define and constitute its own truth, and to take its place in a 'real' world that can nevertheless draw its factual validity from within.

As far as the position of the Gaelic language is concerned, for those who know that 'gu feum ar cànan saothair dha-rìribh' ('our language requires serious effort'), a problem is posed by Crichton Smith, who asks of the Gaels that they 'write of the Highlands as they are, not as they would wish them to be' (I. Crichton Smith, 1961, p. 180). Artistic realism does not provide a guarantee of truth, or a charter for action – Gaels who wish to intervene actively on behalf of their language must ultimately do without the former, and find the latter within a world of loyalties and prejudices where the influence of nineteenth-century thought is still very strong, for all its lack of 'realism'. I have tried to show throughout this book that certain patterns of metaphorical association that have been rendered appropriate to the Gael are very much part of the common grammar of European thought, and will subvert our best attempts to think them away. Crichton Smith says that:

> It is the easiest thing in the world to write what one thinks one feels, or what one ought to feel, but to write what one really feels – that is difficult. Language is a trap: the unimportant writer doesn't realise this, the great writer bleeds within it (I. Crichton Smith, 1961, p. 175).

Who is to say that the Celtic Twilight writers did not 'really' feel what they 'thought' that they felt? Since, by definition, the majority of writers are unimportant, they could perhaps not tell the difference; certainly they were working within ideas that have been proved to have a very enduring appeal and a perennial power to organise the world. Crichton Smith says of Gaelic critics: 'When these writers do not discuss aesthetics and general theory in their own language . . . they will tend to form habits of thought which are in fact English' (ibid., p. 179). That this has happened in many instances, I think the majority, where Gaels have commented on themselves, cannot be denied. The attempt to achieve a clear-eyed and unsentimental realism, welcome as it is, is still unusual. The Celtic Twilight maintains its crepuscular *tristesse*, and the very structure of its constitution renders permanently elusive both bright day and dark night, and the sure ability to distinguish the truth from the lie.

The Gael has many realisms to work with. He has the realism through which Crichton Smith hoped to build 'a spare, vigorous, adaptable language able to take the pressures which will be put on it' (I. Crichton Smith, 1961, p. 180); he has the radical realism through which Comunn na Cànain Albannaich (the Scottish Language Society) were 'ag obair airson na Gàidhlig a chuir air ais . . . air bilean nan Albannaich uile air feadh Alba' ('working to put Gaelic back on the lips of all Scots throughout Scotland' – my translation) (S. Mac a' Ghobhainn, 1974, p. 1); he has the depressed utilitarian realism that asks of the Gaelic learner – 'Why are you learning the language? It has no future.' Between these realisms, various as they are, the Gael has no easy task in knowing himself.

There are two subjects in particular which make it difficult to 'write of the Highlands as they are, not as we would wish them to be'. These concern the place of the Church in Gaelic culture, and the status and survival of the Gaelic language. The problem of language revival is too large to be dealt with here, although I touch upon it in passing, and many of the problems that it faces are implicit in my discussion of other matters. I will deal here with the position of the Church in the Highlands, in so far as it is relevant to the metaphorical, social and political structures that I have been discussing so far.

It is often lamented that all change to Gaelic society comes from outside. This is in part a genuine consequence of the demographic and political weakness of Gaelic society as measured against its immediate neighbour. However, the inability to internalise change and the necessity to see it as an imposition derive ideological strength from the limited capacity (and, at the same time, increased need) for self-definition that Gaelic society has come to have in the nineteenth and twentieth centuries, particularly when it addresses itself in written English. In a situation where everything 'modern' is seen to come from outside, it is easy to see that it would appear to come along with 'English' as a way of life and a language, and that Gaelic would find itself beleaguered not only by the English language but by modernity in all its forms, by urban life, by technology, by rock music. We have seen that the Celt that Arnold designed was constructed out of opposition to the qualities of modern life associated with 'science', 'rationalism' and 'bureaucracy'. This could be a simple description of the facts of differential language use in modern Highland society, where the media, politics, business and education are largely English language domains. It is important to keep in mind that Arnold's picture held its metaphorical coherence within an essentially non-Gaelic discourse. The symbolic status of Gaelic is, as ever, both created by and constitutive of the obvious facts of language use in the Highlands.

We can get some idea of the continued coherence of established symbols for situating what is often titled the 'ancient language of Gaelic' (for example, G. Bruce, 1968, p. 7) from the following, taken from a history of the Gaelic Society of Inverness from 1871 to 1971. Macdonald concludes her history with the following hopes for the future of the society:

> keeping true to its early tenets of saving and publishing everything worth while in Gaelic literature, song and music; of looking after historical monuments; of honouring Gaelic scholars and furthering the teaching of the language; of bringing life to everything connected with the old Highland way of living which today is recognised the world over as having been outstandingly beautiful and worth while – a guiding star to peace, happiness and harmony in a sorely distracted world.
>
> And what of tomorrow, and the second millennium when machines will so reduce man's work that he will enjoy a life of comparative leisure – and study of the arts, languages, travel and general cultural activities take up a large part of his existence? Will not Highland culture then prove to be a rewarding study, and will not future generations feel deeply indebted and grateful to the Inverness Gaelic Society for the storehouse filled and bequeathed them by its members during these hundred years? (M. Macdonald, 1970, p. 20).

Perhaps the future will be so pleasant, and no one could begrudge the Inverness Gaelic Society their gratitude. We notice, however, that the society is concerned with literature, song and music, with monuments, and with bringing to life the old Highland way of life. We also notice that it is only when technology has become so ubiquitous that it has ceased to constitute a discrete and recognisable force, and has become a symbolically neutral feature of the background to life, that Gaelic culture will come into its own once again. This is a common sentiment. Since Arnold gave it its definitive form it has appeared again and again. It has been said of Celtic art that:

> its rhythmic curves and flowing graceful scrolls . . . make an appeal like the rhythm of poetry, or the cadence of some haunting, Gaelic song; they come close to Nature, not in imitating her, but in suggesting her movements – the flight of the birds, the breaking of waves, the undulations of long summer grasses stirred by the wind. This sympathy with the quiet and beautiful rhythms of Nature is a soothing influence, drawing the weary heart of civilised man away from the turmoil, squalor, and ugliness of a mechanised age, and leading him back to the peace and purity of his natural environment (A. Lamont, 1939, p. 54).

Chadwick has written that 'it is not easy for us – the products of centuries of classical education and scientific outlook – to realise the naturalness with which the early Irish mind passed from the reality of the known to the realm of fancy' (N. Chadwick, 1970, p. 235). Echoing Arnold, she says that:

> As we close the pages of the Mabinogion we leave behind the ancient Celtic world. With the Teutonic world which succeeded it we enter an ordered domain, where cause and effect follow one another with mathematical certainty and precision, where events follow one another in logical sequence . . . With the Roman conquest of Gaul, with the encroaching influence of the Teutonic people, the change of outlook was a radical one. The spaces of reality widened and the time limit became fixed. Time and space alike contrasted with the inevitable curtailment of the human imagination, and knowledge became synonymous with precision. We are on the threshold of the modern world (N. Chadwick, 1970, p. 291).

This is from what is probably the most widely read of standard works on the Celts – a work that is, for example, set reading for those Scottish Gaels who go to Aberdeen University to read Celtic studies and learn about themselves. By now, of course, the immiscibility of Gaelic and technology has been rendered not only symbolically apt, but, concretised in the inadequacy of technical language, a veritable fact. Derick Thomson's unique attempt to translate a scientific text into Gaelic (see D. Thomson, 1976a) was a task which he does not, by his own admission, wish to attempt again.[12]

It is not surprising, therefore, considering this attitude towards modernity and the outside as sources of change, that an institution felt to be inimical to the qualities attributed to Gaelic life but which is itself one of its central institutions would be a source of unease. The Protestant Church in the Highlands is in some senses such an institution. This Church, in its rejection of what it considered to be the foolish, wicked and superstitious practices of singing, dancing and story-telling, struck at the very heart of the phenomena that have, by contrast to the majority society, come to be seen as peculiarly Gaelic. Alexander Carmichael quotes the words of a woman from Ness that he met in the course of his enquiries:

> 'A blessed change came over the place and the people,' the woman replied in earnestness, 'and the good men and the good ministers who arose did away with the songs and the stories, the music and the dancing, the sports and the games that were perverting the minds and ruining the souls of the people, leading them to folly and stumbling' (A. Carmichael, 1928, xxx).

Calum MacLean says, 'The preachers, of course, have roundly denounced secular songs and music' (1959, p. 126), and quotes a church elder – 'The Comunn Gaidhealach had a mod in Skye this week. It is supposed to further the Gaelic but in reality it is nothing other than the work of the devil' (ibid., p. 127). MacLean attempts to solve this internal contradiction within the society he admires by reuniting the Free Church and secular entertainment on one side of another duality which has been much used to situate Gaelic culture, the rural/urban. He says:

> The adherents of the Free Church are not dour, solemn and serious minded, as many depict them; on the contrary they have as good a sense of fun, gaiety and humour as anyone else. They have a far greater capacity for creating their own entertainment and enjoying themselves thoroughly than the residents of Morningside Drive or Tottenham Court Road (ibid., p. 132).

He argues that:

> Much has been said about the part that Evangelical Calvinism played in the destruction of Gaelic folktales, folk-music, belief and customs . . . but the fact remains that at most it can only be said to be one of

> several contributory factors. It is by no means the most important factor, and it can now be doubted if it is an important factor at all (ibid., p. 129).

There is ample testimony to the contrary, not least in the wealth of folklore collected in the predominantly Catholic islands of Barra, Eriskay and South Uist by, for example, Alexander Carmichael and Fr. Allan Macdonald. However the important point is that the Church does see itself, and is seen, as being at odds with secular 'entertainments'—music, literature, song and dance. It is not difficult to see how such a Church is inimical to the traditionally drawn picture of the Gael, and how it would come to constitute an ambiguous symbol within the more familiar iconography. This problem is often solved by treating the Protestant Church as an entirely alien imposition. *Guth na Bliadhna* (*The Voice of the Year*), in its first issue, led with an article, presumably by Erskine, which argued that:

> There are parts of the Highlands, and there are isles in the west, to which the so-called Reformation has never penetrated. Moreover, the Protestant religion is even yet somewhat of an innovation, in the Highlands in general. At all events, the history of its establishment entitles us to regard it as such. Presbyterianism is not a plant indigenous to Celtic Scotland, but was an importation which had to be forced on the people, in order to make it take root (*Guth na Bliadhna*, Vol. 1, No. 1 (1904), p. 2).

The relationship of Protestantism to the Gael is further described:

> Protestantism has frowned upon his imagination, and still continues to frown . . . Indeed, how is it possible for a system which was the delight of an alien and hostile race, and which was imposed upon him vi et armis, to be advantageous and pleasing to the Gael (ibid., p. 5).

J.L. Campbell speaks of the:

> imprisonment of the minds of the majority of Highlanders within the bonds of seventeenth-century Calvinism at a time when the rest of Protestant Europe was beginning to free itself from the idea of rigid predestination. The effect of this is apparent in many parts of the Highlands today, for the last-won North-West is now one of the few

> remaining strongholds of fundamentalist Calvinism in Europe (J.L. Campbell, 1950, p. 61).

Thomson says that: 'Religious and secular activities are seen as . . . being in active opposition . . . in parts of Gaelic Scotland' (D. Thomson, 1966, p. 262). He also locates the genesis of this misfortune outside Gaelic society by saying that:

> one section of the religious community adopted a code which was foreign to the Gaelic society, and which in its turn eroded other aspects of that society, as for example the interest in secular literature and entertainment which was characteristic of Gaelic society (ibid., p. 264).

This 'foreign code' within makes the Church an ambiguous symbol for the modern Gaelic poet, particularly when we bear in mind that 'the Gaelic message of the Church (and notably the Free Church following the Disruption) became a significant factor of language conservation' (K. MacKinnon, 1972, p. 381). Language and culture, usually rhetorically entwined in commentary on Gaelic Scotland, are thus felt to be divorced at the hands of the Church. D.J. MacLeod speaks of the Church as 'for long the only sector of High Culture in which Gaelic was much used' (D.J. MacLeod in Derick Thomson, 1976, p. 27). Of the importance of the Church to the Gaelic language he says that: 'dheanadh e cron mór nan cailleadh i an taic seo' ('it would do great damage if this support were lost' – my translation) (ibid., p. 22).

This ambiguity is realised in the treatment of the Church in modern Gaelic poetry. MacLean opposes it uncompromisingly. This is his 'Ban-Ghàidheal' ('Highland Woman'):

v.1 Am faca Tu i, Iùdhaich mhóir,
ri 'n abrar Aon Mhac Dhé?
Am fac' thu 'coltas air Do thriall
ri strì an fhìon-lios chéin?

v.3 Chan fhaca Tu i, Mhic an t-saoir,
ri 'n abrar Rìgh na Glòir,
a miosg nan cladach carrach siar,
fo fhallus cliabh a lòin.

v.6 Agus labhair T' eaglais chaomh

mu staid chaillte a h-anama thruaigh;
agus leag an cosnadh dian
a corp gu sàmhchair dhuibh an uaigh.

(S. MacLean, 1977, p. 77).

v.1 Hast thou seen her, great Jew, / who art called the One Son of God? / Hast Thou, on Thy way, seen the like of her / labouring in the distant vineyard?

v.3 Thou hast not seen her, Son of the carpenter, / who art called the King of Glory, / among the rugged western shores / in the sweat of her food's creel.

v.6 And thy gentle Church has spoken / of the lost state of her miserable soul; / and the unremitting toil has lowered / her body to a black peace in a grave.

(ibid., p. 76).

Thomson, in his poem 'Srath Nabhair' ('Strathnaver'), the Sutherland glen where landlord capitalism made its definitive appearance as a war of Gall against Gael, expresses the ambiguity of the religious image by clothing it with a symbolic duality with which we are already familiar – sophisticated knowledge as opposed to simple truth:

v.2 Agus sud a' bhliadhna cuideachd
a shlaod iad a' chailleach do 'n t-sitig,
a shealltainn cho eòlach 's a bha iad air an Fhìrinn,
oir bha nid aig eunlaith an adhair
(agus cròthan aig na caoraich)
ged nach robh àit aice-se anns an cuireadh i a ceann fòidhpe.

v.3 A Shrath Nabhair 's a Shrath Chill Donnain,
is beag an t-iongnadh ged a chinneadh am fraoch àluinn oirbh,
a' falach nan lotan a dh'fhàg Pàdraig Sellar 's a sheòrsa,
mar a chunnaic mi uair is uair boireannach cràbhaidh
a dh'fhiosraich dòrainn an t-saoghail-sa
is sìth Dhé 'na sùilean.

(D. Macaulay (ed.), 1976, p. 153).

v.2 And that too was the year / they hauled the old woman out onto the dung heap, / to demonstrate how knowledgeable they were in scripture, / for the birds of the air had nests / (and the sheep had folds) / though she had no place in which to lay down her head.

v.3 O Strathnaver and Strath of Kildonan, / it is little wonder that the heather should bloom on your slopes, / hiding the wounds that Patrick Sellar, and such as he, made, / just as time and time again I have seen a pious woman / who had suffered the sorrows of this world / with the peace of God shining from her eyes.

(ibid., p. 152).

We see opposed those who were 'knowledgeable in scriptures' and those with the 'peace of God shining from their eyes', the one amoral, artificial and wicked, the other possessed of a knowledge as natural as blooming heather.

Although the political position of the Church in the Highlands as a tool of the establishment was changed radically by the Disruption of 1843,[13] the philosophy of Calvin remained, for the Gael, an uneasy ally. Thomson gives this apt symbolic expression in his poem, 'Am Bodach-Ròcais' ('The Scarecrow'):

An oidhch' ud
thàinig am bodach-ròcais dh'an taigh-chéilidh:
fear caol àrd dubh
is aodach dubh air.
Shuidh e air an t-séis
is thuit na cairtean ás ar làmhan.
Bha fear a sud
ag innse sgeulachd air Conall Gulban
is reodh na faclan air a bhilean.
Bha boireannach 'na suidh' air stòl
ag òran, 's thug e 'n toradh ás a' cheòl.
Ach cha do dh'fhàg e falamh sinn:
thug e òran nuadh dhuinn,
is sgeulachdan na h-àird an Ear,
is sprùilleach de dh'fheallsanachd Geneva,
is sguab e 'n teine à meadhon an làir
's chuir e 'n tùrlach loisgeach nar broillichean.

(D. Macaulay (ed.), 1976, p. 165).

> That night / the scarecrow came into the ceilidh-house: / a tall, thin black-haired man / wearing black clothes. / He sat on the bench / and the cards fell from our hands. / One man was / telling a folk tale about Conall Gulban / and the words froze on his lips. / A woman was sitting on a stool, / singing songs, and he took the goodness out of the music. / But he did not leave us empty-handed: / he gave us a new song, / and tales from the Middle East, / and fragments of the philosophy of Geneva, / and he swept the fire from the centre of the floor, / and set a searing bonfire in our breasts.
>
> (ibid., p. 164).

The scarecrow ('am bodach-ròcais', lit. 'old man of the crow') and the Presbyterian minister clearly share a sleek blackness, of plumage or dress, and an ability to frighten things away, be they birds or songs. Besides this symbolic affinity, however, it is perhaps not too fanciful to go further, and to see in both symbols of marginality. The scarecrow, man-made but located outside society in the 'wild' of the fields, both internal and external to society; the Church, an alien philosophy, that the people willingly adopted and made their own, even though it turned on them and took the goodness out of the music. Are these external impositions, or creations from within? There is no simple answer to the question of whether the Church is 'a much maligned Calvinism . . . established in the hearts of the people' where it 'found suitable environment' (T. Donn, 1968, p. 352), or the 'foreign code' of which Thomson speaks.

In so far as the Church has consciously suppressed various expressive activities, it has a place in the concern that Macaulay and Crichton Smith share over 'man's propensities to build constructs which diminish life' (D. Macaulay (ed.), 1976, p. 51). Macaulay speaks of his involvement with his native community, saying that:

> In spite of this involvement there are aspects of the place that are strongly criticised. One of these especially is the way in which the community seeks to control the individual. As one of the primary agents of this control, which at times can be repressive and destructive to the individual's human potential, organised religion is criticised (ibid., p. 66).

In his poem 'Féin-Fhireantachd' ('Self-Righteousness') he says:

1.1 Chan iarr iad orm ach

gal aithreachais peacaidh
nach buin dhomh
's gu faigh mi saorsa
fhuadan nach tuig mi:
(D. Macaulay, 1967, p. 21).

1.1 They ask of me only / to weep repentance for a sin / that does not concern me / and I shall get in return an alien / freedom I don't understand:
(ibid., p. 90).

In 'Soisgeul 1955' ('Gospel 1955'), Macaulay describes what his people have got in return for their banished muse:

1.5 dh'èisd mi ris an ùrnaigh
seirm shaorsinneil, shruthach –
iuchair-dàin mo dhaoine.
(D. Macaulay (ed.), 1976, p. 193).

1.5 I listened to the prayer
a liberating, cascading melody –
my people's access to poetry.
(ibid., p. 192).

The position of the Church, in its attitude towards obviously symbolic activity outside its own authority, is interestingly close to that of 'science' as it is often crudely theorised. We could take as an example of such theorisation of science the above cited estimation by Chadwick, where 'fancy' is replaced by 'an ordered domain, where cause and effect follow one another with mathematical certainty and precision', and where, with the 'curtailment of the human imagination, . . . knowledge became synonymous with precision' (N. Chadwick, 1970, p. 291). We could take as an example of such crude theorisation of science almost every definition of 'folklore' that has ever been attempted. Arnold built his picture of the Celt out of those elements that such a science was thought to either deny, reject, or admit incompetence in. I have pointed out how frequently science and technology are seen to be destructive of Gaelic language and culture and contrary to its nature. It can be imagined, therefore, that a religious philosophy like Calvinism, with a system of epistemological exclusions remarkably similar in effect to that of 'Science', would find itself at odds with any traditional picture of the Gael.

One of the aspects of 'Anglo-Saxon Philistinism' that Arnold, the arch-theorist of the Celt, found least likeable was the particular way in which it embraced a puritan Nonconformist religious philosophy. He says, in imagined reply to a Nonconformist evangelist, who argued that without religion the problems of industrial society were insoluble:

> How is the ideal of a life so unlovely, so unattractive, so incomplete, so narrow, so far removed from a true and satisfying ideal of human perfection, as is the life of your religious organisation as you yourself reflect it, to conquer and transform all this vice and hideousness? (M. Arnold, 1969, p. 58).

He elaborates the affinities of 'science' and 'puritanism':

> I say that the English reliance on our religious organisations and on their ideas of human perfection just as they stand, is like our reliance on freedom, on muscular Christianity, on population, on coal, on wealth, – mere belief in machinery, and unfruitful; and that it is wholesomely counteracted by culture (ibid., p. 59).

He says of 'men of culture and poetry' that:

> They have often failed in morality, and morality is indispensable. And they have been punished for their failure, as the Puritan has been rewarded for his performance. They have been punished wherein they erred; but their ideal of beauty, of sweetness and light, and a human nature complete on all its sides, remains the true ideal of perfection still; just as the Puritan's ideal of perfection remains narrow and inadequate (ibid., p. 57).

This affinity of the machinery of the modern state to European Nonconformism was recognised and expressed in a different way by Max Weber. He argued that, with Puritanism, the 'great historic process in the development of religions, the elimination of magic from the world, came here to its logical conclusion' (M. Weber, 1948, p. 105). Calvinist philosophy, which began as a criticism of 'superstitious' elements within organised religion, became:

> The entirely negative attitude of Puritanism to all the sensuous and emotional elements in culture and in religion, because they are of no use toward salvation and promote sentimental illusions and idol-

> atrous superstitions. Thus it provides a basis for a fundamental antagonism to sensuous culture of all kinds (ibid.).

Weber speaks of the 'connection of the spirit of modern economic life with the rational ethics of ascetic Protestantism' (ibid., p. 27), and of the 'utilitarian character of Calvinist ethics' (ibid., p. 109). He argues that, for the Puritans:

> The conceptions of idle talk, of superfluities, and of vain ostentation, all designations of an irrational attitude without objective purpose, thus not ascetic, and especially not serving the glory of God, but of man, were always at hand to serve in deciding in favour of sober utility as against any artistic tendencies (ibid., p. 169).

We have seen that the Gael has commonly been spoken of as a creature of sentiment, emotion, fanciful imaginative powers, artistry and superstition, and that his society and character have been seen to be under threat from the forces of utilitarianism, and economic and scientific rationalism. The location within Gaelic society of a Calvinist Church is thus a clear affront to the coherence of many of the symbolic structures that have been used to situate the Gael. This is reflected in the treatment of the Church in the poems that I have quoted.

We can see that 'science' and Calvinism share a similar attitude to other symbolic systems, other semiotics, although from the point of view of both 'science' and Calvinism the other is an 'erroneous' or 'partial' expression subsumed by a larger truth. The attitude of both to expressive symbolic systems like magic, or less emotive systems like fictional poetry and prose, that is, to all overtly 'metaphorical' or non-utilitarian activity, is in general a negative one. This attitude is, in practice, variously translated. In the main, the authority of science has been protected from its manifest incompetence in these linguistic areas by limiting its claims, grudgingly, to a limited sphere. Attempts have often been made, however, to extend the range of positivist authority to the full range of human thought and activity. Within social anthropology, we can think particularly of functionalist theory, which received one of its most rigorous theoretical statements in Malinowski's *Scientific Theory of Culture* (B. Malinowski, 1944). The impoverishment attendant upon the reduction of human life to a series of materially defined needs that we find in this work is only one example of the reductionist tendency inherent in positivist thinking.

Such attempts to extend the competence of science will continue to be made as long as science interprets metaphorical relationships, symbolic equations, and the like, as propositions of causal connection of the same order as those with which it deals itself. As long as science continues to make this error, then expressive statements can only be interpreted as 'not true, therefore false'. The attitude of the Protestant Church to the rituals of Catholicism paralleled remarkably that of science to non-utilitarian, 'fictional', symbolic systems, and there can be little doubt that this led to a genuine and severe impoverishment of imagery, both within and without the Church (a question not of course related to the spiritual status of these religious disciplines). The Church in the Highlands has attempted, now with less vehemence than formerly, to pursue to its conclusion the conviction that all statements which are not 'true' must necessarily be 'false', and therefore, self-consciously deceitful and wicked. As J.F. Campbell said:

> The strange idea possesses the people in many districts, that to repeat the most harmless sgeulachd [story] is a grievous sin, and that fables, and poems, and novels of every sort ought to be put down and exterminated, because they are fictions. That spirit, if strong enough and put in action, would sweep away much of the literature of ancient and modern times (J.F. Campbell, 1860, cxxx).

We have a clear statement, within the Gaelic context, of the antipathy of Calvinist religious philosophy to other symbolic activity, from the Rev. Thomas Donn. He states that (his emphasis throughout):

> divine revelation is what man *cannot* discover for himself *by the methods of science* (T. Donn, 1968, p. 323).

> *Truth is ultimate meaning* and, therefore, science as such is totally devoid of Truth in *that sense* of the word because it has to deal with the facts of the material universe (ibid.).

Donn is therefore prepared to concede that 'the so-called conflict between science and revelation has been one gigantic delusion. There cannot be any such conflict because both are authoritative within their *own* spheres which are *different*' (ibid.). Revelation and Science, therefore, both have their independent claim to truth, which we can readily accept. However, within this conspiracy to carve up the world of secure knowledge, we find that:

> 'Language is the only truth' in the sense that the Truth must be and only can be proclaimed to men by means of words or languages – it cannot be done *merely* by music, mathematical signs, visual artistic forms, etc. The Word must be preached and written and read by means of language. Many are in favour of Ritualism, Aestheticism and other non-linguistic 'modes of worship' precisely because they wish to escape and avoid the challenge of the Truth and to substitute for the Truth the errors and wishful thinking of man (ibid., p. 326).

This is not written with the overt aim of condemning as wicked music or visual artistic forms, or Ritualism and Aestheticism, but we can see how easily these, by failing to be 'True', can be nothing other than 'errors and wishful thinking', and thus subject to condemnation.

Finlay MacLeod, speaking of a Calvinism that he calls 'undoubtedly a harmful doctrine' (F. MacLeod, 1969, p. 893), neatly sums up the problems that the Calvinist Church presents to an educated and liberal Gael with a knowledge and awareness of his people's history. He argues that the people accepted Calvinism:

> as containing all wisdom and the answer to all things; this was to become the new basis of their world – and they now memorised extracts of Jewish folklore with the same eagerness as the people had earlier memorised the Celtic tales and songs (ibid., p. 91).

The old lore has been displaced, therefore, and the Calvinism that has effected this displacement:

> has become so deeply ingrained into the culture that the people are not aware of it as a separate entity. As with their language, their kin and their birthplace, they do not consider that it could be otherwise. They never conceive of the church as an institution that was introduced from outside (ibid., p. 93).

It only requires one Sunday spent in Lewis to get some idea of the enduring importance to the community of this Church and its teachings. Parman (1972) conveys in her thesis a clear picture of the central position of the Church in much social activity. This institution, then, provides an interesting test case for those many intellectuals who have looked to the 'traditional' Gaelic way of life as a source for all the virtues on the basis of which Gaelic culture could be revived. Is the Church part of that tradition, or is it yet another imperialist imposition?

Feelings run high over religious issues, and the conventions of adherence to one or another established Church will inevitably often preclude a very free discussion of this topic. The Church is not however alone among Highland institutions in having an essentially ambiguous relationship to Highland history as it has been variously constructed. The position of the Church invites comment as a focus of unease for those who would rewrite Highland history towards a particularly desired reconstruction not because it has an essentially unique position in that history, but because it presents a peculiarly acute tension between the practices of the Highlanders and the intellectual fashions among the educated.

The course of the twentieth century has not, so far, seen any conscious evangelical trend in the wider intellectual world, but rather the opposite. The general trend towards sexual and social licence (however real this is, and independent of whether it is treated as a liberation or as an undesirable decadence) is clearly in conflict with the teachings of Calvinism. It is this conflict which makes of the Church an ambiguous symbol. Other obvious features of Gaelic life – subsistence farming, small community life, extended family sentiments, and even minority status have on the other hand a relatively high value in many contemporary considerations of the life that we all ought to live. This has not always been true, and we cannot imagine that these valuations are immutable. Their present currency, however, means that the relationship of these institutions to an imaginatively objectified history of the Highlands need not be seriously considered in the same way as that of the Church. The problems are, however, potentially the same. History is written to serve the ends of those that write it, and the Highlands have come to have a sufficiently important place in Scottish history to make them subject to a historicity whose trajectory changes according to rules laid down not in Stornoway but in Edinburgh. There is no simple truth awaiting innocent enquiry, but at the same time those who imagine that their enquiry is innocent have a power to add to the complexity of the simple truth that they are trying to apprehend. We might perhaps ourselves conclude with a simple, if vital, truth – that history tells us as much about those who write it as it does about those silent objects of history to which it ostensibly gives voice.

7 ANTHROPOLOGISTS, FOLKLORE AND COMMUNITY

In the last part of the nineteenth century the occupations of Celticist, folklorist and anthropologist were sometimes found happily united, in such figures as Alfred Nutt and Andrew Lang. Since then there has been a considerable institutional and intellectual separation of these subjects, coinciding for social anthropology with the growing emphasis on intensive first-hand field experience. As Dorson says, 'In England the cause of folklore has languished since the generation of Lang; British social anthropology has severed its once intimate relations with ethnologically minded folklorists' (R. Dorson, 1961, p. 302). Since this separation there has been little work done by social anthropologists on the Highlands, or on Gaelic material, which have been largely the preserve of Celticists and folklorists. Several reasons for this lack of interest suggest themselves. In the first place, the Highlands were probably not felt to be either distant enough or exotic enough to be the location of the professional 'rite de passage' that field-work came to be for British social anthropologists. This field-work was largely carried out in those areas of the world to which colonialist hegemony still kept an open door, and British social anthropology, particularly in the 1940s and 1950s, was very strongly influenced by African material. It came to be accepted wisdom that social anthropology concerned itself with 'primitive' societies, and that 'complex' societies were outside its competence. It is perhaps worth noting, when we consider this tendency on the part of British anthropologists to look overseas for their 'exotic', that two of the few anthropological studies of Gaelic-speaking areas in the British Isles have been the work of Americans (see C.M. Arensberg, 1937, and S. Parman, 1972). Arensberg apologised for his temerity in overstepping the obvious professional boundary of the social anthropologist, saying: 'It may seem presumptuous that an anthropologist should profess to discuss the life of a modern nation' (C.M. Arensberg, 1937, p. 2). When European anthropologists began to turn their attention to European societies, they tended to choose areas that approximated in 'primitive' status to those that their Africanist colleagues had studied. Davis has said, in a comparative study of anthropological work on Mediterranean peoples:

> it is perhaps a consequence of their sense of professional insecurity that mediterraneanists have tended to under-emphasise those qualities of the mediterranean which might distinguish their work and lead them to differentiate themselves from their colleagues: they have ignored or abused history, and ignored those millennia of intensive interaction which have made mediterranean societies (J. Davis, 1977, p. 7).

He points out that 'Mediterraneanists have chosen to work in the marginal areas of the region – in the mountains, in the small peasant communities' (ibid.), which he ascribes to 'the desire to be as primitive as every other colleague' (ibid.). I am personally extremely sceptical of the kind of comparativism and cultural correlation that Davis hopes to find within the historical dimension, but his criticism of Mediterraneanists is not without foundation, and could be extended to other areas of European anthropology. The search for a timeless peasant traditionalism is by no means over. Du Boulay, for example, chose her area of study in Greece because her interest 'lay largely in the more traditional aspects of village society' (J. Du Boulay, 1974, p. 4), to which end she had been looking for 'a village without regular transport, and thus without too constant communication with the more urban-oriented world' (ibid.). This was in spite of the fact that 'while within the village much of the traditional way of life and thought has been preserved, the desire to remain in such a way of life has been, among the younger people at any rate, almost entirely eradicated' (ibid., p. 5). With such traditionalist sentiments animating social anthropological enquiry it might seem strange that there should be anything but an easy affinity between anthropology and folklore. That there has not been cannot be explained simply by the different area interests deriving from the tendency of the folklorist to look for his 'primitive' within and the anthropologist to look for his 'primitive' abroad. To find an answer to this problem we must look to the theoretical revolution that overtook social anthropology in the first two decades of this century, when a pervasive evolutionist historicism was replaced by the ideally timeless systemic concerns of structural-functionalism (for a typical rejection of 'conjectural history' see A.R. Radcliffe-Brown, 1950). We have seen that 'folklore' studies are still primarily concerned with ideas like tradition, survival, decay into modernity and the like. They therefore have a clear affinity to the evolutionist and diffusionist schools of anthropology that flourished in the late nineteenth century and in the early decades of the twentieth.

Within Scotland the Gaelic-speaking areas have been much used as a source of historical virtue and the starting-point of a trajectory of development into the modern. These historicist and historical associations would have been enough to repel a nascent structural-functionalism, which not only renounced historicism but preferred, if possible, to renounce history as well. As Radcliffe-Brown said, defining a professional boundary and a cast of mind rather than stating an obvious fact: 'In the primitive societies that are studied by social anthropology there are no historical records' (A.R. Radcliffe-Brown, 1968, p. 3). Finnegan locates the disjunction between folklore and social anthropology as follows:

> In England 'folk-lore' (and thus the study of 'folktales') was from the start closely associated with evolutionary anthropology, and the early members of the Folklore society included such well known anthropologists as Tylor, Lang and Frazer. 'Folk-lore' was evolutionist and was, in fact, often described as 'the study of survivals' (R. Finnegan, 1969, p. 62).

She says, therefore, that 'When this concept of unilinear evolution came to be rejected, the whole foundation of the "science of Folklore" collapsed with it' (ibid.). She goes on:

> Those 'folklorists' who clung, and still cling, to the old theoretical framework and write, for example, about 'the folklore of the British Isles' in terms of odd local customs, by-ways, 'survivals', old superstitions, or 'ancient fertility cults', are regarded with scorn by modern professional anthropologists – often rightly so – as dilettante, uncritical and addicted to a totally outdated theoretical framework. It is not surprising in view of this that 'folklore' has become almost a term of abuse among social anthropologists (ibid.).

This prejudice is in several ways unfortunate. Nevertheless it is not without justification. Remembering the importance to a sense of Scottish national identity of the Gaelic-speaking Highlands, and the easy association of the Gaelic world with 'folklore', we can note with interest Davis's general remarks concerning 'the relation between linguistic, sociological, folkloric and physical anthropological studies and nationalistic movements' (J. Davis, 1977, p. 3). He says that:

> In some countries the work of providing a scientific basis for nationalist claims took on such symbolic significance that anthropology ceased to be a developing academic activity altogether but was rather fossil-

> ised so that a contemporary ethnographer from France or England or America . . . may be suddenly confronted by a Tylorean or Frazerian professor appearing like a Japanese corporal from the jungle to wage a battle only he knows is still on (ibid.).

Certainly there has been an interesting and notable academic conservatism in much consideration of Scottish folklore, and in so far as 'folklore' is collected as historical authentication of a national identity, then conservation of a historicist or evolutionist outlook is clearly encouraged.

Social anthropology, therefore, came to disavow thoroughly the theoretical presuppositions that underpinned folklore studies. This disavowal was not, however, a thoroughly unflawed theoretical advance. Radcliffe-Brownian structural-functionalism, while it represented for British social anthropology the important general theoretical advance towards the synchronic analysis of systems, brought with it an uncritical and reductive empiricism derived from an attempt to imitate the innocent observationalist practices of natural science. An assessment of the appeal, origins and limitations of this approach can be found in, for example, E. Leach, 1961, E.W. Ardener, 1971a, and M. Crick, 1976. Crick argues that the 'scientific' observationalist model that was inherited by the social sciences was in any case 'a hopelessly inadequate positivistic view of scientific method (derived not from the actual practise of natural science but largely from philosophers like Mill)' (M. Crick, 1976, p. 89). This 'hopelessly inadequate view' led to the relegation of symbolic systems like myth, ritual, literature, and even, from a strictly behaviourist point of view, language (see E.W. Ardener, 1973) to the realm of social ephemera, whose only place was as validation or affirmation of the more obviously 'concrete' systems that went under labels like 'politics', 'economics' and 'kinship'. This empiricism, coupled with the previously mentioned mistrust of the theoretical preconceptions of most folklore studies, led social anthropology to abandon not only 'folklore' as an academic discipline, but also 'folklore' as an object of study. As Finnegan says:

> when anthropologists rejected folklore in the sense of the customs of 'the folk', a study steeped in evolutionist ideas, they also lumped together with this any study of what could be regarded as the literature of 'the folk', i.e. folktales. They therefore turned away from any serious study of the oral literature of non-literate peoples (R. Finnegan, 1969, p. 63).

This ejection of both baby and bath-water was by no means logically required, but it seemed appropriate enough, and it was a long time before the oversight was noticed.

It should be clear from recent developments in social anthropology towards the analysis of symbolic systems and away from the common-sense positivism of functionalist anthropology, and from what I have said in Chapter 5 concerning the analysis of folklore, that there is no clear necessity for the division of function between folklorist and anthropologist. The School of Scottish Studies in Edinburgh hoped in 1950 to effect some integration of these subjects (see J. Orr, 1957, p. 1). The time is now even more ripe to try to achieve at least partially the easy unity of function that we find in the late nineteenth century, while allowing for the radical change in the theoretical basis of such unity. British social anthropology has begun, in the African context at least, to pay some attention to the literature, written and oral, of those societies that it has studied. This interest owes much to the influence of Evans-Pritchard, who was also significantly the principal force in a general reassessment of British social anthropology, rescuing it from the status of aspirant to natural science, and placing it among the humanities (see, for oral literature, E.E. Evans-Pritchard, 1967, and, for a general theoretical consideration, 1969). This interest in oral literature found published form in, for example, the *Oxford Library of African Literature* under the general editorship of Evans-Pritchard, G. Lienhardt, and W.H. Whiteley (see, for example, W.H. Whiteley, 1964). The editors, in the first volume of this venture, were still anxious to avoid any tarring with the 'folklorist' brush, saying, 'our intention is not to be misunderstood as the conservation, merely, of archaic conventions or of passing forms of social experience. On the contrary, we think it harmful to African literary studies to divide the past from the present' (W.H. Whiteley, 1964, v). We might think in any case that there was little danger that continental Africa could be held for long in the bondage of a historicism in which it became the validation of somebody else's history, a view that we can hold with less confidence regarding the relationship of Gaelic culture to its academic interpretation. The relevance of literature, both oral and written, to the modern anthropologist, and the problematical nature of the relationship of that literature to the society from which it springs, are discussed in *Text and Context* (R.K. Jain (ed.), 1977). The status of literature expressed here is not, however, that of simple evidence, but rather we are told that 'the anthropologist, the writer of the text, and the society to which it refers make a fascinating triad' (ibid., p. 2), of whose interaction we must be aware.

This interacting triad is nicely portrayed in the Scottish Gaelic context by H. Robertson (1976), in his study of the relationship of the folklorist Alexander Carmichael to Gaelic society and the literature that he collected from it, where we are shown the creative and distorting intervention that Carmichael's innocent collecting became. This is not any peculiar reflection on Carmichael, but rather a recognition of the inevitable complexity and difficulty presented by the 'fascinating triad' of which Jain speaks. Herzfeld discusses the kind of problems that a modern approach to oral and literary traditions raises, saying:

> we have seen the dangers peculiar to classifying the products of oral tradition. They may be summarised thus: a tendency to assume irrationality in the processes of oral tradition, the application of a unilineal model of textual evolution, the use of philological criteria alone and the neglect of sociological data, and unwillingness to criticise academic taxonomy in the light of 'folk-taxonomy'. These dangers derive from well-established habits of thinking; but they must be squarely faced if the anthropological study of oral tradition is to avoid becoming enmeshed in the methodological gimmicks of other disciplines (M. Herzfeld, 1977, p. 46).

Certainly if these methodological strictures were taken to heart by both folklore studies and social anthropology, then there would be little room for the maintenance of institutional or intellectual separation.

We have seen that the renunciation of historicism led social anthropology to the ideally 'timeless' primitive world, where the lack of historical documentation permitted, for a time, the illusion of changeless harmony, and that this same bias led anthropologists who turned their attention to Europe to its more 'traditional', 'primitive' communities. While we might argue now that this bias was in a sense theoretically arbitrary, it was not necessarily a theoretical limitation but rather a convenient concentration of attention, and many monographs have been written in this tradition that showed considerable sensitivity to the historical dimension within which their 'synchronic' study was located (see, for example, J.A. Pitt-Rivers, 1954; R. Paine, 1957; J.K. Campbell, 1964; J. Cutileiro, 1971; and P. Loizos, 1975). The tension between synchrony and diachrony in the works of modern social anthropologists has many levels and many forms of expression, and one of these is undoubtedly that high moral valuation of the undisturbed peasant community, expressed by Du Boulay when she says of a Greek mountain village:

> whatever may have been its limitations and its defects, there is no doubt that when it was integrated to a living tradition it gave to life both dignity and meaning—qualities which are conspicuously lacking in the type of society that threatens to succeed it (J. Du Boulay, 1974, p. 258).

Often accompanying this is the assumption that the currently observable phenomena in peasant societies represent 'the decay of some . . . system which is itself taken to have been ancient and unchanging' (J. Davis, 1977, p. 6). This attitude is essentially an artefact of a synchronic view which, assuming timelessness for the purposes of analysis, comes to confuse model with reality and attempts to temporalise a permanent synchronicity. This confusion has often been made in the study of Gaelic-speaking areas. Crofting, for example, in its present form, is an institution which does not pre-date the nineteenth century, but it is now often defended as representative of an ancient way of life with the same emotionality that is attached to the other ancient institutions of Highland life (see E. Condry, 1977, p. 66).

The first works on Highland Scotland that fit unambiguously into the mainstream anthropological tradition are those of Vallee (see F. Vallee, 1954 and 1955) on the community of the Outer Hebridean island of Barra. Vallee was working within a functionalist tradition attempting, after the example of Evans-Pritchard (see E.E. Evans-Pritchard, 1937 and 1956), to come to terms with the analysis of symbolism in its relation to the apparently more 'empiricist' field of social structure as it was conceived by Radcliffe-Brown (see A.R. Radcliffe-Brown, 1968 and, for a concise critique, R. Needham, 1974). Vallee says that:

> Two aspects of the relation between ritual and social structure have been stressed by anthropologists: the functions of ritual activities, or the contribution they make to the maintenance of a system of social relations; and the way in which social relations and values are expressed in symbolic form (F. Vallee, 1955, p. 127).

Various criticisms can be made of such a formulation, not least the observation, springing from the general criticism to which functionalism was subjected in the late 1950s and 1960s, that the division of human activity, or of human society, into such dualities as social structure/ritual expression, or social relations/symbolic form, was an arbitrary prejudice deriving from a persuasive empiricism rather than a simple and natural ordering to be found in all societies. However, the relation of the logic of human activity as evidenced in the phenomena labelled 'social structure' and as evidenced in the phenomena labelled 'ritual and symbolism' provided, in the Hebridean case, a discussion of the internal rationality and contemporary relevance of ritual activity that had often previously been consigned to the sphere of the quaint, outmoded and materially irrelevant. Vallee shows how 'mourning and burial rituals provide one of the most frequent occasions upon which community members meet to express their unity and to reaffirm the values upon which that unity is based' (ibid., p. 128). He argues, quite rightly, that 'the systematic investigation of ritual, generally accepted as essential to the proper study of primitive groups, is of equal value in the study of groups in our own society' (ibid., p. 130). We no longer, therefore, have the assumption, implicit in much work on folklore, and, indeed, in much anthropology, that ritual is something that a modern society might be expected to do without. Vallee shows the 'ritual' significance in what might appear to be the perfectly ordinary activity of, say, communal drinking at times of bereavement.

In spite of this advancement of ritual to a position of contemporaneity, however, Vallee is primarily interested in ritual in so far as it represents an age almost gone. He says:

> An outstanding feature of the history of Barra has been its steady absorption into the economic, politico-legal, and social systems of Britain. In the expressive sphere also there has been a gradual assimilation to the surrounding society. Many of the traditional cultural practices, extant less than a generation ago, have disappeared or are only rarely observed. It is in the prevalence of the Gaelic language and in the persistence of certain ritual observances that the Barra of today resembles most closely the community of old. Of the ritual practices, none contain more traditional elements than those associated with death and mourning (ibid., p. 121).

We see counterposed the traditional and the modern, the one rich in cultural practices, the other devoid of them. There is implicit in Vallee's assessment a conflation of imagery that Du Boulay makes specific, when she describes the absorption of Greek village communities into the larger society as 'the change from traditional and symbolic thinking to modern and secular thinking' (J. Du Boulay, 1974, p. 6). The opposition traditional/modern is often related to the oppositions sacred/secular and symbolic/literal, but it is a particularly interesting (and common) confusion that leads to the elision of these last two oppositions, and makes of them an opposition of the symbolic to the secular, with the weight of history draining the symbolic of its mystery and replacing it with modern literal secularity. This confusion of imagery is, of course, basic to much Arnold-inspired appreciation of the Celt, and is the foundation of the folklorist's fear that his object of study will soon disappear. Modern social anthropology, which has spread the aura of symbolism over every human activity under the title 'semiology' that Saussure (1949, p. 33) gave to the science of signs, need have no such fear, even if the mystery of otherness that 'symbolism' evidently has for many is thereby somewhat devalued. Arensberg, while in many ways sentimental about the ancient Celtic life whose fragments he saw around him, was driven by the demands of functional synchronicity to ask, 'What do the old customs alive today mean for the countryman? What is the way of life of which they are still a part after centuries of existence?' (C.M. Arensberg, 1937, p. 12). Although the place of tradition was, in the functionalist idiom, to give 'sanctity to his conventions, his needs, and his goods. It infuses them with emotional associations far beyond their normal capacity to carry sentiment' (ibid., p. 199), and although the people were argued to 'preserve an unbroken ancient tradition that goes back, perhaps long into pre-Christian times' (ibid., p. 16), Arensberg reaches a balanced conclusion concerning the survival of 'symbolism'. This is largely because of the necessary position that symbolism was held to occupy in the functionalist idiom as that which validated the norm. If symbolism withered, how else was the norm to be validated? Nevertheless Arensberg's conclusion is worth quoting since it demonstrates that the functionalist attitude to symbolism did not always lead to dismissal, even if the emphasis, and the suggested causalities, now seem quaint:

> Today the young are sceptical and a little rebellious; they repudiate much of the older imagery . . . Today folk-belief is undergoing marked change like all else in this world, like all else in Ireland. But that does not mean the death-knell of folk-lore, as some students of folklore seem to think. Far from that, it means only that a symbolic order like any growth in human life must change and grow onward. New forms and new imagery will grow up to clothe in emotional terms the necessary reformations of habit and sentiment in social life, and new syntheses will fashion new belief, changing the old or supplanting it inch by inch (ibid., p. 212).

Arensberg provides a fascinating compromise of Celtic sentimentalism and functionalist necessity, which is worth quoting at length for the density and diversity of the imagery that he uses, consciously and unconsciously, to establish the point that symbolism will survive. Arnold, Tönnies, Yeats, Malinowski and Radcliffe-Brown conspire as the New World looks upon the oldest of the old:

> In retaining older custom and a more intense emotional and purely social organisation of life, Ireland may well have preserved better than most nations of western civilisation that unity of spirit which, underneath the surface of superficial strife, welds a nation into a single crucible. If the rationale of economic and social individualism with its attempted divorce between sentiment and logical self-interest seems lacking, the matter is no cause for lamentation or disdain. Who knows ultimately which is the better way? Each people seeks its own better union; unconsciously in social habit, consciously through religion, through politics, through detached and enlightened social thought. Either the conscious or the unconscious may be the more congenial, to nations as well as to individuals.
>
> But danger lies in neglecting one entirely for the other. In the so-called Anglo-Saxon lands one feels that the unconscious organisation of social habit has been neglected for the conscious. The logical has been too often mistaken for the ultimate. The all-powerful force of human sentiment has been neglected and too lightly regarded. We are prone to forget, with many an economist, that man not only does not, but cannot and will not, live by bread alone (ibid., p. 169).

It has often been observed that any kind of change constituted a theoretical affront to functionalist anthropology (for an attempt to cope with the problem of compromising perfect functional harmony with change see M. Gluckman, 1955 and 1968). There was more to the functionalist attitude to change, however, than theoretical disquiet. Although functionalism had attempted to renounce history, it had retained an implicitly moral attitude towards an undisturbed original harmony of society, as Condry shows in the Highland context (see E. Condry, 1977, pp. 137-52). This tacit moralism, and the traditional/modern duality from which Vallee constructs his picture of Barra, clearly open the door to the kind of sentimentality towards the 'community' that Tönnies had elaborated. Whether expressed or not, the innocent term 'community' invokes, as I have tried to show, a variety of metaphorical associations. What is particularly interesting for our present purpose, however, is not that Vallee operates, consciously or unconsciously, with a traditional/modern, *Gemeinschaft/Gesellschaft* model of society, but rather the evidence that he offers that the Gaels of Barra operate with precisely such a model. Vallee says that:

> the economy of Barra is in no sense a peasant one. Living in rural surroundings and according to codes of behaviour we usually associate with the farm-family ethos, Barra folk are nevertheless caught up in an industrial technology and economy with whose culture they must be familiar in order to gain a livelihood (F. Vallee, 1955, p. 120).

The model where 'community' and 'society' are opposed thus finds observational confirmation in the eyes of the ethnographer. We also find, however, that 'Most Barramen are almost aggressively egalitarian in their attitudes towards community relations, although they apparently accept the legitimacy of the status structure of British society as a whole' (ibid., p. 129). The people of Barra would thus appear to operate with a dual model of society which has certain affinities to that which the folklorist or anthropologist from 'an industrial technology and economy' might bring to them. This suggestion of a native theory of 'Gaelic democracy' (F. Vallee, 1954, p. 190) in opposition to a hierarchised outer world finds interesting confirmation in studies of other European communities. Pitt-Rivers, for example, in his study of an Andalusian village, says that:

> A structural tension exists between the sanctions devolving from the local community and those devolving from the central government of the country. In this instance the tension is visible in every social sphere . . . It corresponds to a conflict between the values of authority and those of equality (J. Pitt-Rivers, 1954, p. 213).

Loizos, describing the relationship of a small Cypriot village society to the wider political world, says that 'political commitment . . . in some ways runs counter to an important village norm, the norm of village solidarity' (P. Loizos, 1975, p. 291). The villagers themselves 'define the administration of the village as "unrelated to politics"' (ibid., p. 294). These examples are drawn from very different contexts, but the comparison with Vallee's observations is worth making. It is notable that the potentially divisive forces of modern politics and economics, with their tendency to introduce locally uncontrollable ambitions and sympathies, are not seen by the people as simply invasive and destructive, but are positively defined out of certain social spheres. This dual model clearly has affinities to the many theorisations that the impact of modernity on, for example, Gaelic society, has had, although it presents a much more robust picture than the cowering retreat of fragile tradition before an economicist juggernaut with which we are often presented.

I have been concerned with the various theorisations that Gaelic society has received, and I have tried to show that the relation of such theorisation to Gaelic society exists at many levels. This relationship is not simply a question of the relative accuracy of an academic discourse to its object. We might note, for example, that the industrial society in which Arnold lived shared with Highland society a similar social determination of the appropriate areas of activity of woman – around family, hearth and home. Consequently, the femininity of Arnold's Celt and the restriction of the usage of the Gaelic language to 'feminine' domains are both, by different processes of mediation, linked to a common social form. Their apparent independence is, of course, a potent source of their capacity for mutual validation.

This suggestion of a common social origin does not, however, exhaust the subtlety, beyond simple representation, of the relationship of Gaelic society to its academic theorisation. The problem is further complicated because, as I have suggested in Chapter 6, those who are theorised cannot now fail to be aware to some extent of their representation in such theorisation. Consequently we have to view the relationship between the theories of the academic concerned with Gaelic life and that life itself as a relationship of mutually effectivity, not least when we consider that academic and native Gaelic informant are often united in the same person. There is certainly no cold and objective gaze on which we can rely. Davis takes note of the mutuality of this relationship, arguing that 'Mediterranean people have been affected, sometimes in important ways, by the anthropological works which have been written about them' (J. Davis, 1977, p. 3). Clearly there is no simple point at which it could be said that a native Gaelic theory of democracy had become transmuted into, say, a Tönnies-inspired idealisation of the community, but we should certainly bear in mind the extent of literature concerning the Highlands, its intellectual origins, and its likely readership within the community that it concerns. The Highlands have come to occupy, since the eighteenth century, a particularly important place in Scotland's historical self-image. The Scottish Gaels, therefore, who have long filled the role of 'noble savage' for the first industrial nation, must be considered as affected by that role in a way that can perhaps be disregarded in the consideration of other minority communities.

J. Campbell, in writing of a Greek nomadic shepherd community, says that 'The affairs of unlettered shepherds were not considered important by classical, Byzantine, or mediaeval writers' (J.K. Campbell, 1964, p. 4). Just as for the Scottish Highlanders, who did not themselves surface clearly into anybody else's recorded history until the eighteenth century, we find that the Sarakatsani only became of importance to the larger world during the Balkan wars, as 'folklorists and historians struggled with patriotic inventiveness to provide historical and ethnological evidence for the advance or validation of their various national frontiers' (ibid., p. 5). Campbell does not, however, feel the need to examine the effect of those folklorists and historians on the society that he is studying, arguing that he is 'a social anthropologist not concerned with the problem of origins' (ibid., p. 6). While this is acceptable in the study of a barely literate community faced with an academic tradition concerning them with a depth of only half a century, we cannot ignore this relationship in the case of Scottish Gaelic society, since, even if the anthropologist is not concerned with the problem of origins, the people are, and have many sources to turn to for enlightenment if the anthropologist refuses to discuss the question. If we remember the political and religious conservatism of women, the 'femininity' of the Celt, the differential use of Gaelic, the location of the 'community' as a source of 'folklore' and the sentiments associated with these, and the opposition of Gaelic democracy to the intrusive mechanics of industrial inequality, then we can look at Vallee's description of ritual activity in Barra after a bereavement, where:

> The death garments . . . are usually made by . . . women from material supplied by the bereaved household. Alternatively, the garments are purchased from one of the island shops . . . The older people strongly object to this practice, insisting that these *sacra* should be fashioned by the hands of the women of the neighbourhood (Vallee, p. 122).

Such a fact can provide us with simultaneous confirmations along several diverse axes of metaphorical aptitude, both native and academic. The weaving of cloth has, of course, its traditional division of labour in Gaelic society. At the same time, however, women could be said to be appropriately involved in ritual practice because they, rather than the men, represent the internal rather than the external face of Gaelic society. The reluctance of women to buy ritual material from a business concern could be argued to arise from the controversion that this would provoke of a series of disparate dualities – home/business, personal obligation/cash nexus, village/town, male/female, and so on. Both the concept of 'ritual' and of the 'traditional', and the role attributed to women, have, as I have tried to show, a wider mutual congruence than can be contained within Gaelic society. We have no clear competence, therefore, to enter this metaphorical diversity and arrive at any simple 'explanation' of such ritual phenomena that is purely and unambiguously internal to Gaelic society.

Vallee also tells us that within the overtly ritual context of the funeral procession there is a contrast between the:

> almost random way in which men distribute themselves in the procession compared with the distribution of women, which tends to follow kinship alignments. This suggests that men have a wider range of interaction than women, and that the sexes are oriented in different ways to the kinship system . . . The interaction of women is limited to kinsfolk to a greater extent than is that of men (ibid., p. 129).

Having raised the suggestion of a conscious duality of the community/society type in Barra society, it is possible to suggest that this division of ritual function derives not from any simple contrast between man and woman on the basis of more or less limited access to a wider society, but is rather a symbolic expression of dualities within which the people of Barra feel themselves to be poised. They are not, after all, so different from the folklorist in their attitude to their own traditions. Vallee mentions the custom practised in some houses of covering pictures and stopping clocks after a death, and says that 'It is claimed by many who are regarded as tradition bearers that this custom is alien to Barra, having been introduced into the community only a generation or so ago by an incomer' (ibid., p. 123). Such a purist attitude to alien influence is a common enough feature of external commentary on Highland society, and although it might have a different affective basis in Barra than in Edinburgh (a kinship-based jealousy as opposed to a sentimental nostalgia, say), the two pictures are clearly ripe for conflation, not only by the analyst, but by the actor.

Susan Parman, in her thesis on socio-cultural change in the Lewis township of Shawbost, has supplied another work which springs from an obviously anthropological tradition. She is concerned to explain the 'seemingly anomalous survival of crofting and crofting communities' (S.

Parman, 1972, p. 1), a survival that she regards as 'inconsistent with what we would expect given our conceptions of the conditions of a modern, urban-industrial nation state' (ibid.). She says, therefore, that 'the expectation that township members will manifest values and beliefs congruent with those prevalent in larger British society, and that patterns of economic specialisation and individualisation will be found among persons working in the available industries, is not fulfilled' (ibid.).

Parman employs a theoretical orientation based on the work of Barth and his transactionalist anthropology (see especially F. Barth, 1966 and 1968). While some of the theoretical language that comes with this approach seems to add little to the argument other than an air of authority, Barth's work has clearly provided an interest in the way the community defines itself. Consequently the society that Parman shows us is not simply an existence to be observed but rather an entity with an awareness of, and an interest in, its own identity. She says that 'The relationship of a community to the larger society of which it is a part may be investigated not by trying to place it on an urban-rural continuum, but by investigating its state of boundedness' (ibid., p. 192). Parman does not, in common with other transactionalist work, much investigate the ideological structure which underlies the events into which 'strategy' is read, and by which structure is thought to be perennially reconstructed. She does, however, provide some fascinating clues as to the nature of that structure, which would lead us to think that the 'anomalous, strongly-bounded sociocultural system' (ibid.) of which she speaks is not bounded by virtue of any simply unitary sense of identity, but rather through an ideology that consciously orders the rural and urban, minority and majority, by use of the imagery that I have been discussing. She tells us, for example, that 'People come and go from the township, but this appears to maintain rather than weaken township boundaries because behaviour different from that prescribed within the township can be performed outside it' (ibid., p. 188). We are also told that 'Township members who have settled away from the island come back periodically for recreation and a sense of belonging. They increase the value of the township and its way of life in the eyes of the inhabitants' (ibid.). This is no simple forced emigration from a dearly loved native community. Parman says that:

> Although young villagers and emigrants often describe the village as 'dull' and 'dead', the emigrants are happy enough to return to the island for short periods of time, during which they participate in those situations in which expressiveness and limited license are

accepted (ibid., p. 142).

We find a suggestion that in some cases the village society exists only because the outside society requires it to, not in the rhetorical sense of metaphorical necessity but in the actual retention of people in the village. These two necessities are, I would argue, now intimately linked. Parman says of the islanders who choose to live away:

> The 'exiles' prefer to return at such times as New Year's, or during the summer months when the beaches are inviting and the gales absent. They remember the 'characters' and other features of village life which give it color, often forgetting the drab background out of which the color was forged. Some villagers whose siblings have married and left the island continue to live alone in the house mainly to keep the house in order for their return. 'I wouldn't close the house on them. They come back every summer' (ibid., p. 147).

This society, which is required to exist by those who have left it, has a value that Parman expresses as follows:

> The 'exiles' sing the old songs with vigor, drink heavily during their visits, and praise the island for that 'special quality' which is unmatched by life in the dirty, crowded, unfriendly city. Some plan to retire in the village. The villagers take up the tune that their society is eminently worthwhile. When talking to strangers, they ask questions pertaining to this image of themselves, such as, 'Don't you think this place has something which you will never find in a city?' 'People come here during the summer and they love it; they can't keep away. So they must find something here. What would you do in a city anyway? Out here you're freer.' (ibid., p. 148).

She locates immediate sources of this kind of sentiment: 'The image of the island as spiritual home is fostered by The Stornoway Gazette, and by nostalgic songs, most of which were written by islanders who emigrated to Canada in the first quarter of the century' (ibid., p. 149).

It is clear that there is more to the relationship of Lewis society to the urban majority society than could be expressed in economic terms, or explained as a consequence of geographical marginality. The sense of 'boundedness', the sense of identity, that Gaelic society has is clearly to some extent found within metaphorical structures which are only complete in so far as they subsume both the minority and majority society.

Ardener has expressed the mutual relationship of two such societies, showing the way in which, despite great disparity in obvious 'size' or 'power', they can stand, from certain points of view (regarding, say, the capacity for 'self-definition') on equal terms. The 'world' in which a minority lives is not simply a politically and demographically inadequate or reduced version of the 'world' in which the larger society subsumes it. The parentheses with which we must surround 'world' in such a context stem not merely from the respect of the relativist who is prepared to grant to widely different ideologies an equal status, but rather from the need to express the capacity for the definition of meaningful reality that societies have, a capacity that is, with respect to any notion of the plenitude of the 'real' world, at once reality-reducing and totalising. Ardener illustrates this, using the example of the apparently ephemeral and shifting gipsy society and its relationship to the architectural solidity of the majority society with which it coexists. The term 'world-structure' in the following (see also E. Ardener, 1975b) is that parenthetic world that I have referred to above. We are told that:

> all world-structures are totalitarian in tendency. The Gypsy world-structure, for example, englobes that of the sedentary community just as avidly as that of the sedentary community englobes that of the Gypsies. The englobed structure is totally 'muted' in terms of the englobing one. There is then an absolute equality of world-structures in this principle, for we are talking of their self-defining and reality reducing features (E. Ardener, 1975, p. 25).

What is said of the relationship of gipsy society to the majority society applies equally to the position of Hebridean or Gaelic-speaking society to its majority neighbour.

This power of 'englobing' is no simple economic relationship, and would give us grounds for criticising the often simplistic, if refreshingly radical, analyses of the relationship of Hebridean society to the majority society which treat it as only about economic oppression (see, for example, the *West Highland Free Press*, a radical weekly newspaper printed in Skye). As Ardener says:

> That this approach is not simply a marxist one lies in our recognition that the articulation of world-structures does not rest only in their production base but at all levels of communication: that a structure is also a kind of language of many semiological elements,

which specify all actions by its power of definition (ibid.).

The 'muting' of which Ardener speaks is 'a technically defined condition of structures – not some condition of linguistic silence' (ibid., p. 22). It is an inability to speak other than through a structured discourse whose organisation is centred elsewhere – a group 'is muted simply because it does not form part of the dominant communicative system of the society' (ibid.).

This condition of 'mutedness' can be clearly related to the organising power, at both an intellectual and a social level, of the imagery that I have been discussing – an imagery that is, in origin, of the English language. Much of the imagery used in the self-assessment of the Gaelic community has a full existence within a simply English-speaking community, and the relationship of Gaelic to English society is expressible in terms which the average city-dweller in England would use to assess, for example, the relationship of rural to urban society. Dualities like rural/urban, community/society and the like have, I have tried to show, an intimate relationship to less obviously 'social' dualities such as woman/man, and Celt/Anglo-Saxon. It is within the metaphorical fabric of such dualities that the relationship of 'Gaelic' to 'English' society is imagined.

The problem, however, is not one of understanding the relationship between two societies discrete in their personnel, but between two ideas. Discussion of the relative merits, qualities and 'nature' of the two societies would often provoke the belief that the Highlands were exclusively Gaelic-speaking and the Lowlands exclusively English-speaking, not because this is ever asserted, but by the polarisation of metaphorical dualities along an axis between the two societies as represented by their languages. Such a simplicity is of course thoroughly subverted both by bilingualism and by the dispersion throughout Scotland of its Gaelic speakers. The figures from the 1971 census tell of only 477 persons over the age of 3 in the whole of Scotland who speak only Gaelic (for these, and all the following figures, see Census 1971, Scotland: Gaelic report). The exclusively Gaelic mind and culture is therefore effectively no longer either in existence or in any simple way open to inspection. Of the 88,415 claiming to be bilingual in Gaelic and English only 50 per cent professed a reading knowledge of Gaelic, and fewer still a reading and writing knowledge. Figures for literacy in English are not given in the 1971 Census Gaelic report, but can be assumed to be approaching 100 per cent. Consequently, in so far as an idea of what society is like comes from reading about it, the idea of what Gaelic society is will be transmitted predominantly through the English language.

We have seen from Parman's evidence that the Gaels outside the traditional Gaelic-speaking areas exert some force in the self-definition of those areas. This weight is both socially and demographically considerable. Socially, one aspect of that force is that urban living standards are higher and middle-class sophistication more easily achieved, which will lend to the voice of the emigrant at least some kind of authority. Demographically it is effective in that the third-largest Gaelic-speaking population by gross statistical unit in the 1971 census was in Glasgow city. The five largest were, in decreasing order of magnitude, the county of Ross and Cromarty (22,000), the county of Inverness (20,000), Glasgow City (12,800), the county of Argyll (9,800) and the county of Sutherland (2,400). This demographic and social weight of the Glasgow Highlander is even more considerable when we note that, in the Central Clydeside Conurbation, the highest figure for Gaelic-speakers arranged by age in five-year groups is for those aged 20–24, with a fairly steady distribution over five-year groups between the ages of 20 and 50, after which there is a decline. By contrast, in Scotland as a whole the highest five-year group figure is for those aged 75 and over, with all the higher figures clustered above the age of 40.

Parman gives us some insight into the relationship of the minority to the majority society as it is evidenced in the lives of those that live in both. She mentions that:

> A girl who teaches Gaelic in Glasgow and comes home to the island only for holidays never goes to the island dances, but loves going to the dances sponsored by the Lewis and Harris Society in Glasgow. All the young people from the islands come, and dance away accumulated insults in a fiery sense of belonging (S. Parman, 1972, p. 131).

She also speaks of 'Associations which sponsor Highland dancing and the opportunity to get together with other Gaelic speakers' (ibid.), which thrive 'everywhere but in the Gaelic-speaking Highlands' (ibid.). These, she says, 'serve important functions in situations of interaction between Gaelic speakers and members of the dominant society; they provide identity and self-defense against those who react to them as members of a lower-status minority group' (ibid.). It is clear, however, that this minority status and its attributes are not, whether or not they once were, simply imposed from without.

Macaulay has written of the influence and aims of the Gaelic community in the Galltachd, calling it: 'urban, with an "artificial" structure in the form of a set of Gaelic (etc.) societies, and parasitic upon the urban community within which it operates' (D. Macaulay, 1966, p. 136). He speaks of the 'crucial position it occupies in Gaelic culture' (ibid., p. 137). What he says of the relationship of the rural and urban communities is worth quoting at length, since it touches upon crucial issues that are not, out of motives ranging from piety to simple inability to perceive any difficulty, often raised. He says of the 'urban Gaeltachd':

> Whereas the declared aim of its organised existence is to preserve and promote Gaelic culture, it, in fact, does not serve as a bridge-head, but rather as a bridge. The traffic on this bridge is very largely in the wrong direction. This is an undeniable fact and is inherent in its existence as an organised community, and the fact that it refuses to admit that its situation makes it different, in an essential way, from Gaelic communities in the Gaidhealtachd. So it is busy reinterpreting Gaelic culture and recreating 'the image of the Gaidheal' in its own image (ibid.).

This passage occurs in a discussion of the difficulties associated with innovation in the literature of a minority culture, and the relationship of the urban Gael to the rural Gael over this issue is described. Macaulay says of the urban reaction to verse such as that written by Ian Crichton Smith:

> It is interesting that the most vocal resistance to the kind of poetry that we get in *Bìobuill is Sanasan-Reice* comes from this organised community. This is not simply because it is vocal but because the poetry does not coincide with or promote its 'ideals'; or, indeed, recognise its self-appointed role as guardian of Gaelic culture (ibid.).

We can see that, along this rural/urban axis, 'symbolic appropriation' is given a new dimension which is at first appearance internal to Gaelic society, in that it is internal to those who speak its language. This we have seen in another form in the lives of those who, as Parman says, maintain a house in the Gaidhealtachd so that the exiles will have somewhere to return.

The polarity of which Macaulay is treating is not, however, simply one between two discrete societies, one in Glasgow and one in Stornoway, but is of course internal to them both and internal to the bilinguality of every Gael. Language use in a bilingual situation permits of a whole system of 'linguistic' communication independent of the ostensible meaning of the words spoken. The choice of language itself is a message, and we have seen some of the likely sources for imagery by which that choice will be described and according to which it will inevitably be made. Parman confirms that 'Gaelic is the language of hearth, home, family and community. English is the language of education, the business world, and various transactions with the larger society' (S. Parman, 1972, p. 132). She observes that 'If a Gaelic speaker chooses to speak English in a village situation where there are no officials present or other cues which make English-speaking appropriate, this indicates that he considers himself a cut above everyone else' (ibid., p. 136). Parman interprets this simply as a consequence of differential social status attached to the two languages. This is obviously an important factor. However, once we introduce Lowland Gaels, the Highland Societies, and the like, it is clear that, for them at least, the issue is not so simple. Parman argues that the sanctions against speaking English when all present speak Gaelic 'increase the emphasis on uniform behaviour within the marginal group' (ibid.). Vallee has, as we have seen, suggested the existence of a dual model of self-definition within which the emphasis on the use of Gaelic in certain contexts is more than the defensive reaction of a 'socially marginal group' (ibid.), and is rather a conscious assertion of the relative nature of Gaelic and English society, the latter being class-stratified and the former not.

We have seen that the 'community' became in the nineteenth century a locus for a variety of socially desirable characteristics. We have also seen that there were those who saw its disappearance as a potential emancipation from limiting and stunting restrictions. Folklore studies have on the whole adopted the former view, and many Gaels who choose to live in Glasgow have apparently accepted the latter before leaving, and the former upon having left. The essentially fictional nature of the idea of 'community' in this context is expressed by Plant, who says that (his emphasis) 'the notion of community is . . . implicitly defined in a conservative way in terms of a way of life which has been *lost*' (R. Plant, 1974, p. 28). Argument about it is therefore not a simple regret for the passing of a well observed phenomenon, but rather 'a debate fundamentally about the kind of society in which we *ought* to live' (ibid.). The tension between the two very different valuations of small-scale society as both humanly valuable and intolerably oppressive is clearly shown by Parman. She describes (see above, p. 195, S. Parman, 1974, pp. 142-8) those who choose to live on the mainland, in part at least to escape from the community in its undesirable aspects, who are happy to return to celebrate a picture of community life which they construct while they are away.

Ian Crichton Smith gives these paradoxical sentiments literary expression in his *An t-Aonaran* ('The Recluse'), a novel set in a small Hebridean community, where the relationship of the individual to the society about him is discussed. Crichton Smith gives us some idea of the potential for moral tyranny that such a community has, and the limitations imposed upon a lone intellectual by the limitations of the surrounding society. The subtle modes of moral censorship that exist in the watchful and knowing silence of village life are quietly suggested, and the picture painted is neither happy nor optimistic. In one scene the principal actor is talking to two Gaelic 'exiles' who are visiting relatives on the island:

> Dh'fhaighnich mi de'n dithis eile dé mar a bha an làithean-saora a' cordadh riutha 's thubhairt iad gu robh glé mhath, gu robh iad air a bhith muigh air eathar ag iasgach.
>
> 'B'fheàrr leam gum bithinn a' fuireach an seo fad na tìde,' arsa bràthair Dhougie–Eachann is ainm dha–'s a' bhriag 'na ghuth. Thubhairt a bhean an aon rud. Bidh an luchd-turais an còmhnaidh ag ràdh an aon rud, gach bliadhna, gum b'fheàrr leotha gum biodh iad a' fuireach an seo, ach chan eil duine gun creidsinn. Oir bidh iad a' falbh dhachaidh 's cha chluinn duine bhuapa airson bliadhn' eile.
>
> (I. Crichton Smith, 1976, p. 47).
>
> I asked the other two how they were enjoying their holidays and they said very much, that they had been out fishing in a boat.
>
> 'I would prefer to stay here all the time,' said Dougie's brother–Hector his name was–with the lie in his voice. His wife said the same thing. The tourists always say the same thing, every year, that they would rather live here, but nobody believes them. Because they go home and nobody hears anything from them for another year (my translation).

Parman says of the uneventful life of Shawbost that 'The generally low level of stimulation derives in part from values which restrict opportunities for self-expression. People are ready to gossip, i.e., to participate vicariously in the escapades of others, but are less eager to act' (S. Parman, 1972, p. 140). Recent studies of gossip have tended to emphasise some positive social aspect in order that such a ubiquitous social phenomenon should not be forever consigned to the realm of unpleasant social malfunction. E. Colson (1953) showed how the most slanderous of gossip among the Makah Indians could be seen as a process of self-definition of the Makah group against wider American society, and she places the nature of this self-definition within the context of the old potlatching prestige system and the modern financial advantages of being a credited Indian in modern America. Frankenberg (1957), in his study of a Welsh village, showed that gossip served as a means of group definition, and that the right to gossip was reserved to a small in-group which thus defined itself by this right. Frankenberg also, however, showed how the fear of gossip led to a lack of initiative in village affairs that caused the continual breakdown of organised activity within the village, as potential leadership was cut down to size by gossip and scandal. Gluckman (1963), with characteristic functionalist vigour, finds in gossip the function of maintaining group cohesion and solidarity, of defining the social unit, of controlling potentially intrusive influences, and the like. Even within a social unit that is collapsing, gossip can have the function of speeding that collapse.

R. Paine (1967) attempts to find a fresh direction away from the inevitability of the functioning social unit, but the only direction that he can find is towards the Barthian individual, maximising his information gain in gossip transactions (for the theoretical inspiration of such argument see F. Barth, 1966). He argues that 'investigation of gossip is best kept on an instrumental plane' (R. Paine, 1967, p. 282), and that gossip is best seen as a medium of competition for scarce information. Whether we take function or transaction as our explanatory vehicle, it is clear that gossip is not 'idle chatter'. We are also made aware of its controlling and restrictive aspects, where social control grows from a benign functionalist abstraction into an oppressive threat. Parman says that 'In the everyday life of the village, a style of indirectness and restricted communication is encouraged' (S. Parman, 1972, p. 140). This is effective at all levels of socialisation. We are told that 'A major feature of practices of child-rearing on the island is inconsistency, which develops a style of guarded watchfulness and hesitance to act or express oneself' (ibid.). We also find that:

> Villagers engage with each other in constant, quiet game-playing. They are dependent on each other for many things, but try to minimise the control that others have over them while improving their own positions . . . Such training allows little room for the development of close friendships in which the individuals involved are sympathetic with each others' idiosyncrasies. A constant joking keeps people at arm's length and discourages the development of empathy (ibid., p. 141).

In accord with this picture of the Gaelic community as inimical to the 'emancipation of the self-conscious, self-directing individual' (R. Plant, 1974, p. 31), Finlay MacLeod writes that a Lewis person's:

> interactions with others are coloured by his prime concern not to bring shame on his family through anything he does or says. He avoids doing anything which may draw attention to himself and his family, and to protect his reputation he shuns social responsibility and keeps others at a distance from him. This individualism and lack of leadership are striking characteristics of such a culture (F. MacLeod, 1969, p. 77).

The relationship of gossip to competition within an 'Honour and Shame' structure is discussed in, for example, J.K. Campbell (1964), J.G. Peristiany (1965) and P. Loizos (1975). There is no clear evidence that the field of honour and shame in the Highlands is either as morally and semantically sophisticated, or as totalitarian, as it is in many traditional Mediterranean communities. However the tendency towards conservatism and lack of leadership that such concepts can provoke can be demonstrated from otherwise diverse societies. Vallee's 'native theory of Gaelic democracy' in this light looks less like the simple equality of freedom and more like the Hobbesian equality of permanent competition. As Loizos says of a Cypriot community, 'The coin that has solidarity on one face has social control on the other' (P. Loizos, 1975, p. 101).

The moral duplicity of Crichton Smith's 'exiles' is comprehensible in such a context. People leave a Lewis community because 'There is nothing to do. The place is dead' (S. Parman, 1972, p. 140). At the same time we have seen that Parman quotes islanders saying of emigrants who return summer after summer that 'they love it; they can't keep away. So they must find something here. What would you do in a city anyway? Out here you're freer' (S. Parman, 1972, p. 148). This tension between two opposed valuations of the small community is, of course, generalised throughout the British Isles in the sustained increase of urban as opposed to rural population, and the emptying of remote areas, which has as its converse the migration of the urban middle class to the part-time alternative society of the weekend cottage. The same paradox in the Scottish Gaidhealtachd is, however, permitted a fuller expression than it is elsewhere, in that it comes to incorporate the symbolic dualities of language difference. The relationship between the rural and urban societies in this respect is, as Macaulay says, 'a fascinating sociological case "deserving of the closest scrutiny"' (D. Macaulay, 1966, p. 137). Davis says that, within Mediterranean studies, 'the study of the links of rural populations with urban ones has not been seriously undertaken' (J. Davis, 1977, p. 8), and he complains of a 'paucity of information about immigrants' associations in cities' (ibid., p. 35). I have tried to explore some of the ideological background within which the relationship of rural to urban society might be conceived, and by which we might, in Scotland at least, understand the activities of immigrants' associations.

MacKinnon, in an important socio-linguistic study of Harris based on field-work in Harris of a duration that would be conventionally acceptable for a social anthropologist, has provided a work which, while not self-consciously anthropological, and drawing its inspiration primarily from Bernstein (see, for example, 1971), nevertheless provides a confirmation of the picture that we have already drawn. MacKinnon takes the Durkheimian duality of mechanical/organic solidarity to express the relative nature of the Gaelic and English features of Harris life. He says that:

> In terms of a folk-society such as that of Harris, solidary relationships within the community are chiefly of a mechanical character whereas solidary relationships with the 'outside' or mass-society of English-speaking modern Britain are chiefly of the organic type whereby individuals relate to each other through a complex interdependence of social function (K. MacKinnon, 1977, p. 29).

He argues that Harris society 'possesses many of the distinctive attributes of a folk-society: smallness, isolation, solidarity, co-operation, homogeneity, moral consensus' (ibid., p. 30). He quotes Redfield to the effect that 'the folk-society is that society in which the technical order is subordinated to the moral order' (ibid.). There is a clear if unstated moral attitude towards the community and its affective solidarity, and we have seen that Vallee has suggested that this moral attitude is one that Gaelic speakers themselves share.

MacKinnon clearly shows, as I have argued above, that the language confrontation in this situation is no simple dominance of one language over another. He argues that it is rather a question of 'legitimate occupancy of social space by the two languages' (ibid., p. 170). Bilinguals, he argues 'see both of their languages as having their proper place and do not necessarily themselves see language-contact in terms of power, domination or conflict' (ibid.). He also points out that the boundary of differential language use is both intra-communal and intra-personal (ibid., p. 171) and must be understood in these different but intimately related dimensions. We must also remember, however, that the 'folk-society' and the 'community' have a place in MacKinnon's vocabulary, and probably increasingly in the vocabulary of the Gael (especially the urban exile), which is of considerable moral weight, and that MacKinnon's work is directed ultimately towards the 'transformation of Gaelic society' (ibid., p. 192), which seems to involve the restoration of all the virtues of Durkheimian mechanical solidarity without any of its vices.

We are faced with an intellectual structure whose capacities for gathering and ordering reality, and for generating internal coherence, are convincingly total. We should avoid the trap of imagining that we have contributed an external and learned commentary on this system if we simply draw one set of metaphors from the basket and line them up against the others, posing the first as data and the others as analysis, and then announce our rectitude through observing a congruence. It is an artefact of the 'near bewitching self-verification' (M. McDonald, 1978, p. 27) of this system that any critique of it appears inevitably like the espousal of one or other of its permissible polarisations. If, therefore, we seem to be questioning the communal beauty of Gaelic life our vision immediately becomes the harsh gaze of rationalist utility. If, on the other hand, we deny to science the capacity to encapsulate, englobe, or invade Gaelic folk-life, then we appear to be advocating a retreat into the meaningful womb of the alternative society.

It should be clear, therefore, that my examination of the imagery by which the virtues of Gaelic society are expressed is not in any simple sense a denial of those virtues. At the same time, I think that there is a great deal more to be said.

8 CONCLUSION

I have tried, in previous chapters, to relate the often congruent imagery used to express dualities such as Celt/Anglo-Saxon, woman/man, and folk/sophisticated. To this end I have quoted Tönnies, who brings together many of these images in his *Gemeinschaft und Gesellschaft*, a work which Plant calls 'a classic of sociology, . . . from which most modern discussions of community start' (R. Plant, 1974, p. 24). Remembering the central importance of Ossian in the formation of an image of the Celt, and also the great popularity of Ossian in Germany, we can establish Tönnies's ideas of 'community' and Arnold's Celt as constructs deriving from the same period, the same historical movements, and, at one level, from substantially the same people. Plant argues that Tönnies's book 'is indebted to the works of the German romantics which were really the fountainhead of this disposition of thought about man and society' (ibid.).

Plant is concerned primarily with the idea of 'community' and its moral connotations as it is used in the context of social work, within which Tönnies's typology 'has dominated thinking' (ibid., p. 23). This influence has, however, undoubtedly been felt within other areas of intellectual life concerned with the social, not least within social anthropology. As I have tried to show, the symbolic richness of what we think of as morally neutral or simply analytical terms can be pervasive, often barely noticeable, and impossible to wish away. I have been attempting, through a study of this often tacit symbolic background, both to understand 'the extent to which the historical career of a concept structures our present understanding of it' (ibid., p. 28), and to contribute to a study of the symbolic structure within which the 'strategic scientific value' (M. Crick, 1976, p. 57) belonging to our 'more ordinary terms of human self-understanding' (ibid.) might be found.

Plant argues that:

> terms which are usually taken to stand at the opposite pole to that of community, with its emphasis on rootedness, cohesion and belonging, are part of the stock in trade of cultural Jeremiahs on both the left and the right: alienation; estrangement; anomie; rootlessness; loss of attachment are all, we are so often told, part of the crisis of modern mass society. Salvation and redemption are to be found in

the community, but what is it? (R. Plant, 1974, p. 1).

Before the establishment of this high valuation of the community there were those such as Hobbes, Hume and Bentham who 'were not at all sympathetic to the notion of community' (ibid., p. 31). For eighteenth-century rationalism:

> The loss of community . . . was . . . a necessary condition of the emancipation of the self-conscious, self-directing individual and, as late as the end of the eighteenth century, by which time the reaction in favour of the reformulation of community had set in, Jeremy Bentham, the great utilitarian philosopher, attempted to build up a whole social and moral philosophy out of a set of statements about the necessary trajectory of individual motivation (ibid.).

We have seen that this tension between the virtues of the solidary community and the virtues of the free individual are manifest, in various forms, in the lives of Scottish Gaels. We find that those Gaels outside the traditional Gaidhealtachd show a tendency to applaud the 'community' while those inside it, particularly the young, are often keen enough to escape from it. Students of Scottish Gaeldom have, on the whole, treated it as an example of a 'community' declining inevitably into modernity. This treatment has often been largely informed by those metaphors with which Tönnies cut the world in two.

It is worth noting the prevalence within sociological thought of dualities that are congruent with Tönnies's *Gemeinschaft/Gesellschaft*. Durkheim, in his formulation of the notions of mechanical and organic solidarity (see E. Durkheim, 1948) was much influenced by Tönnies. Maine's expression of the evolution of modern European law, the temporalised duality of status and contract (see H. Maine (1861), 1950), is an opposition of the same order. Louis Wirth, one of the leading figures in the group of Chicago empiricist sociologists who profoundly influenced modern sociology in the 1930s and 1940s, constructed a typology of the characteristics of rural and urban society which now appears like 'common knowledge'. He argued that, in urban society:

> Our acquaintances tend to stand in a relationship of utility to us in the sense that the role which each one plays in our life is overwhelmingly regarded as a means for the achievement of our own ends. Whereas the individual gains, on the one hand, a certain degree of emancipation or freedom from the personal and emotional controls

> of intimate groups, he loses, on the other hand, the spontaneous self-expression, the morals, and the sense of participation that comes with living in an integrated society (L. Wirth, 1964, p. 60).

We see, therefore, that there is a remarkable unity of imagery within several apparently diverse expressions. The often persuasive congruence of these apparently independent pictures, while it seems to provide a sense of stability and a surety of assessment, should perhaps rather make us suspicious that what stability there is lies in the nature of the imagery itself, and not in any shared qualities of the 'Celt', the 'folk', 'woman' and the 'community' which can be abstracted for innocent comparison. The qualities attributed to the Celt have occasionally been subverted (e.g. S. MacLean, 1938, and G.B. Shaw, 1912), and the stereotype of femininity has been under increasingly vigorous attack throughout the twentieth century. It seems likely that the aptitude of the same imagery in its more obviously sociological applications to the 'folk' and the 'community' is no less problematical, and in part dependent on the confirmation that it has received from elsewhere.

The questionable nature of the whole edifice is suggested by its appearance in a context which is familiar enough in modern anthropology as it concerns itself with alien thought systems, but which seems odd and rather laughable when introduced into our own. The binary symbolism of left and right has drawn considerable academic attention since Robert Hertz's work (see 1960), and its more common associations have almost become a cliché within modern social anthropology (for the most comprehensive work on the subject to date, see R. Needham (ed.), 1973). In our own culture, however, this is a rather attenuated and rarefied symbolic sphere (hence perhaps the interest it provokes), but it is not without interest that the qualities attributed to the Celt, and often eagerly accepted, like imagination, nervous sensibility and the like, were considered, at least from the example of my early school career, to be qualities particularly associated with left-handed children. The right-handed were, by comparison, sober, matter-of-fact, and straightforwardly competent.

This left/right binarism is given another expression in works on the analysis of handwriting, where (and we should remember the feminine, mysterious, archaic Celt) a leftward trend in the slope of letters is said to be representative of passivity, femininity, the past and the inner world. A rightward trend, not unexpectedly, is representative of activity, masculinity, the future and the outer world (see K.G. Roman, 1961, p. 138). We are told that:

> Rightward extensions . . . represent alert mental activity, intellectual ambition, drive and planning. A leftward trend . . . represents on the other hand an emphasis on the inner life, a tendency toward contemplation or introspection, a preoccupation with one's imaginings, or a brooding on memories (ibid., p. 142).

The graphological niceties are unimportant for our present purpose, which is simply to present these ubiquitous dualities in another context. Their appearance in the context of left/right symbolism, which we do not tend to regard in modern Britain as having great powers of signification, does not of course render them necessarily insubstantial in their other applications, but it does provoke a certain scepticism.

It might be appropriate here, speaking of scepticism, to raise one or two classificatory anomalies that this system of dualities can create within itself. We have seen that the Celt has been accredited with a mystical incompetence that is read as an essentially feminine characteristic. On the other hand, the kilted bare-legged Highlander can readily pose as the essence of aggressive and unfettered masculinity (see, for example, the Gaelic quarterly, *Gairm* (Autumn 1976), No. 96, 318-19). This is not, however, quite the crippling contradiction that it might appear. I have tried to show that none of the dualisms with which I have been dealing, even the physiological and corporeal dimensions of sex and bodily laterality, have any essentially definitive status in relation to the rest. The male/female dimension, therefore, only acquires its substance in an already rich metaphorical context. Let us remember, for example, that the Highlands have been accredited with a naturality, and the Highlander with an emotional spontaneity. If these characteristics are given a sexual content, there is no doubt that the qualities attributed to the Highlander are feminine. On the other hand, the intrusion of a male/female dimension is not essential to the creation or understanding of the system of oppositions. If we leave women and femininity out of things altogether, and look at the natural, spontaneous, emotional Highlander within a strictly male symbolic context, then it is clear that he, rather than the Lowlander, represents an unrestrained masculine sexuality. The Lowlander is cultured, mannered and not given to display of feeling; the Highlander is naturality unchained. For this purpose, therefore, we give the opposition nature/culture a priority over the lesser defining power of the female/male opposition. It should, however, be remembered, as I have stressed, that any simple priority will remain elusive, and that the system as a whole has an integrity that single manifestations or lone dualities might themselves lack. It is only thus that we can explain the femininity of the Celt, and yet at the same time appreciate the Highlander's hairy legs and the continuing preoccupation with what he wears under his kilt.

One of the problems in much of the preceding argument will appear, I think, to be the apparent absence of any immutable structure, any solid grounding, by which statements about the Gael, or statements about those statements, could be located and rendered secure (one thinks, for example, of the physiological immutability of race, the infrastructural reliabilities of Marxist economics, or even the warm safety of untainted 'historical fact' itself). I am personally reluctant either to try to find or to give the appearance of having found any such security, either from anthropological theory or Gaelic life. The metaphors and habits of mind which brought anthropology into existence in the nineteenth century are so like those through which the Gael has been interpreted that any confirmation or interpretation of one through the other runs the risk of merely being an internal congruence, a self-validation, however it might appear like something intellectually more detached. The metaphors from which the literary Celt has been built have no clear priorities, and there is no clear relationship of dependence either way between the Celt and, say, theorisations of 'science' and 'art', or of the ideal 'woman', both of which can be shown to partake of substantially the same imagery.

Since my research has been largely literary, it might be felt that my position was itself a literary artefact, an intellectual balancing act that could only be performed in the ideality of a library, and which lacked inevitably the rigorous materiality that an injection of real life would supply. This is a problem potentially provocative of a considerably longer discussion than I have room for, and I can only suggest some of the possible areas of debate. In the first place there is no *a priori* reason for regarding a 'culture', be it pre-literate, non-literate or aliterate, as any more solidly based or intransigent than a literary tradition, since both must continually reinterpret their own performances to themselves, and thus provide a point of departure for future performance that is more than a simple neutral presence of, or awareness of, 'history', whether this history takes the form of a library of books or an unwritten 'tradition'.

The often-remarked conservatism of the oral tradition of Gaeldom does not, in this sense, mark it radically apart from the consciously innovative literary tradition of the nineteenth and twentieth centuries with which it has coexisted, since both contain, within different media, the same potential for internal development. The concretisation that the written word represents can be argued to promote a conservatism, to be an immutable reality that will constrain future development. The written word can also be argued to permit of studied reflection, and thus encourage novelty and innovation. In the same way the necessary impermanence of the performances of an entirely oral tradition can be argued to encourage chaotic and random change. It can, on the other hand, be argued to demand a conservatism. We might expect that a written tradition would grow to be more aware than an oral tradition of processes of change and development as they occurred within its own fabric. We might also expect that an oral tradition would find it more easy to sustain a fiction of changelessness in the face of continuous innovation. Even so, an oral tradition offers us no more security of unaffected truth to its past than does a literary discourse. The same point can be made for a 'society' or a 'culture', neither of which are immutable and constraining external realities, immune to internal and reflective development. In the case of Gaelic culture this is particularly evident, since Gaelic culture has emerged into literary discourse largely through the medium of the English language, and at the hands of those outside the culture, from whom it has then drawn its modern capacity for reflection.

We have, therefore, to consider the problem of the relationship of Gaelic society to the literary discourse concerning it not as a problem of the relative accuracy of representation (within which we might say, for example, that the Gael is no longer considered to be a mystical gloomy creature, as if this were an observational error now rectified by closer inspection) but as a problem of mutual effectivity. The bulk of literary commentary on Gaels and Gaelic has been made, by both Gaelic and English speakers, in English, and the language of literacy for the reading public has been English. The media are still almost entirely English-dominated. At the same time many features of the relationship of the Gaelic-speaking areas to the English-speaking areas have conspired to render Gaelic culture, at least in so far as it represents itself in the written word, extremely conscious of the threat to itself posed by the larger community and therefore extremely self-conscious. Thus we can expect that the relationship between Gaelic society and commentary on that society (irrespective of the 'accuracy' of that commentary) will be one of the problems that will have to be considered in a study of Gaelic culture. The problem is made the more complicated when we remember that 'There is now no linguistic hinterland to which the Gaelic writer can retire, except for that hinterland of the imagination' (D. Thomson, 1974, p. 250), and that consequently no Gael can fail to be aware of at least some aspects of the position that he and his culture have come to occupy in the larger community.

Gaelic culture must now, perforce, be conscious of its identity in a way different to the consciousness of identity of a monoglot English-speaker. G.B. Shaw, while supporting the cause of Irish home rule, recognised that the conscious drive towards a national identity was a kind of cultural pathology, saying that a healthy nation was as 'unconscious of its nationality as a healthy man of his bones' (1912, xxiii). The same could be said for a healthy culture. Gaelic culture has now to face the great paradox that to revive itself it must become more self-conscious, and that its self-consciousness will be based in part on an authenticity which derives from an alien discourse rather than from fidelity to itself. And pursuit of fidelity, the more so the more vigorously it is carried out, will provoke that self-consciousness that is at the heart of the problem.

I have not discussed the subject of language revival at any length in this work, although I think that there is much that can be said about it within the general context of this discussion. The subject is large and would require extended treatment to do it any justice. However, since I have raised the problem of the 'self-consciousness' of a culture, there are one or two points about language revival that I would like to make. Many people in Scotland are now learning Gaelic, and *An Comunn Gaidhealach* puts considerable effort into running language courses and encouraging publication of teaching texts. I have some personal experience of this aspect of the Gaelic revival, and I think that it would be fair to say that the results of all this effort are, at one level at least, disappointing. Inevitably, for most learners, the enthusiasm for Gaelic is very much a part-time affair, finding its chief expression through Gaelic records, ceilidhs and the Gaelic choir competitions organised by *An Comunn.*

The attendance at Gaelic language courses consists of four recognisable groups: those with an academic interest in Gaelic (myself included); those who learn it to sing in Gaelic singing competitions, especially the Annual National Mòd, where a degree of linguistic fluency is a requirement for those competing for the highest prizes, the coveted gold medals; those who are seeking their Highland roots, often people from countries like Canada, South Africa, Australia and so on, where Caledonian and Highland societies have, of course, their most abundant existence; and, lastly, students who are pursuing a radical or romantic yearning, or who are studying Celtic at university, and for whom a certain knowledge of Gaelic is a course requirement. There are learners who fall into none of these categories, and those who fall into several, but these four groups are usually represented, and for all four the learning of the language is a gesture whose validity is not entirely dependent upon how much is learnt. English-speakers who actually live in Gaelic-speaking areas and who might be expected to feel the need to learn Gaelic for use as a daily tool are, on the whole, conspicuous by their absence at Gaelic courses. There are, however, a few of this rare and valuable breed, with whom the future of *learnt* spoken Gaelic might be expected to rest.

An Comunn has tried to make its courses effective and intensive, and it has found it necessary to wage a tacit campaign against those who attend its language courses merely for a cheap and slightly exotic holiday. At the same time it feels that it cannot afford to alienate the goodwill of those whose linguistic ambitions are slight, but who nevertheless add enthusiasm, substance and finance to the notion of a Gaelic revival. It cannot be doubted that genuinely exacting standards and the demand for rigorous application would evaporate much of this revival, and expose a rather more depressing reality. Learning Gaelic is essentially a 'holiday' pursuit, with all that that entails. It is perhaps not surprising that many feel that their pleasure in learning and the very essence of their attitude towards Gaelic are threatened by any excessively intellectual demands. Scholastic rigour does not attune readily with the very agreeable mixture of singing, laughter and ceilidh-going that constitutes the attraction of an intensive course in the Gaelic language.

It would not be unjust to argue that the essential message of a Gaelic course is contained in the attendance and the intention, and achievement comes as an added but not entirely necessary bonus. Furthermore, the message of this intention to learn, this public proclamation of the value of the Gaelic, is one that is articulated within the kind of symbolic structures that I have been discussing, and does not make obvious sense within the realities of Gaelic use in the Gaidhealtachd. Although these realities and Lowland enthusiasms have, as I have tried to show, interesting homologies, this does not alter the fact that the incompetent Gaelic-learner presents a fragmentary and somewhat inexplicable intrusion into the day-to-day structure of Gaelic use. Gaelic-learners use their Gaelic, on the whole, in conversation among themselves.

All this may sound unnecessarily gloomy and critical. I should add that I have every gratitude to those who have helped me learn Gaelic, and that I have found Gaelic courses a valuable and enjoyable educational facility. On the other hand, I do not think that the picture is hopeful, and

I do not think that there is any point in allowing ourselves to pretend that it is. The issues that I have raised above are not much discussed, and this silence permits the illusion that Gaelic-learners are on a straight and unproblematical, if lengthy, route towards being Gaelic-speakers, which is simply not true. It might be felt that my appeal for a more rigorous approach to the learning of Gaelic was profoundly innapropriate to the sea-girt Hebrides, to the dignity of an older and less hurried way of life, and to the pursuit of the spiritual substance of the Scottish nation. This is in a conventional sense perfectly true, and provides us with yet another reason for questioning the virtue of such assessments of the Gaidhealtachd. It is not possible to learn a difficult language simply by soaking up an atmosphere, however drenched in atavistic yearnings that atmosphere has come to be. The formal complexities of idiom and pronunciation, however much they evoke dreary memories of schooling, and however inimical they seem to the Gaelic ideal, have to be learnt and taught in all seriousness. Nothing would be lost by assuming that Gaelic-learners really do want to learn Gaelic. It might as well be accepted that there is no cultural renaissance lurking in an ability, however widely spread, to phrase the Gaelic greeting 'Ciamar a tha sibh?' (How are you?). The Gaelic language can only answer, 'Thank you for your kind and well-intentioned enquiry. I am still dying.'

It is my personal feeling that to attempt to advance the Gaelic language through the pursuit of a rather rustic populism, however appropriate this might seem to a greater Scotland as it turns its eye to the Gaidhealtachd, will not do the Gaidhealtachd much good, and will not much further the cause of serious Gaelic-learning. Scotland will only thereby find itself in the same situation as Ireland, where 'a greater percentage of the people . . . now declare themselves to have a knowledge of Irish than at any time since the founding of the Gaelic League' [1893] (S. O Tuama, 1972, p. 103) and where, nevertheless, 'The Gaeltacht is in its death-throes, and neither the people of Ireland nor the State are really agitated about it' (ibid., p. 100).

I have stressed that learning Gaelic is a part-time activity for many, with the implication that while commitment may be present, it is hardly something that is lived and breathed. People do, after all, have other things to do. With this in mind, it is interesting to note that several Gaelic scholars have lamented the absence of enthusiasm for the Gaelic language that most of its native speakers display. Calum MacLean says:

That there is widespread devotion to the language throughout the

> Highlands is beyond all doubt, but it is not the enthusiasm of zealots whipped up by propaganda, for there is no effective propaganda; it is the spontaneous devotion of a disinterested but unfortunately inarticulate mass to something they feel is a very vital part of their spiritual lives (C. MacLean, 1959, p. 116).

We also often read of the necessity that a Gael should be 'perfervid' (for example, H. Macdiarmid, 1968, p. 305; F.G. Thompson, 1970, p. 80) in his attitude to his language and his heritage. Indeed it seems logical that if the indifference and scorn of the Lowlander have put Gaelic on the retreat, then it will require devotion and fervour to restore its place. I think, however, that this easy assumption should be scrutinised with some care. Fervour in this context is something that it might be rather difficult to sustain, and is something, like the Lowland enthusiasm for Gaelic, that we might expect to be necessarily part-time. We might, indeed, ask ourselves what it would be like to get up every morning and have to become 'perfervid' in order to carry out the trivial daily round, and having to muster 'devotion' to every linguistic expression.

While it is quite appropriate that non-Gaelic-speakers should espouse 'devotion' to the language, it is naïve to expect that more than a handful of native speakers will do so, at other than the most trivial level. The English language is, on the whole, a neutral, unselfconscious medium of expression. This is usually true at least within, if not always across, its dialectal variations. The English-speaker does not self-consciously define himself as such with every word that he speaks. Whether or not this is a universal attitude to language (and for some doubts about this, see M. Crick, 1976, pp. 66ff), it is one that we can expect the Gaelic-speaker to extend to many at least of his uses of Gaelic. To ask him to define and affirm his status as a Gael with every statement that he utters is perhaps to impose a burden on the language that it will not wish to bear.

This is not, of course, to deny that the use of Gaelic does not sometimes carry a message beyond the obvious meaning of the words employed, or that Gaelic is not sometimes used as a means of self-definition (see above, p. 201). These meta-linguistic messages are not, however, readily understood in a context of devotion, commitment or fervour.

I should make it clear that my sympathies are entirely with those who wish to effect a renaissance of Gaelic as a spoken language, and those who wish to see Gaelic given its rightful place in the school curriculum, particularly as a teaching medium. This is, however, a battle that will be won, if at all, in schools and families in the traditional Gaelic-speaking areas, even if it draws strength from the enthusiasm and goodwill that the Lowlander can give to it. The use of Gaelic in the education of Gaelic-speakers is at present a fairly lively and innovatory field, and judgement on its success must wait on events (for a now rather outdated, but still useful summary of the situation, see Scottish Council for Research in Education, publication XLVII, Gaelic-Speaking Children in Highland Schools, 1961).

One of the most worrying evidences of the status that Gaelic has among its speakers is that Gaelic-speaking children, particularly at school, prefer to talk between themselves in English. We have seen that Gaelic has become associated with the familial, domestic, expressive and essentially 'non-serious' aspects of life, and that English is by comparison associated with business, economics, education and the hard and rational outside world. We can also note that for many Lowlanders the western seaboard of Scotland is the location, *par excellence*, of the 'holiday', that Western European categorical antithesis of the dull and demandingly serious business of daily life. Bearing all this in mind, we can note that Gaelic courses in Stornoway are housed in hostels that during school term-time accommodate children from distant islands who spend the school week, or even the whole term, boarding away from home. During the school holidays English-speaking Gaelic-learners walk the corridors conversing in Gaelic (on holiday), and during term-time Gaelic-speaking schoolchildren walk the same corridors conversing in English (on business). This is at the same time unfortunate, slightly comic, and extremely interesting. It also requires that we seriously question the virtue of the symbolic structures within which the Lowlander articulates his enthusiasm for Gaelic if, as it indeed turns out, they allow Gaelic-speaking schoolchildren to be so utterly and blithely dismissive of the language that we would have them speak.

It is often maintained that learning Gaelic is an educational process of many dimensions, and that regardless of whether fluency is achieved, the learner gains a sympathy for a valuable and rich minority culture that is in danger of being lost. This is doubtless true, although I have tried to show that its modes of expression are not always the beneficent and complimentary statements that they are imagined to be. I cannot doubt, however, that the peculiarity of the position of the Gaelic-learner has made me more sensitive than I might otherwise have been to the difficult problem of 'self-consciousness' of a culture, and to the problematical and uneasy relationship between 'authentic' Gaeldom and its representation, whether that representation is in nineteenth-century literature, the publicity efforts of the Highlands and Islands Development Board, or in the activities of Gaels themselves.

Due to the near-universality of bilingualism in the Gaidhealtachd it is not possible to learn Gaelic in the way that we traditionally expect to learn a language like, say, French or German, by going to an area where only that language is spoken and thus being forced to speak it in order to be understood. Learning to speak Gaelic requires a commitment beyond the utilitarian on the part of both the learner and those who assist him, and the learner unfortunately requires a good answer to the question (that we would scarcely think to ask of somebody learning English) 'Why are you learning it?' It was in part through a discovery of the permissible replies to this question, of the permissible modes of expression of commitment to the Gaelic, that the questions that I have been concerned with in this work first presented themselves to me.

My emphasis on what might be considered the histrionic aspects of Gaelic life might be thought both misplaced and belittling. I hope that it is neither. An intimate and dialectical relationship between what we might choose to call fact and fiction, or reality and illusion, and so on, is something that we can demonstrate in all historicist self-representations. The relationship is, perhaps, in the case of Gaelic Scotland, both more than usually intimate and obvious, since Gaelic Scotland, now virtually without monoglots of its own, stands right on the doorstep of the English language and the international power of the English written word, and has been an easy candidate for symbolic appropriation by that word. Thomson says, 'a minority culture can be treated in many different ways: it can be fostered, recognised, tolerated, ignored, or persecuted' (D. Thomson, 1966, p. 258). These treatments are not at all mutually exclusive, and to them I have added, not with any great verbal felicity, 'symbolically appropriated', which bears no necessary relationship to the others. It caused little apparent concern, for example, to those Scots who were proud to dress up in Highland clothes, that the culture whose clothes they wore was being destroyed by Clearances to serve short-term commercial ends. A letter to the editor of the *Scotsman*, 14 June 1817, puts the matter quite succinctly:

> You know, sir, that, a few years ago, a number of enlightened and benevolent persons in the Southern *Lowlands* of Scotland, instituted a society for promoting and maintaining Gaelic schools . . .
>
> You may naturally suppose that the Highland proprietors would be desirous of affording encouragement to an institution so well calculated to promote every species of improvement. But the lament-

> able truth is, that it is almost exclusively to the benevolence of Lowlanders that we owe the existence of Gaelic schools; and (shameful to relate), that but very few of our Highland Lairds have contributed a shilling to the funds of the Society! Here is a specimen of the boasted 'amor patriae' of Highlanders! and at a period too, when some of our own chiefs and gentry are attempting, by means of an association called the Society of True Highlanders, to preserve the distinctive peculiarities of the Gaelic nation! There may, perhaps, be no harm in wearing feligs, breacans, or bonnets, nor in listening to the martial notes of the piobreachd, nor in beholding scenes of fencing with the claihde mor, or the performance of gymnastic exercises, but these exhibitions and performances, however much they may gratify the long-titled descendants of the leaders of Creachs, are of little or no importance in comparison with the propagation of divine and moral truths. Let us hope that . . . every landholder in the Highlands will, even for his own sake, contribute liberally to the support of the Gaelic schools; . . . This would indeed be acting the part of true Highlanders ('Abriensis', *Scotsman*, No. 24, 191, 1817).

The point is well made, even if we would now hope to see in the Gaelic language more than a vehicle for the 'propagation of divine and moral truths'.

It is not the carefully preserved idiosyncrasies of Lowland religious and legal institutions, enshrined in the treaty of Union, that define Scotland in the popular imagination, but overtly Highland institutions, the pipes, the kilt, whisky, the clan and so on. The surprise of the tourist on finding that the mountains do not leap suddenly out of the plain on crossing the Tweed, and the conviction on the part of several young Scots that I have met that England is without hills are only a projection into topography of the many symbolic manipulations to which Highland life has been subjected.

In dealing with an overt continuity of discussion in a literature over a considerable time period, however problematical the relationship of that literature to its ostensible object, we have to consider the problem of the internal relationships within that literature. The citation of a few crucial texts over a two-hundred-year period can provide us with the security of a linear succession of ideas, and by placing these texts within the chronology of the annual calendar we can temporally authorise derivation and development. To what extent this is justifiable is very difficult to say, and to what extent we can treat authors as 'creative' or 'derivative' must depend on factors of which we frankly have little knowledge. To make such decisions we need to know not only who wrote what, whom they were addressing, and by whom they were read, but we also need to know who read what, and, more importantly, *how* they read. There can be no doubt, for example, that my reading of Arnold's *Celtic Literature* is quite different from that of those who first heard the lectures when they were given in Oxford. I can understand this particular example with some insight, but the same problem arises with every reading of every article concerning the Celts and Gaels.

We cannot do much with this problem other than raise it before ourselves, but a suggestion of possible complications is possible. Within, say, Celtic studies, within that discourse constituted by articles and books concerning 'Celts', there is, through succession of citation and derivation of phrases and ideas, an apparent unity of commitment in retrospect that might, at any one period of time, seem much more difficult to establish. We might, for example, note that there was a strong element of satire coexistent with the more fanciful products of Celtic studies, and more people might have read of the Celts with an awareness of this than we could possibly imagine or discover by going back through what appears to be the mainstream of serious consideration of the 'Celt'. Our gravity in approaching certain texts might, therefore, be seriously misplaced in so far as we wish to effect a similitude of popular understanding within ourselves.

I cannot demonstrate this better than by quoting G.B. Shaw on the Celt and Anglo-Saxon, from the introduction to his play *John Bull's Other Island.* The play concerns the business co-operation of an Englishman called Broadbent and an Irishman called Doyle, and Shaw describes them as follows, with a refreshingly materialist subversion of Arnold's dualities:

> Broadbent's special contribution was simply the strength, self-satisfaction, social confidence and cheerful bumptiousness that money, comfort, and good feeding bring to all healthy people; and . . . Doyle's special contribution was the freedom from illusion, the power of facing facts, the nervous industry, the sharpened wits, the sensitive pride of the imaginative man who has fought his way up through social persecution and poverty (G.B. Shaw, 1912, xi).

He then collapses the conventional racial dualities entirely, amid, one would imagine, laughter:

> when I see the Irishman everywhere standing clear-headed, sane,

> hardily callous to the boyish sentimentalities, susceptibilities, and credulities that make the Englishman the dupe of every charlatan and the idolater of every numskull, I perceive that Ireland is the only spot on earth which still produces the ideal Englishman of history. Blackguard, bully, drunkard, liar, foulmouth, flatterer, beggar, backbiter, venal functionary, corrupt judge, envious friend, vindictive opponent, unparalleled political traitor: all these your Irishman may easily be, just as he may be a gentleman (a species extinct in England and nobody a penny the worse); but he is never quite the hysterical, nonsense-crammed, fact-proof, truth-terrified, unballasted sport of all the bogey panics and all the silly enthusiasms that now calls itself 'God's Englishman'. England cannot do without its Irish and its Scots today, because it cannot do without at least a little sanity (ibid.).

> Roughly I should say that the Englishman is wholly at the mercy of his imagination, having no sense of reality to check it. The Irishman, with a far subtler and more fastidious imagination, has one eye always on things as they are (ibid., xii).

When we think of the pious reverence of Arnold and Renan before the Celt, and the often sanctimonious and self-congratulatory way in which their ideas were used, it is as well to remember that what people think fit to say and what they think fit to write may be entirely different things, and what they laugh at may be more important than either.

Macdiarmid makes a complaint very similar to Shaw's, when he quotes Anna Ramsay, saying:

> the Highlander, a dreamer and a poet, a mystic and a romantic, is contrasted with the shrewd, keen, pushing practical lowlander . . . Nothing could be more remote from the facts of everyday life, as it appeared in the pages of history . . . The Highlander excelled in practical work: he made a good colonist, pioneer, soldier, scientist, engineer. But for poetry, romance, idealism – one must go to the Lowlands . . . (cited H. Macdiarmid, 1968, p. 306).

We can sympathise with this to an extent. It is certain that most of the romance that is now located in the Highlands has had its origin in the Lowlands. On the other hand, the powers of definition have lain with the Lowlander, and he did not generate his romance for use at home but for use in the hills. There is no doubt that it is his story that the rest of the world has believed.

This work has been concerned with the different representations that Gaelic society has been subjected to, and found for itself. I have been concerned to display the various complexities of relationship that can exist between a 'people', the real Gaels on the ground, and their appearance in literature. I have tried to show that this simple dualism of the fact and the fiction obscures to us the very real congruence that the 'social structures' and the 'symbolic structures' display. Recent years have seen attempts to wake the public image and self-image of the Highlands out of its Romantic sleep, and the young and the radical have pursued a realism that would put to rout the centuries of false consciousness and mystification which an exploitative external society has imposed. This is in many respects welcome, but it has its own concealments and silences. We can briefly discuss two of these.

The Highland Clearances have long been justly deplored by local tradition that remembers the suffering and misery caused, and by scholars fearing the blow dealt to Gaelic culture and life. The problems of interpretation involved here are not normally approached with any great subtlety, and at a first level the Clearances provide a pleasingly unambiguous picture of external oppression and of native suffering and resistance. Although people are no longer easily dispossessed of their land or burnt out of their houses, it is now fashionable, within a radicalism purchased rather more cheaply from the paperback shelf, for a wider public to regret and deplore these Clearances. The blame for these now regretted social upheavals is frequently located outside Gaelic society, among landlords who are 'alien', 'Anglo-Saxon', or 'English'. This is in clear but comfortable disregard of the fact that many of the Clearances were imposed by an aristocracy that shared the blood of those that were evicted. Even this truth is often racialised by those that would argue that such an un-Gaelic irresponsibility was only made possible because the aristocracy had been 'Anglicised'.

We should not forget that the Clearances were invariably represented at the time as an enlightened social reform, conducive to the greatest good of the greatest number. While we might disagree in retrospect with this judgement, it is a rather shallow moral exercise to render this whole aspect of 'political economy' morally defective, reify its proponents as villains, and thereby assume our own moral rectitude, complacently imagining that we would have done any better.

We should also remember that the kind of publicity that the Highland Clearances received was very much one to encourage the belief that all was happening for the best.

Those that have been 'blamed' for the Clearances could quite genuinely have been unaware of what was going on. Certainly there were brutal compulsions at work beneath the comfortable façade. Even so, the relationship of this façade to the reality, the problem of understanding how information was handled, the problem of understanding how cottar, tacksman and landlord represented the Clearances to themselves and to one another, are scarcely penetrated by any simple model of economic exploitation or racial and cultural animosity. Most of the contemporary accounts (we might now call them 'justifications') of the Clearances now read like bare-faced propaganda, fairy-tale like in their suppression and distortion of cruelty and suffering, and insufferably patronising in their talk of a child-like, indolent and worthless (albeit picturesque) peasantry. If we have so much difficulty in entering into the educated mind of the early nineteenth century, then we must exercise some humility in projecting into the mind of the Highland peasant our contemporary understanding of his grievances, and we must remain sceptical, in all sympathy, of accounts that purport to tell his story for him.

A similar point can be made about the decline of the Gaelic language. Many people nowadays wish to see a resurgence of Gaelic as a vigorous modern language. It seems that the most morally convenient way to imagine this resurgence is to argue that Gaelic has only fallen from the lips of the Gael because it has been forced off by external oppressions and maltreatments. Rather than accept that Gaelic is dying because people have stopped using it, we are presented with a less problematical and more easily resolvable problem if we imagine that Gaelic is dying because its speakers have been killed, shipped overseas, or beaten whenever they uttered a Celtic word. Remove this oppression, it might seem, and the language will blossom. The language is not blossoming, however, and it is still convenient to recall tales of children being thrashed for speaking Gaelic (e.g. J.L. Campbell, 1950, p. 68; C. MacLean, 1959, p. 51). Why else would they have stopped speaking it? This physical compulsion is easily understood and equally easily removed, and offers an easier hope of revival than does the need to penetrate the imponderable complexities of the bilingual psyche. It is not, however, credible that any widespread derision of Gaelic or any sustained campaign of corporal punishment could be carried through without the complicity of the local community. If we are to use emotive terms, it makes as much sense to speak of 'linguistic suicide' (D. Greene, 1972, p. 11) as it does to speak of 'genocide' (J.L. Campbell, 1950, p. 68). As Greene says of the practice in Ireland of flogging children for speaking

Gaelic:

> No British Government prescribed these brutalities, any more than did the landlords or the priests, . . . it is clear that the system of policing and flogging was planned and carried out by the parents and schoolmasters working in co-operation. Over a quarter of the Irish people was bent on linguistic suicide (D. Greene, 1972, p. 10).

The desire to find outside the Highlands the source of all its problems is one that we can understand, and such a pursuit is not without historical justification. Even so, all those problems now have an internal dimension of some complexity, that is only trivially expressed by simple models of external influence, imposition or imperialism. It sometimes seems that a new generation of unambiguously cruel and hostile schoolmasters would be welcome as a focus of blame, and a continued justification to ignore or dismiss the internal dimensions of the problem.

There is no doubt that the Highlands and Islands have been tossed around by economic, social and political movements that had their origin outside. At the same time there is little contemporary comfort to be found in seeking an inviolable Highland integrity that has been only superficially distorted or overlain by history. The searcher after the undisturbed Highland world, yet to be confronted by the external world and all its problems, must go back a long way before he has exorcised all the imagined defects in Gaelic society that he would like to treat as external impositions. He could go back to time without record, to an heroic age where we can assume everything to have been beer and skittles. He could go back to an early medieval Scotland where Gaelic was the language of learning and of the Court, and where displaced and rustic older tongues were doubtless jeered into silence. Would that help?

It is not difficult for those with radical pretensions (among whom I include myself) to get agitated about the history of exploitation and ignorant indifference that the common man of the Highlands has suffered at the hands of the powerful. It is, however, fanciful to imagine that the system that engendered this would go away if the Highlands were united as an entirely Gaelic world, freed at last of English and the Anglo-Saxon. Gaelic is the language of the family, of friendship, of religion and of the common man. It is, however, the language of a half-world, and it would cease to occupy this space of simple virtue if Gaelic society became complete within itself, and engendered its own power structure, divisions of labour and so on.

This might seem obvious. It is not, however, difficult to discover plans for Gaelic-based political action founded on the hope that since Gaelic excludes the world of business, of class stratification, of exploitative capitalism, of harsh go-getting education, of materialism and of utilitarianism, then these unpleasant aspects of life would disappear if the world became entirely Gaelic. A similar ambition is frequently articulated by those concerned with the other areas of the Celtic fringe (see e.g. the journals *Crann-Tàra, Carn*, or the *Celtic League Annual*). A politically benign Gaelic autonomy is now often invoked by pursuing a resentment of the 'English' as the cause of all the troubles. Such a judgement is compounded of a multitude of discursive inevitabilities whose structure I have tried to expose. Comfortable though such a position surely is, it is politically myopic.

I have pursued in this work the interrelationship between various expressions of metaphorical, political and social structures. My treatment of these has been fragmentary, but this has only been made possible by the ubiquity and essential continuity of an imagery over a considerable period. Thoroughly to establish continuity would require an enormous work, and I hope to have in part achieved the same end by examining a limited, fragmentary sample of the emergence into literary expression of this continuity. It is easy in discussion to appear to give to these 'symbolic' or 'metaphorical' phenomena an independent life that deprives the author of any competence other than that of sitting with pen in hand waiting to be written. We would be justified, I think, in treating many of these images as having more vigour, more creativity and more independence (although the language of moral approbation is of course entirely inappropriate here) than many of the authors from whose pens they flow with such ease. It is within this world of the tyranny of the word and the inevitability of forms of expression and the formation of ideas that the Highlanders have come to occupy their place in the Scottish consciousness. I have tried to provide an understanding of the intellectual and metaphorical automatisms involved in this process. I would like to think that such an understanding can help to create the possibility of a political reading of the problem that would transcend the invocation of resentment, or the simple and unreflective attribution of blame.

We have seen that there are multiple reasons why Gaelic should find itself excluded from the harsh world of politics, and why those concerned with the public image of Gaelic should remain 'stubbornly apolitical' (H. Macdiarmid, 1968, p. 306). I should make it clear that my criticism of a particular political use of Gaelic does not mean that I think, along with many past members of *An Comunn*, that Gaelic should stay out of politics. On the contrary, I think that Gaelic has a potential political importance of great strategic value. There is also no doubt that the question of the use of Gaelic in schools, in bureaucracy and in the media is in all respects a political question. On the other hand, an ostensibly radical political engagement is quite easily come by through very traditional intellectual and symbolic structures. It is now possible and even fashionably easy to deplore events like the 'Gathering of the Clans' as merely advertising phenomena, packaged culture and identity for mass-media consumption. Even the annually donned public face of Gaeldom, the National Mòd, can now be heavily criticised, particularly by the young, for its inauthenticities and its lack of political involvement. It is not possible, however, by virtue of such criticism, to go back to a simple beginning, to remove the veneer and expose the reality. Levels of involvement, achievement and commitment in such spheres render some enterprises radically different from others (we could contrast the Gathering of the Clans with, say, the Gaelic publishing programmes of *An Comunn* and Glasgow University), but the attempt to restore the origin, to go back to the beginning of the story, cannot now be more than the addition of the next, most recent chapter.

Scotland in general, and Gaelic Scotland in particular, is very used to finding its identity and the validation of its present by looking to its past. I have shown how this backward gaze has been created by the present, and how no amount of visual acuity can penetrate the fogs of representation and re-representation that constitute the history and the image of Gaelic Scotland. For a culture traditionally supposed committed to its own history, this is a hard pill to swallow. The general criticism is not, however, one aimed solely at Highland historiography. We must simply agree with Foucault, in his denunciation of those that wish:

> that beyond any apparent beginning, there is always a secret origin – so secret and fundamental that it can never be quite grasped in itself. Thus one is led inevitably, through the naivety of chronologies, towards an ever-receding point that is never itself present in any history; this point is merely its own void (M. Foucault, 1972, p. 25).

We are absolved, therefore, of the pursuit of an origin that retreats as we pursue it, but at the same time we are obliged to take seriously the organising power and structure of the 'mere ideas' that we study. Foucault asks:

> Has not the practice of revolutionary discourse and scientific discourse

> in Europe over the past two hundred years freed you from this idea that words are wind, an external whisper, a beating of wings that one has difficulty in hearing in the serious matter of history? (ibid., p. 209).

It has been suggested that I should give some idea of what Gaelic or Hebridean society is really like – behind the mask of representation and self-presentation. I would rather be inclined to argue, however, that this is something that I cannot do, and that the whole burden of this work has been to show the difficulty (indeed, the impossibility) of achieving any untroubled and clear-eyed vision. If I were to direct the reader to popular fiction in search of the Hebrides he might find, for example, the works of Lillian Beckwith (see, for example, 1968), and read there of charming, happy and simple people untroubled by the sordid anomie that besets urban man. In doing so, however, I would be referring the reader to a representation of the Hebrides that provokes mingled amusement and wrath among Gaels that I have met, and that I have heard called 'pornography' for the disservice that they do to the Gael in thus inserting him into the Scottish and British consciousness. I could, on the other hand, refer the reader to a multitude of reports on the economic situation in the Highlands and Islands, all speaking of gloom and misery and social decay. Who is right, Lillian Beckwith or the Highlands and Islands Development Board? Which of these pictures is true, or if they are indeed both true, at what level of reality can they possibly interrelate?

I should, perhaps, be able to go beyond the literature and tell what Gaelic Highland society is like, in so far as I have experienced it. Even here, however, the same problems arise. Tourists who go to the west of Scotland for the beauty of sunsets over the ocean, for the mountains, and for the tranquillity of an older way of life (all of which they doubtless find) can go home without knowingly having heard a word of Gaelic. On the other hand those learning Gaelic are drawn into a somewhat ambiguous fraternity in which they become a party to secrets that are not shared with the common tourist. They do not, however, by virtue of this, become in any simple sense a part of Gaelic society. Indeed, Gaelic-learners are often subject to another kind of dismissive derision from those for whom Gaelic is as ordinary as white bread, and for whom the part-time pieties of the would-be Gael are somewhat grotesque. Gaelic is, in many different ways, representative of the intimate interiority of the society of the Highlands and Islands. It is not surprising that outsiders learning or knowing Gaelic would present to that society a rather more complex problem than does the tourist, who can be discreetly and politely excluded (usually without his knowing it) from more intimate affairs. Gaelic society is not yet in any immediate danger of finding itself having to deal with an influx of fluent Gaelic-speakers who have learnt the language – who are, as it were, Gaels by self-adoption. If it ever is faced with such an influx, then we cannot doubt that the necessities of self-definition will find a way of dealing with the problem.

If we cannot rely on the external observer to supply us with an unbiased picture of what Gaelic society is like, then we might still expect to get such a picture through the works of someone who actually belongs to that society. Even here, however, we are disappointed. There are few books written by the Gaels about the Gaels, and as I have tried to show in earlier chapters, many Gaelic scholars have only written what has been expected of them, which does not help us very much in our search for hard reality. This is not merely a criticism of bias, or lack of acuity. The decision on the part of a Highlander to write about the Highlands is almost necessarily preceded by another decision – the decision to remain a Highlander. Those who elect to forget where they come from do not, reasonably enough, bother to write about it. For a stimulating, if sometimes confused, assault on these problems, I would refer the reader to C. MacLean's *The Highlands* (1959).

It might be imagined that we could turn to the camera for an objective salvation. Even there, of course, we find that although the camera cannot lie, it can tell all manner of truth. The scenic tradition of photography in the Highlands is a long and strong one, and it is not difficult to take breathtakingly beautiful pictures of the mountains, with little houses nestling into their flanks in a perfect and peaceful integration. We could, however, take a photograph of some of the streets of Stornoway or Oban or Inverness in black and white on a rainy day and come out with a depressing picture of urban blight in the best tradition of realist documentary.

The visitor to Lewis finds himself confronted with a landscape that is, even for those accustomed to the Highlands, astonishingly bleak. He can drive through the island and pass bare and stark modern houses designed in the dullest tradition of council-house utility, set in straggling rows in a featureless landscape. Photographs of townships so constituted might tell him that he was in some as yet unfulfilled corner of a dispersed industrial new town. Even so, he could take photographs of the smiling people, the picturesque shepherd at his sheep, the house-tops giving off wreaths of peat smoke against a blue horizon of distant moor, glittering sea, and a sky alive with the glorious colours of a Hebridean sunset. What other reality are we prepared to see? There is no doubt that the tourist and travel books on the Highlands and Islands tell a very particular kind of photographic story. We could, if we chose, balance this with photographs of Stornoway bars at closing time, of the piles of household rubbish that surround every township, of rusting caravans and abandoned cars, of long-forsaken black houses in all states of decay. The moral, perhaps, is to remain sceptical, and to read every story that purports to completion with the other half of the story in mind.

I have spent considerable effort in pursuing to the death certain well established and conventionally acceptable ideas and images through which Highland society has been expressed to the outside world. It might be felt that all I had done was wrestle with illusion, and that reality had somehow escaped me, tangled as I have been in webs of scholastic abstraction. It is not difficult, however, to establish that the authority of the word is not confined to the library shelf, or to the mind of the dilettante, the intellectual, and the bibliophile. I have suggested, in the Scottish Gaelic context, some ways in which the authority of the word is evidenced, and some of the power that imagery has for rendering itself apt. This is no simple idealist emphasis, however. Although it is in the spare-time pleasurings and leisured musings of Scottish intellectuals that we can most conspicuously see expression of the imagery by which the Gael takes his place in Scottish life, it is not only in such 'dubious ephemera' that the imagery under discussion exerts itself. Two of the most conspicuous features of the organisation of Hebridean economic life, two of its most firmly economic realities, can be argued largely to owe their form to such 'ephemeral', 'non-economic' determinants. The crofting legislation of the late nineteenth century, although it appeared to many to represent a radical blow on behalf of the common man (for a history of the crofting institution see J. Hunter, 1976), was no facet of a class struggle, in that: 'the socialists and the landlords failed. It was the Celtic scholars, and the members of the Gaelic and Highland societies that won the day' (E. Condry, 1977, vii).

The isolation of the Highland smallholder within an economic system of his own, self-consciously constructed according to the demands of an archaic past (see E. Condry, 1977, Chapter 3), with a security of tenure and a rent stability that would be the envy of many, while it might appear like a blow for radicalism, can just as easily, particularly when we consider the relatively small scale of the Highland economy, appear to be a simple process by which the Highlands were defined out of the sphere of modern economics. Whatever we might think of the morality of the economic system within which we find ourselves, it can be argued that isolation from it, while it might confer immunity of a kind, also represents a confirmation and maintenance of a wider economic impotence. As women have found, isolation from the dirty world of politics and economics is not a bed without thorns. The crofting laws have in a sense operated to keep the crofter in precisely that idealist half-world to which Arnold blithely consigned him, economically and politically irrelevant. The crofting legislation of the 1880s was predicated upon the desirability of keeping the stout Highland stock working the land, and upon the often sentimentally expressed love that he had (and became required to have) for that land. It is of interest that the gardens of modern Lewis council houses, provided in the best garden-city fashion, are often full of grass and nettles growing wild. Donald Macaulay, in pointing this out, said that if you asked the tenants why they did not, for example, grow vegetables, they would reply that they and their families had had quite enough of that sort of thing, having been crofters for long enough.[14] J.S. Blackie would be shocked, but we have no more right to our urban indignation than he.

The production of Harris Tweed is organised, like the crofting institution, on lines which make it quite self-consciously an archaism in the modern world. The decision of the tweed-makers in 1976 to continue producing single-width cloth on 'hand' looms rather than convert to a more centralised production of the now more usual double-width material was a decision to maintain that authentic historical validity that genuine Harris Tweed, however much it costs and however wide it is, has. The weavers' decision was in part based on a shrewd assessment of the likely manpower requirements of a reorganised and more efficient industry. Even so, in cornering the market in the historically authentic product, while they are using to their advantage the historical status accorded to them, they are also renouncing a potential effectivity in a wider and more vigorous economic world.

Probably every point that I have made concerning crofting and Harris Tweed is capable of being hotly contested, and I only introduce the topics at all, which demand much fuller attention than I have time or competence to give, in order to demonstrate that the kind of analysis I have been doing is not a mere literary indulgence, and that the imagery I have been discussing has a modern and material effectivity, and is no 'beating of wings that one has difficulty in hearing in the serious matter of history' (M. Foucault, 1972, p. 209).

The imagery that I have been discussing can be considered, at one level, as a manifestation of an asymmetrical power relationship. Its denunciation in the context of modern feminism treats it as precisely that. Nevertheless the problem is more than one of simple political disequilibrium. The use throughout Scotland of Highland symbolism is not mere theft, but part of a process whereby the social space that the Gaelic-speaking Highlander occupies is defined. I have discussed in Chapters 6 and 7 the complexity of the relationship that binds the majority and minority together in this respect. The minority society remains capable of subsuming the majority in its definition of its social world, despite demographic and cultural attenuation. However, in doing so, it finds, in the Highland context, that in seeking imagery to express itself, to define its world, it is reduced to borrowing back its own clothes, often without noticing the alteration of fit.

The literary Celt that sprang from Arnold's imagination is, as I have suggested, not yet a dead figure gathering dust on the library shelves. In a recent popular anthropology magazine series entitled *Family of Man*, Anne Ross (see also A. Ross, 1970) supplies the section on Celts. She tells us that:

> The Celts . . . had a highly-developed religion, and this passion for the supernatural has remained one of the most deeply-rooted Celtic traits (A. Ross, 1974, p. 463).

> they have always been a people of unstable temperament, quick to anger, much given to humour and wit, and both bravery and cowardice (ibid.).

> The Celts were a vain people – they loved to deck their bodies (ibid.).

> The Celts were not concerned with material things (ibid.).

We note the past tense, and we see pictures of Welshmen with coracles, of 'Killarney's Ross castle, an ancient relic of the early Celtic civilisation' (ibid., p. 461), of Breton women who 'wear the traditional costume of their ancestors and speak the ancient Celtic Breton language' (ibid.), of 'Celtic peasants' (ibid., p. 463) who 'dig peat from a moor in a remote part of western Ireland' (ibid.), and of a little wind-blown red-haired girl from the Scottish Gaidhealtachd, from which 'it is likely that both the language and the culture will soon vanish from everyday use' (ibid., p.

464). Archaeology, pre-history, spurious ethnology, folklore and modern census data jostle together in the same paragraphs in a way that is familiar enough in descriptions of the Celts, but would seem outrageously unlikely for many of the other 'peoples' of western Europe. The only young man photographically present as a 'Celt' remains a 'peasant', in spite of his wellington boots and cloth cap. 'The picture that the Celts offer us today is that of an ancient and distinctive culture in the final stages of disintegration' (ibid.).

As part of my attempts to learn the Gaelic language I went, in the summer of 1976, to Sabhal Mór Ostaig,[15] to attend a course intended to teach the spoken language. There were people from all over the world there, and we were well looked after and well entertained. Almost every evening had its *ceilidh*, its dancing, its singing, or its drinking. One of the teachers there, a girl from one of the smaller islands of the Outer Hebrides, expressed some concern that we were in danger of getting a totally false idea of what Gaelic life was like. 'It isn't like this,' she said, 'normally nothing happens for weeks on end.' Yet there we all were, Gael and Gall alike, drawn into a common conspiracy to celebrate the Gaelic world that we all felt should exist. Where did that Gaelic world of our imagination have its origin? What compulsion was it that drew us all into willing complicity to celebrate it? At whose direction were we dancing and singing? It is to questions like these that I have been trying, implicitly, to provide an answer.

NOTES

1. The 'Gaidhealtachd' is a term ambiguously employed, sometimes to refer only to the area where Gaelic is still spoken in strength, and sometimes to refer to the Highlands in general.

2. The Statutes of Iona of 1609 were acts designed by the central authorities to draw the Highlands securely into the larger political system. One of the clauses demanded that 'every gentleman or yeoman possessed of over sixty heads of cattle should send his eldest son or daughter at least to the Lowlands to receive an English, and Protestant, education' (J.L. Campbell, 1950, p. 49).

3. The number of Gaelic-speakers in Scotland actually rose between 1961 and 1971 according to the census data, which give 80,004 speakers in 1961 (1.6 per cent of the Scottish population), and 88,415 in 1971 (1.8 per cent of the Scottish population). It is widely suspected that this rise is at least to some extent illusory, deriving from a change in the form of the question, and from positive answers from those who are, with varying degrees of success, learning the language. The number of Gaelic-speakers in Scotland as a percentage of the total population has fallen as follows: 1891 (5.2 per cent), 1901 (4.5 per cent), 1911 (3.9 per cent), 1921 (3.1 per cent), 1931 (2.7 per cent), 1951 (1.8 per cent).

4. For published extracts from this work see N. Ross (ed.), 1939.

5. Macpherson is referring here to two prominent seventeenth-century Irish historians. Geoffrey Keating (*c.* 1570-*c.* 1644) was a Roman Catholic priest who wrote a history of Ireland, entitled *Foras Feasa ar Eirinn* (*Foundation of Knowledge on Ireland*) (see G. Keating, 1908). This work, probably dated 1629, was the first connected history of Ireland in the Irish language, and was widely read. The work 'shows an extensive knowledge of Irish literature, but is devoid of all historical criticism' (*Dictionary of National Biography*).

Roderic O'Flaherty (1629-1718) published in London in 1685 a volume entitled *Ogygia, seu rerum Hibernicarum chronologia*, which was the first work in which Irish history was placed in scholarly form before readers in England (*Dictionary of National Biography*).

6. Sorley MacLean, the most eminent of modern Gaelic poets, has been until recently similarly unavailable. Between the publication of *Dàin do Eimhir* in 1943 and of *Reothairt is Contraigh* in 1977, MacLean's work was available only in limited selection in a few anthologies and magazines.

7. The Society for the Propagation of Christian Knowledge, see also above, p. 29.

8. Thomson claims that this attempt to derive Gaelic from Eden is merely a 'humorous bonus' to the poet's main concern, which is to 'emphasize the larger Scottish relevance of the language' (D. Thomson, 1974, p. 158). While there is certainly room for debate about just what an eighteenth-century writer 'meant' by philological references to Eden, we are not justified in dismissing these as humorous. Until the recognition of the importance of Sanskrit, which can be traced to William Jones in 1786 (see W.B. Lockwood, 1971, p. 22), and the emergence of the idea of the Indo-European language family (ibid., pp. 23-33), references to Hebrew, Eden or Babel were the most important underpinning of philological enquiry. Gaelic scholars were solemnly establishing the Old Testament origin of Gaelic until well into the nineteenth century (see, for example, Lachlan Maclean, 1837 and 1840; Donald Macintyre, 1865).

9. 'The Mòd' is the term used by An Comunn Gaidhealach (The Highland

Association) to describe their annual festival, which is the Scottish equivalent of the Welsh Eisteddfod. The Mòd, sometimes known as the 'whisky olympics', has come under severe criticism in recent years from the more youthful and radical members of An Comunn for its lack of political commitment and content. The Gaelic word *mòd* means court, assembly, or meeting.

10. This was first published in *La Revue des Deux Mondes* in 1854.

11. John Francis Campbell of Islay (1822-85) was the eldest son of Walter Campbell of Islay and through his mother, grandson of the Earl of Wemyss. Educated at Eton and Edinburgh University, the collection of Highland folklore occupied much of his leisure time, although he had interests in many other fields. He died at Cannes in 1885.

Alexander Carmichael (1832-1912), a native Gaelic-speaker who worked as a customs and exciseman in the Highlands, gathered a large body of oral literature, much of which was published by others after his death (see A. Carmichael, 1928-71).

12. This topic was treated by Thomson at a one-day conference on Scotland's languages at Glasgow University in autumn 1976.

13. 'The Disruption' is the term given to the break-up of the General Assembly of the Church of Scotland in Edinburgh over the issue of the right of a congregation to have a say in their choice of minister. This was a serious political question, since ministers chosen by the landlord were morally and economically bound to him, thus depriving the common people of their potentially most literate and respected representative. The Disruption led to the formation of the Free Church, now a distinctively Highland and Gaelic institution.

14. This was said in an address to the Hebridean Studies summer school in Stornoway in summer 1977, a course that was running concurrently with a Gaelic course that I was attending.

15. Sabhal Mór Ostaig is a recently founded Gaelic college, in Sleat, in the south of Skye.

REFERENCES

Abbreviations

JASO	*Journal of the Anthropological Society of Oxford*
SGS	*Scottish Gaelic Studies*
SS	*Scottish Studies*
TGSI	*Transactions of the Gaelic Society of Inverness*

Dates refer to editions that I have used. Bracketed dates indicate, where necessary, date of first publication.

'A.E.' (George Russell) *The Nuts of Knowledge, Lyrical Poems old and new.* Dundrum, The Dun Emer Press, 1903

_____ *By Still Waters, Lyrical Poems old and new.* Dundrum, The Dun Emer Press, 1906

Alexander, E. *Matthew Arnold and John Stuart Mill.* London, Routledge & Kegan Paul, 1965.

Allen, Grant. 'Are We Englishmen?' *Fortnightly Review* (n.s.), CLXVI (1880), 472-87

Althusser, L. and Bálibar, E. *Reading Capital.* London, New Left Books, 1970

Anderson, M.O. *Kings and Kingship in early Scotland.* Edinburgh and London, Scottish Academic Press, 1973

Ardener, E.W. (ed.). *Social Anthropology and Language.* London, Tavistock, 1971

_____ 'The New Anthropology and its critics', *Man* (n.s.) 6 (1971a), 449-67

_____ 'Belief and the Problem of Women' in La Fontaine (ed.), 1972, pp. 135-58

_____ 'Behaviour: A Social Anthropological Criticism', *JASO*, 4 (1973), 152-4

_____ 'The Problem Revisited' (1975) in S. Ardener (ed.), 1975, pp. 19-27

_____ 'The Voice of Prophecy. Further Problems in the Analysis of Events'. *The Munro Lecture.* Edinburgh, unpublished, 1975a

_____ 'The Cosmological Irishman', *New Society*, 14 (8) 1975b, 362-4

Ardener, S. (ed.). *Perceiving Women.* London, Malaby Press, 1975

Arensberg, C.M. *The Irish Countryman. An Anthropological Study.*

London, Macmillan, 1937
Arensberg, C.M. and Kimball, S.T. *Family and Community in Ireland.* Cambridge, Mass., Harvard University Press, 1940
Arnold, M. *The Study of Celtic Literature* (1867). (Popular edition) London, Smith, Elder, 1891
——— *Letters* in G. Russel (ed.), 1895
——— *Culture and Anarchy* (1869). Cambridge, Cambridge University Press, 1969
Austin, J.L. *Sense and Sensibilia.* Oxford, Clarendon Press, 1964
Bannerman, J. 'The Dal Riata and Northern Ireland in the sixth and seventh centuries' in J. Carney and D. Greene (eds.), 1969, pp. 1-11
——— *Studies in the History of Dalriada.* Edinburgh and London, Scottish Academic Press, 1974
Barth, F. 'Models of Social Organisation', *Royal Anthropological Institute.* Occasional Papers, No. 23, 1966
——— (ed.). *Ethnic Groups and Boundaries.* London, Allen and Unwin, 1968
Beckwith, L. *The Sea for Breakfast.* London, Arrow Books, 1968
Bernstein, B. *Class, Codes, and Control.* London, Routledge & Kegan Paul, 1971
Black, G.F. *Macpherson's Ossian and the Ossianic Controversy: a Contribution towards a Bibliography.* New York, New York Public Library, 1926
Blackie, J.S. *The Gaelic Language. Its Classical Affinities and Distinctive Character.* Edinburgh, Edmonston and Douglas, 1864
——— *Language and Literature of the Scottish Highlands.* Edinburgh, Edmonston and Douglas, 1876
——— *Gaelic Societies, Highland Depopulation, and Land Law Reform. Inaugural Address to the Gaelic Society, Perth.* Edinburgh, David Douglas, 1880
——— *The Language and Literature of the Scottish Highlands.* Royal Institution of Great Britain, Weekly Evening Meeting, 29 April 1881
——— *The Union of 1707 and its Results. A Plea for Scottish Home Rule.* Glasgow, Morison Brothers, 1892
Blackwell, T. *An Enquiry into the Life and Writings of Homer* (2nd edition). London, 1736
Blair, A. 'The Way of the Celt', *Guth na Bliadhna* (*The Voice of the Year*), xii (4) (1915), 411-24
Blair, H. Preface to *Ossian.* 1760
——— *A Critical Dissertation on the Poems of Ossian*, subjoined to

Ossian, 1765

Boswell, J. *Life of Johnson*, Vol. II, 1766–1776 (1791). Oxford, Clarendon Press, 1934

Boulay, J. Du. *Portrait of a Greek Mountain Village.* Oxford, Clarendon Press, 1974

Brody, H. *Innishkillane. Change and Decline in Western Ireland.* Harmondsworth, Penguin, 1974

Bromwich, R. *Matthew Arnold and Celtic Literature. A Retrospect. 1865-1965.* Oxford, Clarendon Press, 1965

Brooke, S. *Chambers Cyclopaedia of English Literature*, Vol. 1, 1901, pp. 1-4

BRSM. 'The Late Calum MacLean', *SS*, 4 (1959), 121-3

Bruce, G. (ed.). *The Scottish Literary Revival.* London, Collier-Macmillan, 1968

Burnet, J. (Lord Monboddo). *Of the Origin and Progress of Language.* Edinburgh, 1773

Burton, J. Hill. *Life and Correspondence of David Hume.* Edinburgh, William Tait, 1846

Calder, G. (ed.). *Gaelic Songs by William Ross.* Edinburgh, Oliver and Boyd, 1937

Campbell, J.F. (ed.). *Popular Tales of the West Highlands orally collected.* Vols. 1 and 2. Edinburgh, Edmonston and Douglas, 1860

——— (ed.). *Popular Tales of the West Highlands orally collected.* Vols. 3 and 4. Edinburgh, Edmonston and Douglas, 1862

——— (ed.). *Leabhar na Féinne.* London, 1872

——— (ed.). *Leabhar na Féinne.* Shannon, Irish University Press, 1972

Campbell, J.K. *Honour, Family, and Patronage.* Oxford, Clarendon Press, 1964

——— and Sherrard, P. *Modern Greece.* London, Ernest Benn, 1968

Campbell, J.L. *Highland Songs of the 'Forty-Five.* Edinburgh, John Grant, 1933

——— *Gaelic in Scottish Education and Life.* Edinburgh, W. and A.K. Johnston for the Saltire Society, 1950

——— *Fr. Allan Macdonald of Eriskay 1859-1905, Priest, Poet, and Folklorist.* Edinburgh and London, Oliver and Boyd, 1954

——— (ed.). *Tales of Barra told by the Coddy.* Edinburgh, for the editor by Johnston and Bacon, 1960

——— and Thomson, D. *Edward Lhuyd in the Scottish Highlands 1699–1700.* Oxford, Clarendon Press, 1963.

——— and Hall, T.H. *Strange Things.* London, Routledge & Kegan Paul, 1968

______ and Collinson, F. *Hebridean Folksongs.* Oxford, Clarendon Press, 1969.

______. 'The Expurgating of Mac Mhaighstir Alasdair' *SGS*, XII(1) (1971), 59-76

______ (ed.). *A Collection of Highland Rites and Customs.* Folklore Society, 1975

Carlyle, T. *Critical and Miscellaneous Essays,* Vol. 1. London, Chapman and Hall, 1899

Carmichael, A. *Carmina Gadelica* (2nd ed.), Vols. 1 and 2 (1900). Edinburgh and London, Oliver and Boyd, 1928

______. *Carmina Gadelica*, Vols. 3 and 4 (J. Carmichael Watson (ed.)). Edinburgh and London, Oliver and Boyd, 1940-1

______. *Carmina Gadelica*, Vol. 5 (A. Matheson (ed.)). Edinburgh and London, Oliver and Boyd, 1954

______. *Carmina Gadelica*, Vol. 6 (A. Matheson (ed.)). Edinburgh and London, Scottish Academic Press, 1971

Carney, J., and Greene, D. (eds.). *Celtic Studies*. London, Routledge & Kegan Paul, 1969

Census (Scotland: Gaelic Report). Edinburgh, HMSO, 1971

Chadwick, N. *The Celts.* Harmondsworth, Penguin, 1970

Chapman, M. 'What Science is saying about the Celts'. *JASO*, VIII(2) (1977), 85-94

______. 'Reality and Representation', *JASO*, IX(1) (1978), 35-51

Chesson (*née* Hopper), N. *Selected Poems.* London, Alston Rivers, 1906

Christiansen, R.Th. 'Scotsmen and Norsemen: Cultural Relations in the North Sea Area', *SS*, 1 (1957), 15-37

Cole, J.W. 'Anthropology Comes Part-Way Home: Community Studies in Europe', *Annual Review of Anthropology*, Vol. 6 (1977), 349-78

Colson, E. *The Makah Indians.* Manchester, Manchester University Press, 1953

Condry, E. 'The Impossibility of Solving the Highland Problem', *JASO* VII(3) (1976), 138-49

______. 'The Scottish Highland Problem: Some Anthropological Aspects'. Unpublished B.Litt. thesis, Oxford University, 1977

Cregeen, E. 'The Changing Role of the House of Argyll in the Scottish Highlands' in I. Lewis (ed.), *History and Social Anthropology*. London, Tavistock, 1968

Crick, M. *Explorations in Language and Meaning.* London, Malaby Press, 1976

Curtis (Jr.), L.P. *Anglo-Saxons and Celts: A Study of Anti-Irish Prejudice*

in Victorian England. Connecticut, University of Bridgeport, 1968
Curwen, E. 'The Hebrides: A Cultural Backwater', *Antiquity*, XII (47) (1938), 261-89
Cutileiro, J. *A Portuguese Rural Society.* Oxford, Clarendon Press, 1971
Daiches, D. *The Paradox of Scottish Culture: The Eighteenth Century Experience.* Oxford, Oxford University Press, 1964
——. *Charles Edward Stuart.* London, Thames and Hudson, 1973
Davies, E. *Celtic Researches on the Origin, Traditions, and Language of the Ancient Britons.* London, 1804
Davis, J. *People of the Mediterranean. An Essay in Comparative Social Anthropology.* London, Routledge & Kegan Paul, 1977
Dearden, R.F. 'Education as a Process of Growth' in R.F. Dearden, Hirst and Peters, *Education and the Development of Reason.* London, Routledge & Kegan Paul, 1972
Dickens, C. *Hard Times* (1854). London, Oxford University Press, 1974
Domhnallach, M. *The West Highland Free Press*, No. 304, 24 February 1978
Donn, T.M. 'Semantics of the Gaelic Language', *TGSI*, XLV (1968), 319-53
Dorson, R.M. 'Folklore Studies in England', *Journal of American Folklore*, 74 (1961), 302-12
—— (ed.). *Peasant Customs and Savage Myths.* London, Routledge & Kegan Paul, 1968
Dresch, P. 'Economy and Ideology: An Obstacle to Materialist Analysis', *JASO*, VII(2) (1976), 55-77
Durkheim, E. *The Rules of Sociological Method* (1895). New York, The Free Press, 1938
——. *The Division of Labour in Society* (1893). Illinois, The Free Press, 1948
——. *The Elementary Forms of the Religious Life* (1915). London, George Allen and Unwin, 1957
Eliot, T.S. *Selected Essays.* London, Faber and Faber, 1966
——. *The Complete Poems and Plays.* London, Faber and Faber, 1969
Erskine, R. 'The Two Cultures', *The Scottish Review*, 37 (1914), 283-306
——. 'Celt, Slav, Hun, and Teuton', *The Scottish Review*, 37 (1914a), 315-25
Evans-Pritchard, E.E. *Witchcraft, Oracles, and Magic Among the Azande.* Oxford, Clarendon Press, 1937

_____. *The Nuer.* Oxford, Clarendon Press, 1941

_____. *Nuer Religion.* Oxford, Clarendon Press, 1956

_____. *The Zande Trickster.* Oxford, Clarendon Press, 1967

_____. *Essays in Social Anthropology.* London, Faber and Faber, 1969

Evans-Wentz, W.Y. *The Fairy Faith in Celtic Countries.* London, Oxford University Press, 1911

Faverty, F.E. *Matthew Arnold the Ethnologist.* Evanston, Illinois, Northwest University Press, 1951

Ferguson, A. *An Essay on the History of Civil Society.* London, A. Millar and T. Caddel; Edinburgh, A. Kincaid and J. Bell, 1767

Finnegan, R. 'Attitudes to the Study of Oral Literature in British Social Anthropology', *Man* (n.s.) 4(1) (1969), 59-69

_____. *Oral Literature in Africa.* Oxford, Clarendon Press, 1970

Fitzgerald, R.P. 'The Style of Ossian', *Studies in Romanticism*, 6 (1966), 22-33

Flower, R. 'Byron and Ossian'. Byron Foundation Lecture, University College, Nottingham, 1928

Foerster, D.M. 'Scottish Primitivism and the Historical Approach', *Philological Quarterly*, XXIX (4) (1950), 307-23

Forbes, R. 'Lyon in Mourning', Vol. 1. *Scottish History Society*, XX (1895)

Foucault, M. *The Archaeology of Knowledge.* London, Tavistock, 1972

Frankenberg, R. *Village on the Border.* London, Cohen and West, 1957

Frazer, J.G. *The Golden Bough, A Study in Magic and Religion* (abridged edition). London, Macmillan, 1949

Freeman, E.A. *Four Oxford Lectures.* London, Macmillan, 1888

Freer, A.G. *Outer Isles.* Westminster, Archibald Constable, 1902

Gadamer, H.-G. *Truth and Method.* London, Sheed and Ward, 1975

Gaelic Society of Glasgow. *The Old Highlands.* Glasgow, Archibald Sinclair, 1908

Galand, R.M. *L'Ame Celtique de Renan.* New Haven, Yale University Press; Paris, Presses Universitaires de France, 1959

Geipel, John. *The Europeans: An Ethno-Historical Survey.* London, Longmans, 1969

Gibbon, Lewis Grassic (J.L. Mitchell). *A Scots Quair.* London and Sydney, Pan Books, 1973

Giddens, A. *Capitalism and Modern Social Theory.* Cambridge, Cambridge University Press, 1971

Glen, D. *Hugh MacDiarmid and the Scottish Renaissance.* Edinburgh and London, W. and R. Chambers, 1964

Gluckman, M. *Custom and Conflict in Africa.* Oxford, Basil Blackwell, 1955

———. 'Gossip and Scandal', *Current Anthropology* 4(3) (1963), 307-16

———. 'The Utility of the Equilibrium Model in the Study of Social Change', *American Anthropologist*, 70 (1968), 219-37

Goethe, J.W. von. *The Sorrows of Werther* (1774). London, George Bell, 1885

Gomme, G.L. in D. Macinnes, 1890, appendix

Green, J.R. *History of the English People*, Vol. 1. London, Macmillan, 1877

Greene, D. 'The Founding of the Gaelic League' in S. O Tuama (ed.), 1972, pp. 9-19

Grieve, C.M. (Hugh Macdiarmid) (ed.). *The Scottish Chapbook* 1(3) (1922)

———. *Lucky Poet, A Self-Study in Literature and Political Ideals.* London, Methuen, 1943

———. 'Scotland' in O.W. Edwards, G. Evans, I. Rhys and H. Macdiarmid, *Celtic Nationalism.* London, Routledge & Kegan Paul, 1968, pp. 229-358

———. *More Collected Poems.* London, Macgibbon and Kee, 1970

Grimm, J. *Deutsche Grammatik.* Göttingen, 1822

Guest, C. *The Mabinogion* (3 vols). London, Longman, Brown, Green and Longmans, 1838-49

Gunn, N. *Whisky and Scotland.* London, George Routledge, 1935

———. *The Green Isle of the Great Deep.* London, Faber and Faber, 1944

———. *The Well at the World's End.* London, Faber and Faber, 1951

———. *Butcher's Broom* (1934). London, Souvenir Press, 1977

Guth na Bliadhna. 'The Church and The Highlands' 1(1) (1904)

Hartland, E.S. *Folklore: What is it and what is the good of it?* London, David Nutt, 1899

Hay, G. Campbell. 'Feachd a'Phrionnsa' ('The Prince's Army'), *The Voice of Scotland* (Hugh Macdiarmid (ed.)), III(1) (1946), 14-15

———. *Fuaran Slèibh.* Glasgow, William MacLellan, 1947

Henderson, W. *Folklore of the Northern Counties of England and the Borders* (2nd ed.). London, Folklore Society, 1879

Henson, H. *British Social Anthropologists and Language.* Oxford, Clarendon Press, 1974

Herder, J.G. 'Auszug aus Einem Briefwechsel Uber Ossian und die Lieder alter Volker' in *Werke*, Vol. 2. Aufbau-Verlag Berlin und Weimar, 1964

Hertz, R. *Death and the Right Hand* (1907/9). London, Cohen and West, 1960
Herzfeld, M. 'The Advent of Spring in Rural Greece' (1977) in R.K. Jain (ed.), 1977
Hobbes, T. *Leviathan* (1651). Oxford, Clarendon Press, 1909
Home, H. (Lord Kames). *Sketches of the History of Man.* Edinburgh, W. Creech; London, Strahan and Cadell, 1774
——. *The Gentleman Farmer.* Edinburgh, W. Creech; London, T. Cadell, 1776
Home, J. *Douglas: A Tragedy.* London, A. Millar, 1757
Hopper, N. (see also Chesson). *Songs of the Morning.* London, Grant Richards, 1900
Hudson, W.M. 'Ossian in English before Macpherson: Hanmer's *Chronicle of Ireland* 1633', *Studies in English*, XXIX (the University of Texas) (1950)
Hueffer, F. Madox. 'Introduction' to N. Chesson, 1906, Vol. 1.
Hull, E. *A Text Book of Irish Literature.* London, David Nutt, 1906
Hume, D. *Essay on the Authenticity of Ossian's Poems* in J. Hill Burton (ed.), 1846
Hunter, J. *The Making of the Crofting Community.* Edinburgh, John Donald, 1976
Jackson, K. *A Celtic Miscellany.* Harmondsworth, Penguin, 1971
Jain, R.K. (ed.). *Text and Context. The Social Anthropology of Tradition.* ASA Essays in Social Anthropology, Vol. 2, 1977
——. 'Introduction' to R.K. Jain (ed.), 1977
Jenkins, T. 'Review Article: Perceiving Women', *JASO,* VII(1) (1976), 35-41
Johnson, Dr S. *A Journey to the Western Islands of Scotland.* London, W. Strahan, 1775
Jones, D.M. 'The Celtic Twilight', *The London Quarterly Review*, CLXXXVII (1900)
Journal des Sçavans. Review of Macpherson's Ossian. Tome LXXI (1762), 49-64
Julius Caesar. *The Gallic Wars.* London, Heinemann, 1914
Kant, I. *The Critique of Judgement* (1787). Oxford, Clarendon Press, 1952
Keating, G. *The History of Ireland* (*c.* 1633). Irish Texts Society, VIII and IX, 1908
Keltie, J.S. (ed.). *A History of the Scottish Highlands, Highland Clans and Highland Regiments.* Edinburgh and London, A. Fullarton, 1875
Kennedy, J. 'Alexander Macdonald, The Poet', *The Celtic Magazine*,

XIII (1888), 265-71, 302-10, 337-43

———. 'Duncan Bàn Macintyre', *The Celtic Magazine*, XIII (1888a), 385-93, 433-8, 481-6

Kenward, J. *The Keltic Element in England.* Birmingham, Birmingham Philosophical Society, 1881

Kingsley, C. *Life and Works of Charles Kingsley.* London, Macmillan, 1901

Kirk, R. *The Secret Commonwealth of Elves, Fauns, and Fairies* (1691). Folklore Society, 1976 (ed. and intro. S.F. Sanderson)

Kreager, P. 'Malthus and Formal Analysis', *JASO*, VIII(2) (1977), 63-73

La Fontaine, J.S. (ed.). *The Interpretation of Ritual.* London, Tavistock, 1972

Laing, M. *The Poems of Ossian etc. Containing the Poetical Works of James Macpherson.* Edinburgh, Archibald Constable, 1805

Lamont, A. 'The History of Celtic Art', *Scottish Anthropological Society Proceedings*, VIII(2) (1933), 29-55

Lang, A. 'Introduction', *The Folk Lore Record*, Vol. II (1879), i-viii

———. 'The Celtic Renascence', *Blackwood's Magazine*, DCCCCLXXVI (1897), 181-91

Leach, E. *Rethinking Anthropology.* London, The Athlone Press, 1961

Lévi-Strauss, C. *The Savage Mind.* London, Weidenfeld and Nicolson, 1966

Lévy-Bruhl, L. *Primitive Mentality.* London, George Allen and Unwin, 1923

Lhuyd, E., *Archaeologia Britannica* (Vol. 1, Glossography). Oxford, 1707

Lockwood, W.B. *Indo-European Philology.* London, Hutchinson University Library, 1971

Logan, J. 'Introduction' (1904) to J. Mackenzie (ed.), 1904

Loizos, P. *The Greek Gift: Politics in a Cypriot Village.* Oxford, Basil Blackwell, 1975

Lovejoy, A.O. 'The Meaning of Romanticism for the Historian of Ideas', *Journal of the History of Ideas*, II (3) (1941), 257-78

Mac A'Ghobhainn, S. Editorial in Crann-Tàra, 1, p. 1 (Newsletter of Comunn na Cànain Albannaich, The Scottish Language Society) (1971)

Macaulay, D. 'On Some Aspects of the Appreciation of Modern Gaelic Poetry', *SGS* XI(1) (1966), 136-45

———. *Seobhrach as a'Chlaich.* Glasgow, Gairm, 1967

———. (ed.). *Nua bhàrdachd Ghàidhlig* (*Modern Scottish Gaelic Poems*).

Edinburgh, Southside, 1976
Macbain, A. 'Macpherson's Ossian', *The Celtic Magazine* XII (1887), 145-54, 193-201, 241-54
_____. *Celtic Mythology and Religion.* Stirling, Eneas Mackay, 1917
Macdiarmid, H. See under C.M. Grieve
Macdonald, A. *Leabhar a Theagasc Ainminnin no A Nuadhfhocloir Gaoidheilg & Beurla,* Dun-Edin, Le Raibeard Fleming, 1741
_____. *Aiseirigh na Sean Chanain Albannaich.* Edinburgh, 1751
Macdonald, A. and Macdonald, A. (eds.). *The Poems of Alexander Macdonald (Mac Mhaighstir Alasdair).* Inverness, The Northern Counties Newspaper and Printing and Publishing Company, 1924
Macdonald, J. (ed.). *Voices from the Hills (Guthan o na Beanntaibh). A Memento of the Gaelic Rally 1927.* Glasgow, An Comunn Gaidhealach, 1927
Macdonald, M. 'History of the Gaelic Society of Inverness', *TGSI,* XLVI (1970), 1-21
McDonald, M. 'Language "At Home" to Educated Radicalism', *JASO,* IX(1) (1978), 13-34
MacInnes, D. (ed.). *Folk and Hero Tales from Argyllshire.* London, Folklore Society, 1890
MacInnes, J. 'Clan Unity and Individual Freedom', *TGSI,* XLVII (1972), 338-73
_____. 'The Gaelic Literary Tradition', *Scottish Literature in the Secondary School.* Edinburgh, HMSO, 1976, pp. 56-68
Macintyre, Donald. *On the Antiquity of the Gaelic Language.* Edinburgh, MacLachlan and Stewart, 1865
Macintyre, Duncan. *Orain Ghaidhealach.* Dun-eidinn, A. Mac Dhónuil, 1768
_____. *Songs and Poems in Gaelic* (5th ed.). Edinburgh, MacLachlan and Stewart, 1848
_____ *The Songs of Duncan Bàn Macintyre* (A. Macleod (ed.)). Edinburgh, Oliver and Boyd, 1952
Mackay, J.G. *More West Highland Tales* (transcribed and translated from the original Gaelic by J.G. MacKay). London and Edinburgh, Oliver and Boyd, 1940
Mackenzie, A. *The Highland Clearances.* Inverness, A.W. Mackenzie, 1883
Mackenzie, A.M. (ed.). *Orain Iain Luim.* Edinburgh, Oliver and Boyd, 1964
Mackenzie, H. (ed.). *Report of the Committee of the Highland Society of Scotland appointed to inquire into the Nature and Authenticity*

of the Poems of Ossian. Edinburgh, Archibald Constable, 1805
Mackenzie, J. (ed.). *Sàr-Obair nam Bard Gaelach or The Beauties of Gaelic Poetry* (1841). Edinburgh, Norman MacLeod, 1904
MacKinnon, K. 'The School in Gaelic Scotland. Some Historical and Sociological Perspectives and Suggestions', *TGSI,* XLVII (1972), 374-91
——. *The Lion's Tongue.* Inverness, Club Leabhar, 1974
——. *Language, Education, and Social Processes in a Gaelic Community.* London, Routledge & Kegan Paul, 1977
Mackintosh, D.T. 'James Macpherson and the Book of the Dean of Lismore', *SGS,* VI(1) (1947), 11-20
MacLauchlan, T. *Celtic Gleanings; or, Notices of the History and Literature of the Scottish Gael.* Edinburgh, MacLachlan and Stewart, 1857
MacLean, C.I. *The Highlands.* London, Batsford, 1959
——. 'Traditional Beliefs in Scotland', *SS,* 3 (1959a), 189-200
MacLean, D. *The Literature of the Scottish Gael.* Edinburgh and London, William Hodge, 1912
Maclean, L. *Adhamh agus Eubh, no Craobh Sheanachais nan Gael.* Glasgow, Maclachlan and Stewart, 1837
MacLean, M. *The Literature of the Celts.* London, Glasgow, and Dublin, Blackie, 1902
——. *The Literature of the Highlands.* London, Blackie, 1904
MacLean, S. 'Realism in Gaelic Poetry', *TGSI,* XXXVII (1938), 80-114
——. 'The Poetry of the Clearances', *TGSI,* XXXVIII (1939), 293-324
——. *Dàin do Eimhir.* Glasgow, William MacLellan, 1943
——. *Poems to Eimhir* (translated by Iain Crichton Smith). Newcastle on Tyne, Northern House, 1973
——. *Reothairt is Contraigh* (Spring Tide and Neap Tide). Edinburgh, Canongate, 1977
—— and Garioch, R. *17 Poems for 6^{d}.* Edinburgh, The Chalmers Press, 1940
MacLeod, A. (ed.). *The Songs of Duncan Bàn Macintyre.* Edinburgh, Oliver and Boyd, 1952
Macleod, C. *Sgial is Eachdraidh.* Glasgow, Gairm, 1977
MacLeod, D.J. 'A' Ghaidhlig am Beatha fhollaiseach an t-Sluaigh' ('Gaelic in Public Life') in D. Thomson (ed.), 1976, pp. 12-27
MacLeod, Finlay. 'An Experimental Investigation into Some Problems of Bilingualism'. Unpublished Ph.D. thesis, University of Aberdeen, 1969

MacLeod, Fiona (William Sharp). 'A Group of Celtic Writers', *The Fortnightly Review*, 71 (1899), 34-48

———. *The Writings of Fiona Macleod* (5 vols.) arranged by Mrs William Sharp. London, Heinemann, 1909

Macleod, N. *Clarsach an Doire.* Edinburgh, Norman Macleod, 1902

Macneill, D.H. *The Scottish Realm.* Glasgow, A. and J. Donaldson, 1947

Macneill, F.M. *The Silver Bough* (Vol. 1). Glasgow. William Maclellan, 1957

MacNeill, N. 'Remarks on Scottish Gaelic Literature', *TGSI,* II (1873), 80-92

———. *The Literature of the Highlanders* (1892). Stirling, Eneas Mackay, 1929

Macpherson, J. 'Dissertation concerning the Antiquity etc. of the Poems of Ossian Son of Fingal' in *Ossian*, 1765, i-xvi

Maine, H.S. *Ancient Law* (1861). London, Oxford University Press, 1950

Malinowski, B. *A Scientific Theory of Culture.* Chapel Hill, The University of North Carolina Press, 1944

Markale, J. *Women of the Celts.* London, Gordon Cremonesi, 1975

Martin, H. *Histoire de France* (Tome 1). Paris, Furne Libraire-Editeur, 1855

Meek, D.E. (ed.). *Màiri Mhòr nan Oran.* Glasgow, Gairm, 1977

Mill, J.S. *Utilitarianism, Liberty, Representative Government* (1861). London, J.M. Dent, 1968

Mitchell, J. *Psychoanalysis and Feminism.* New York, Pantheon Books, 1974

Mommsen, T. *The History of Rome.* London, Richard Bentley, 1894

Mott, L.F. 'Renan and Matthew Arnold', *Modern Language Notes,* XXXIII (1918), 65-70

Müller, F.M. *Address to the Anthropological Section of the British Association.* Cardiff, 1891

Nakamura, T. 'Neil Miller Gunn: a Spiritual Survey', *Studies in Scottish Literature* XII(2) (1974), 79-89

Needham, R. (ed.). *Right and Left, Essays on Dual Symbolic Classification.* Chicago, University of Chicago Press, 1973

———. *Remarks and Inventions. Skeptical Essays about Kinship.* London, Tavistock, 1974

Nisbet, J. 'Bilingualism and the School', *SGS*, X (1963)

Nutt, A. *Ossian and the Ossianic Literature.* London, David Nutt, 1899

———. 'The Critical Study of Gaelic Literature Indispensable for the

History of the Gaelic Race', *The Celtic Review*, 1 (1904), 47-67
——. (ed.). 'Introduction to M. Arnold' in *The Study of Celtic Literature.* London, David Nutt, 1910

Okun, H. 'Ossian in Painting', *Journal of the Warburg and Courtauld Institutes*, XXX (1967), 327-56

O'Rahilly, T.F. *Early Irish History and Mythology.* Dublin, Institute for Advanced Studies, 1946

Orr, J. 'The School of Scottish Studies', *SS*, 1 (1957), 1-2

Ossian. *Fragments of Ancient Poetry Collected in the Highlands of Scotland and Translated from the Gaelic or Erse Language* (2nd ed.). Edinburgh, 1760

——. *Fingal, an Ancient Epic Poem in Six Books composed by Ossian the Son of Fingal*, translated from the Gallic Language by James Macpherson. Dublin, 1762

——. *Temora, an Ancient Epic Poem in Eight Books*, translated from the Gallic Language by James Macpherson. London, 1763

——. *The Works of Ossian Son of Fingal in Two Volumes* (3rd ed.). Dublin, 1765

——. *The Poems of Ossian in the Original Gaelic* with a literal translation into Latin by the late Robert Macfarlan together with a dissertation on the authenticity of the poems by Sir John Sinclair, Bart. and a translation from the Italian of the Abbé Cesarotti's dissertation on the controversy respecting the authenticity of Ossian, with notes and a supplemental essay, by John M'Arthur. London, published under the sanction of the Highland Society of London, 1807

——. *Dana Oisein mhic Fhinn*, air an cur amach airson maith coitcheannta muinntir na Gaeltachd (Ewen MacLachlan (ed.)). Edinburgh, Tearlach Stiubhart, 1818

O'Suilleabhain, S. Contribution to *Four Symposia on Folklore*, S. Thompson (ed.). Indiana University Publications, Folklore Series 8-9, 1953

O Tuama, S. (ed.). *The Gaelic League Idea* (The Thomas Davis Lectures). Cork and Dublin, The Mercier Press, 1972

——. 'The Gaelic League Idea in the Future' in S. O Tuama (ed.), 1972, pp. 98-109

Owen, T. 'The "Communion Season" and Presbyterianism in a Hebridean Community', *Gwerin* 1 (2) (1956), 53-66

Paine, R. *Coast Lapp Society: A Study of Neighbourhood in Revsbotn Fjord.* Trømso Museum, 1957

——. 'What is Gossip about? An Alternative Hypothesis', *Man* 2(2) (1967), 278-85

Parman, S. 'Sociocultural Change in a Scottish Crofting Township'. Unpublished D.Phil. thesis, Rice University, Houston, Texas, 1972

Pattison, T. *The Gaelic Bards.* Glasgow, Archibald Sinclair, 1890

Pearce, R.H. 'The Eighteenth Century Scottish Primitivists: Some Reconsiderations', *Journal of English Literary History*, 12 (1945), 203-20

Peristiany, J.G. (ed.). *Honour and Shame. The Values of Mediterranean Society.* London, Weidenfeld and Nicolson, 1965

Piggott, S. 'Prehistory and the Romantic Movement', *Antiquity*, XI (1937), 31-8

———. 'Celts, Saxons, and the Early Antiquarians'. Oxford, The O'Donnell Lecture, 1966

———. *The Druids.* Harmondsworth, Penguin, 1977

Pinkerton, J. *A Dissertation on the Origins and Progress of the Scythians or Goths.* London, 1787

Pitt-Rivers, J. *The People of the Sierra.* New York, Criterion Books, 1954

Plant, R. *Community and Ideology.* London, Routledge & Kegan Paul, 1974

Powell, T.G.E. *The Celts.* London, Thames and Hudson, 1960

Prebble, J. *The Highland Clearances.* Harmondsworth, Penguin, 1969

———. *The Lion in the North.* Harmondsworth, Penguin, 1973

Radcliffe-Brown, A.R. *Structure and Function in Primitive Society.* London, Cohen and West, 1968

——— and Forde, D. (eds.). *African Systems of Kinship and Marriage.* London, Oxford University Press, 1950

Raftery, J. (ed.). *The Celts.* Dublin and Cork, The Mercier Press, 1976

Ralston, W.R.S. 'Notes on Folk Tales'. *The Publications of the Folklore Society, Vol. 1*, 1878, pp. 71-98

Ramsay, A. *The Evergreen* (2 vols.). Edinburgh, 1724

———. *The Tea Table Miscellany.* London, 1730

Ramsay, M.P. *Calvin and Art considered in relation to Scotland.* Edinburgh and London, The Moray Press, 1938

Reid, J. *Bibliotheca Scoto-Celtica.* Glasgow, John Reid, 1832

Renan, E. *Recollections of my Youth.* London, Chapman and Hall, 1883

———. *Life of Jesus.* London, Walter Scott Publishing Co. Ltd., 1897

———. *Oeuvres Complètes* (10 vols.). Calmann-Lévy (eds.). Paris, 1947-64

Rhys, J. 'British Association for the Advancement of Science. Address to the Anthropological Section'. Bradford, 1900. London, 1900

Richards, E. 'How Tame were the Highlanders during the Clearances?' *SS*, 17(1) (1973), 35-50
Roberts, P. *Sketch of the early history of the Cymry or Ancient Britons.* London, 1803
Robertson, A. *Children of the Fore-World.* London and Glasgow, Gowans and Gray, 1933
Robertson, H. 'Studies in Carmichael's Carmina Gadelica', *SGS*, XII(II) (1976), 220-65
Robertson-Smith, W. *Religion of the Semites.* London, Adam and Charles Black, 1907
Roger, J.C. *Celticism – A Myth.* For the author at the Courts of Justice Printing Works, 1884
Roman, K.G. *Handwriting, a Key to Personality.* London, Routledge & Kegan Paul, 1961
Ross, A. *Everyday Life of the Pagan Celts.* London, Batsford; New York, Putnam, 1970
_____. 'Celts', *Family of Man*, 17 (1974), 461-4 (Marshall Cavendish Ltd)
Ross, J. 'The Classification of Gaelic Folk Song', *SS*, 1 (1957), 95-151
Ross, N. (ed.). *Heroic Poetry from the Book of the Dean of Lismore.* Edinburgh, Oliver and Boyd, 1939
Rousseau, J.J. *The Social Contract and Discourses* (1762/50), London, J.M. Dent, 1961
_____. *The Confessions* (1781). Harmondsworth, Penguin, 1965
Russel, G.W.E. (ed.). *Letters of Matthew Arnold 1848-1888*, Vol. 1. London, Macmillan, 1895
Sanderson, S.F. 'The Work of the School of Scottish Studies', *SS*, 1 (1957), 3-13
Saussure, F. de. *Cours de Linguistique Gênérale.* Paris, Payot, 1949
Scotsman, The. 'Abriensis', 24 (1817), 191
Scott, T. (ed.). *Four Points of a Saltire.* Edinburgh, Reprographia, 1970
Scott, W. 'Review of Report of the Committee of the Highland Society on the Poems of Ossian, Drawn up by Henry Mackenzie Esq., And, The Poetical Works of James Macpherson Esq. by Malcolm Laing Esq.' *Edinburgh Review*, VI(XII) (1805), 429-62
Scottish Studies. 'Folk Tales from South Uist', *SS*, 1(1) (1959), 14
Sellar, W.C. and Yeatman, R.J. *1066 And All That* (1930). London, Magnum, 1976
Shairp, J.C. *Aspects of Poetry.* Oxford, Clarendon Press, 1881
Sharp, E.A. (ed.). *Lyra Celtica.* Edinburgh, Patrick Geddes and Colleagues, 1896

Sharp, W. (ed.). *The Poems of Ossian.* Edinburgh, Patrick Geddes and Colleagues, 1896

Shaw, G.B. *John Bull's Other Island* (Home Rule Edition). London, Constable, 1912

Smart, J.S. *James Macpherson, An Episode in Literature.* London, David Nutt, 1905

Smith, Iain Crichton (Iain Mac a'Ghobhainn). 'Modern Scottish Gaelic Poetry', *SGS*, VII (1953), 199-206

——. 'The Future of Gaelic Literature', *TGSI*, XLIII (1961), 172-80

——. *Biobuill is Sanasan-Rêice.* Glasgow, Gairm, 1965

——. *An T-Adhar Ameireaganach.* Inverness, Club Leabhar, 1973

——. *Eadar Fealla-dhà is Glaschu.* Glasgow, Gairm, 1974

——. *An T-Aonaran.* Glasgow University, Roinn nan Canan Ceilteach, 1976

——. 'Scottish Poetry in English' in N. Wilson (ed.), 1977, pp. 29-41

Smout, T.C. *A History of the Scottish People 1560-1830.* Collins, 1969

Snyder, E.D. *The Celtic Revival in English Literature 1760-1800.* Cambridge, Mass., Harvard University Press, 1923

Sterne, L.C. 'Ossianic Hero Poetry', *TGSI*, XXII (1898), 257-325

Stuart, D.M. '"Ossian" Macpherson Revisited', *English*, VII(37) (1948)

Stukeley, W. *Stonehenge, a Temple Restored to the Druids.* London, 1740

——. *Abury, A Temple of the Druids.* London, 1743

——. *A Letter from Dr. Stukeley to Mr. Macpherson on his publication of Fingal and Temora.* London, 1763

Tacitus. *The Agricola and Germany of Tacitus* (English translation). London, Macmillan, 1926

Taylor, I.B.C. 'On Telling the Culloden Story', *TGSI*, XLV (1968), 132-47

Thierry, A. *Histoire des Gaulois*, Tome 1. Paris, A. Sautelet, 1828

Thompson, F.G. 'The Folklore Elements in Carmina Gadelica', *TGSI*, XLIV (1966), 226-55

——. 'Gaelic in Politics', *TGSI*, XLVII (1970), 67-100

Thomson, D.S. *The Gaelic Sources of Macpherson's Ossian.* London and Edinburgh, Oliver and Boyd, 1951

——. *An Dealbh Briste.* Edinburgh, Serif Books, 1951a

——. 'The Gaelic Oral Tradition', *Proceedings of the Scottish Anthropological and Folklore Society*, V(1) (1954), 1-16

——. 'Scottish Gaelic Folk Poetry Ante 1650', *SGS*, VIII(1) (1955), 1-17

_____. '"Ossian" Macpherson and the Gaelic World of the Eighteenth Century', *Aberdeen University Review*, XL (1963), 7-20

_____. 'The Role of the Writer in a Minority Culture', *TGSI*, XLIV (1966), 256-71

_____. *Eadar Samhradh is Foghar.* Glasgow, Gairm, 1967

_____. 'Unpublished Letters by the Poet Ewen MacLachlan', *SGS*, XI (II) (1968), 202-36

_____. *An Introduction to Gaelic Poetry.* London, Victor Gollancz, 1974

_____ (ed.). *Gàidhlig ann an Albainn (Gaelic in Scotland).* Glasgow, Gairm, 1976

_____. *Bith-Eòlas.* Glasgow, Gairm, 1976a

_____. 'Leabhraichean, Litreachas, Foillseachadh' ('Books, Literature, Publishing') (1976b) in D. Thomson (ed.), 1976, pp. 78-86.

Thomson, J. *The Complete Poetical Works of James Thomson* (J. Logie Robertson (ed.)). London, Oxford University Press, 1961

Thomson, W. *Orpheus Caledonius.* 1725

Tocher. Vol. 1. Edinburgh, School of Scottish Studies, 1971

Tönnies, F. *Community and Association* (*Gemeinschaft und Gesellschaft*) (1887). London, Routledge & Kegan Paul, 1955

Vallee, F.G. 'Social Structure and Organisation in a Hebridean Community. A Study of Social Change'. Unpublished Ph.D. thesis, London School of Economics, 1954

_____. 'Burial and Mourning Customs in a Hebridean Community', *Journal of the Royal Anthropological Institute*, 85 (1955), 119-30

Voice of Scotland. 'Notes of the Quarter', 1(3) (1938), 1-6

Warner, F. *Remarks on the History of Fingal and other Poems of Ossian.* 1762

Watson, J. Carmichael (ed.). *Gaelic Songs of Mary MacLeod.* Edinburgh, Oliver and Boyd, 1965

Watson, W.J. 'Introduction' to J.G. MacKay, 1940, xxiv-xxvi

_____. *Bardachd Ghàidhlig* (1918). Stirling, A. Learmonth, 1959

Watts, A. *Nature, Man, and Woman.* London, Abacus, 1976

Weber, M. *The Protestant Ethic and the Spirit of Capitalism* (1904). London, George Allen and Unwin, 1948

Whitaker, I. 'Photographs of Traditional Scottish Life', *SS*, 2 (1958), 211

_____. 'Some Traditional Techniques in Modern Scottish Farming', *SS*, 3 (1959), 163-88

Whiteley, W.H. (ed.). *A Selection of African Prose. 1. Traditional Oral Texts.* Oxford, Clarendon Press, 1964

——— (ed.). *Language and Social Change. Problems of Multilingualism with special reference to Eastern Africa.* London, Oxford University Press, 1971

Whitney, L. *Primitivism and the Idea of Progress.* Baltimore, The Johns Hopkins Press, 1934

Wilson, N. (ed.). *Scottish Writing and Writers.* Edinburgh, The Ramsay Head Press, 1977

Wirth, L. *On Cities and Social Life.* Chicago and London, University of Chicago Press, 1964

Wolfe, B. *Scotland Lives.* Edinburgh, Reprographia, 1973

Wright, D. (ed.). *The Penguin Book of English Romantic Verse.* Harmondsworth, Penguin, 1968

Yeats, W.B. *Essays. Ideas of Good and Evil.* London, Macmillan, 1924

———. *Mythologies.* London, Macmillan, 1959

Youngson, A.J. *After the Forty-Five.* Edinburgh, Edinburgh University Press, 1973

———. *Beyond the Highland Line.* London, Collins, 1974

INDEX